CHARLES TODD'S MAGNIFICENT OBSESSION

The epic race to connect Australia to the world

DAVID DUFTY

ALLEN&UNWIN
SYDNEY • MELBOURNE • AUCKLAND • LONDON

First published in 2024

Allen & Unwin
Cammeraygal Country
83 Alexander Street
Crows Nest NSW 2065
Australia
Phone: (61 2) 8425 0100
Email: info@allenandunwin.com
Web: www.allenandunwin.com

Allen & Unwin acknowledges the Traditional Owners of the Country on which we live and work. We pay our respects to all Aboriginal and Torres Strait Islander Elders, past and present.

NATIONAL LIBRARY OF AUSTRALIA

A catalogue record for this book is available from the National Library of Australia

ISBN 978 1 76147 135 3

Maps by David Dufty
Set in 12/17 pt Adobe Garamond Pro by Midland Typesetters, Australia
Printed and bound in Australia by the Opus Group

10 9 8 7 6 5 4 3 2

MIX
Paper | Supporting responsible forestry
FSC® C001695
FSC
www.fsc.org

The paper in this book is FSC® certified. FSC® promotes environmentally responsible, socially beneficial and economically viable management of the world's forests.

David Dufty is an historian and researcher. He is the author of *Nabbing Ned Kelly*; *The Secret Code Breakers of Central Bureau*, winner of the 2017 Nib Military History Prize; and *Radio Girl*, winner, Best Non-fiction in the 2020 ACT Notable Awards.

'The gripping story of how visionary engineer Charles Todd built over 3000 kilometres of telegraph line between Adelaide and Darwin that connected the Australian colonies to the world's first global communications network—and dramatically cut the time it took to send a message around the globe from many months to less than a day.'
David Hill, author of *The Great Race and Convict Colony*

'A tale of endeavour and perseverance . . . Duffy has dusted off letters, documents and journals, never before seen, to bring us this driving narrative of a determined character who . . . had to overcome the country's killing heat, floods, drought, snakes, crocodiles and nefarious and violent competitors.'
Roland Perry OAM, author of *Bill the Bastard and Monash and Chauvel*

'Meticulous research and Dufty's monster writing skills shape a cracking retelling of Charles Todd's race to stretch a single strand of telegraph wire across 3000km of remote Australia from Port Augusta to Darwin.'
Glenn Morrison, general editor of *Borderlands* journal

'A good read, and speaks of the man and his team, illustrating the talents of a rare achiever' **Mac Benoy, National Coordinator of the Overland Telegraph Sesquicentennial 2022 Committee**

Contents

List of Maps

The Overland Telegraph Line and Cable to Java

Yam Creek
Katherine
Daly Waters
Powell's Creek
NORTHERN TERRITORY
Tennant Creek
Barrow Creek
Alice Springs
Charlotte Waters
QUEENSLAND
The Peake
Strangways Springs
SOUTH AUSTRALIA
Beltana
Port Augusta
Brisbane
NEW SOUTH WALES
Adelaide
Sydney
VICTORIA
Melbourne
TAS
Hobart

Part I
Rising Stars

1

The Lightning Line

England, 1837

On the evening of 25 July 1837, in a dingy little room at Euston Square Railway Station in England, a demonstration of a working electric telegraph was held. Professor Charles Wheatstone sat huddled over his contraption, illuminated by candlelight, twiddling five dials on a board. The dials pointed to letters so that, as Wheatstone turned them, they spelled a message. The machine was connected to five wires that slunk out of the room and loped along poles to Camden Town Railway Station, a mile and a quarter north.

There, Wheatstone's co-inventor, William Cooke, sat by an identical machine. As Wheatstone turned his dials, Cooke watched needles on his own machine swing back and forth like an electric Ouija board.

Behind Wheatstone, two representatives of the London and Birmingham Railway Company stood watching. They were witnessing something wonderful: the birth of the telegraph, which in turn was the precursor to the telephone, and ultimately the internet. This was a unique and magical moment in history.

But the railway men were unimpressed. They doubted the inventors' wild claims about their creation, such as its ability to signal train arrivals and departures from station to station. They walked away from the proposed deal to employ a telegraph on their railway, dismissing it as 'a new-fangled thing'.[1]

For over half a century, men had been looking for ways to send messages along electric wires. Early schemes included pith balls that jumped when hit by voltage; dozens of wires; and tubs of acid that bubbled like a witch's cauldron in response to galvanic shock. Sending a message between two nearby rooms was the limit of most.

Cooke and Wheatstone figured out a way of using only five wires and, instead of jumping pith balls and bubbling vats, they used compass needles. They were sure they were onto a winner.

Undaunted, Cooke and Wheatstone took their invention to a rival, the Great Western Railway Company, whose directors were more receptive. In July 1839, their five-line telegraph commenced operation between London's Paddington Station and West Drayton, thirteen miles west. It was an instant success. For the very first time, railway staff at one station knew exactly when trains had departed from the other station. They knew when trains were delayed, were running on time or were full to capacity—before those trains even arrived.

Electricity was new and strange. The light bulb had not yet been invented, so candles were still the main form of lighting everywhere (although gas lighting was another recent invention that was gaining in popularity). It would be decades before homes would have electric power, and electric appliances such as refrigerators and electric ovens were almost a century away. The public didn't really understand electricity, but they did know that it had something to do with lightning, so they dubbed the telegraph 'the lightning line'.

Cooke and Wheatstone quarrelled, with Cooke accusing Wheatstone of trying to take all the credit. Cooke had learned that Wheatstone sometimes called the telegraph 'my invention', without clarifying each time that Cooke was co-inventor. Their dispute continued on and off for years, but without any detriment to their financial success or to the uptake of their invention. Before long, Cooke–Wheatstone telegraph lines were ubiquitous on the English railway lines.

In America five years later, on 11 May 1844, Samuel Morse sent a telegraph message from the Supreme Court in Washington, D.C. to Baltimore, forty miles north, where the message was received by his colleague Alfred Vail. Morse had an audience of sixteen people, including congressmen. He invited Annie Ellsworth, the daughter of a friend, to compose the inaugural message. Annie's mother suggested a line from the Bible:[2] '*What hath God wrought?*' The Americans, at least, showed more of a sense of occasion than the sceptical English railway executives.

Morse had come up with two stunning innovations. The first was that his telegraph needed only one wire, not five. The messages were sent by just switching the voltage along the wire on and off for either a brief moment or a slightly longer moment, creating a series of 'dots' and 'dashes' in the voltage at the other end. He had devised a code, known as the Morse code, for sending letters and numbers in a string of these dots and dashes. This could be done by holding a metal key down to break the circuit, then releasing it. If you held the key down for a split second, you sent a dot. If you held it down for slightly longer, then it was a dash.

Morse's second innovation was a roll of paper that unfurled, passing under a pen that bobbed up and down to the dots and dashes; it marked the paper and recorded the message. No longer did someone have to sit there watching needles on dials dance about and record their movement. The operator could return from a lunch break and read the dots and dashes from recent messages marked on the coils of paper lying on the floor.

Morse's was not the first telegraph system, but it was the best. The English inventors recognised this, and by 1860 Cooke himself was recommending that Cooke–Wheatstone machines be decommissioned and be replaced by Morse equipment. It did not matter to Cooke because, by then, he was the co-owner of a successful British telegraph system.

The bigger the telegraph network, the more powerful it became. Wires, like the tentacles of an electric beast, spread over England, North America and Europe, then through South America, Africa and Asia. Cables plumbed the oceans, fusing continents into a single, connected whole.

But not Australia. There, ships still brought newspapers and letters from the other side of the world. The fastest means of communication from England and other faraway nations took months. Those newspapers proclaimed the birth of a wondrous technology. Perhaps, sometime soon, it would come to Australia's shores.

2

Samuel McGowan

Melbourne, 1853

Before he even stepped ashore on Melbourne Docks in May 1853, Samuel McGowan was creating commotion in the colonies. As he travelled by steamship from New York, colonial newspapers heralded the imminent arrival of the technological savant; a protégé of Samuel Morse himself.

Despite the Canadian accent, McGowan was Irish by birth, having emigrated as a child with his family to Kingston, Ontario. McGowan, it was said, had been hand-picked by Morse to run the telegraph line between New York and Buffalo. When news of the gold rush in Victoria travelled around the world, many young men arrived to make their riches in the diggings, but McGowan saw a different kind of opportunity. After seeking Morse's advice, he bought passage to Victoria, with a plan to bestow the wonders of telegraph on the newly rich colony, and particularly the major goldfield towns of Ballarat and Bendigo.[1] Everyone had heard of Samuel Morse, but not even the Victorian Governor himself had met the legendary inventor. But the young Canadian who had made his way around Cape Horn carried the status and mystique of having a personal connection with Morse.

The hype was justified, and McGowan did not disappoint.

His luggage included a box of telegraph apparatus, including batteries, coils, transmitting keys and sundry electrical equipment. It was all he needed to start building a telegraph line from scratch. On arriving, he quickly began assembling a consortium of investors. He ran private viewings of his telegraph equipment for journalists, patiently explaining the arcane science behind the wizardry. Melbourne already had a vague plan to build a line a short distance around the bay to the headland at Williamstown, with the idea that this would help with shipping. Given the lack of local expertise, this was more of an aspiration than a plan, but McGowan declared that it was very achievable, and that it would be his first endeavour.[2]

Melbourne's elite were excited by this development, but alarmed that they would lose control to a private operator. McGowan was invited to demonstrate his equipment to Cabinet and senior public servants.

On a blustery winter's morning, McGowan hauled his equipment into the Treasury building on William Street and set it up. Politicians and bureaucrats took their seats. Before them was a roll of thin paper tape coiled around a wheel, the axle of which was held in a wooden frame. McGowan threaded the end of the paper through a small machine sitting on a table, where a motor would feed the tape so it could be embossed with dots and dashes. This was the Morse receiver. Nearby, McGowan sat down with his transmitter, connected by wire to the receiver.

He switched the receiver on and its wheel turned, unrolling the paper and feeding it through the machine, marking it, then sending it dropping in coils to the floor. McGowan tapped out a message on the transmitter's Morse key, sometimes with a quick peck (a dot) and sometimes holding it a fraction longer (a dash). The message travelled along a wire to the receiver, whose embossing needle bobbed up and down and hammered the paper with ticks and clacks. When he was finished, he showed them the embossed paper and explained how to read the code. He had sent a message from one side of the room to the other![3]

He assured his audience—although they already knew—that the messages could travel much longer distances.

In North America, private enterprise was hailed as the vehicle of progress, but McGowan soon learned that colonial governments preferred to run things themselves. Two months after his Treasury presentation, the government announced that it would build a telegraph line from Melbourne to the Williamstown headland—the very route for which McGowan was raising finance—and warned of severe penalties for any private lines built in competition. McGowan had a choice, of sorts: either work for the government or go to war against it. He signed up.

Construction began right away, and the line was finished five months later, the first message being transmitted on 3 March 1854. Ship arrivals in Port Phillip Bay were relayed to Melbourne, where they were posted on a board in the Customs House.

Meanwhile, work began on another exciting new infrastructure project: the colony's first railway line between Sandridge (now known as Port Melbourne) and Melbourne city. By September, steam locomotives were hauling cargo along the line.

The first telegraph and steam trains arrived in Melbourne in the same year. It really must have felt as if they were living in the Age of Wonders.

McGowan commenced work on a telegraph line to Geelong, which he completed in November. Around that time, trouble was brewing on the goldfields, culminating in the Eureka Rebellion in Ballarat, which was brutally quelled by soldiers and police in a violent confrontation. According to legend, the first message transmitted from Melbourne to Bendigo was a report about the Eureka Rebellion. That's possible, but unlikely. It's certainly true that the line was operational by then, but it did not open for business until early the following year, because the station house had not yet been built and fitted out.[4]

McGowan was given the position of 'Chief Telegraphist' for the colony. As a public servant, the problems of raising capital were gone. He found himself showered with funds from politicians who wanted him to succeed.

From Geelong, McGowan built a branch line to Queenscliff near the entrance to Port Phillip Bay, allowing reports in Melbourne of ship arrivals before they even entered the bay.

Within three years, under McGowan's energetic supervision, Victoria was criss-crossed by a network of profitable telegraph lines, stretching from Portland to Wodonga. The pricing was based on the length of the message, and the distance it was sent. For a transmission of ten miles or less, it cost 1 shilling and sixpence per word; but the cost rose steeply for long distances. Annual revenue in the third year of McGowan's burgeoning empire was an impressive £5500.[5]

The other colonies were paying attention. They were not only remote from the rest of the world, they were remote from each other, and even from their outlying settlements. Isolation was a disease and telegraph was the cure. They all wanted their own Samuel McGowans.

The South Australian Governor wrote to the Colonial Office in London, requesting that they send someone of suitable calibre to build a telegraph line between Adelaide and its port, just as McGowan had done in Melbourne.

Enquiries were made in London. The man they chose to send had just as much ability as Samuel McGowan—and he had even bigger, crazier dreams.

3

Charles and Alice

Cambridge, England, mid-nineteenth century

Charles Todd had not been the first choice for the job.

The Governor's letter made its way around the world by ship to England. On receiving it, the Secretary of the Colonies consulted England's Chief Astronomer, George Airy, about whom to appoint. Airy and the secretary received at least one knockback from a formal offer and other promising candidates may have also declined informally. For prominent scientists, the idea of moving to a far-flung little outpost of the Empire was not exactly appealing. But Charles Todd had the right mix to both receive an offer and to accept it: he was young, brilliant and ambitious.

Born in 1826, Todd was the son of a grocer and had grown up in Greenwich, where the British Observatory happened to be located. Each year, George Airy would visit the local schools to recruit a handful of mathematically gifted male students to work at the observatory as 'computers'. These boys were human computers—the modern machines we call computers were a long way off. Todd was selected, freeing him from having to make hard decisions about his future career. If he had not been selected, there were two main choices: either help in his father's grocery business or become a sailor. His older brother Griffith had joined the merchant marine; he lived the hard life of a sailor and died in Calcutta at the age of 36, leaving behind a widow and four children.[1]

So at the age of fourteen, he started working at the British Observatory. He and the other boys calculated astronomical data with pencils and paper, working seven days a week, twelve hours a day during summer, and eight hours a day during winter. Britain was a great seafaring nation. For centuries, it projected its power across the waters of the globe. For centuries, its men built countless ships in which they explored, fished, hunted whales, hauled cargo, traded, colonised, and conquered. The ship was the engine of the British Empire.

Therefore, the science of navigation was critical. For Britain, astronomy was not just about scientific curiosity. It was part of the machinery of commerce and war.

As well as studying the stars and planets, the British Observatory was also the nation's weather bureau and its official timekeeper. Airy's boys took hourly measurements of thermometers and rain gauges, recorded the positions of celestial bodies, and oiled the gears of clocks and astronomical devices.

Todd rose through Airy's hierarchy of acolytes. When he completed his apprenticeship in 1848, he moved to Cambridge to work as an assistant astronomer at the Cambridge Observatory. One of his responsibilities was maintaining the imposing machinery of the famous Northumberland telescope. He gained a reputation for trustworthy calculations and, although he was neither a student nor a member of the faculty, his contributions were acknowledged in scholarly publications.

Three years before Todd's arrival in Cambridge, a rail line had opened, connecting this picturesque little town to London, and the locals were still adjusting to the influx of city day-trippers. Steam engines were leviathans of the English countryside, hauling towns and villages into the modern age. And running alongside every rail line was a telegraph line. These engineering wonders travelled like twin prophets over hill and dale, proclaiming the arrival of the future.

Through his church, Todd met the Bell family and seems to have courted their daughter, Charlotte. The Bells, like the Todds, were not wealthy. They lived by the fish market in the business district, where Mr Bell was a seed seller. Mrs Bell was a bonnet maker. Todd gave

Charlotte a Bible as a present, with the inscription 'To Charlotte, from her sincere friend'. And as further evidence of courtship, on the evening of the 1851 Census, Charles was visiting Charlotte and her parents.[2] By then, the Bells had moved to a house in Free School Lane, a district where tradesmen and students lived, and they had a young woman living with them as a servant. Having a servant was hardly the sign of wealth and status that modern depictions of the time suggest. Orphans and rural poor abounded in Victorian England; servants were so cheap that even humble households could afford them.[3]

His own family had moved to London, his father now working as a bookkeeper. They had adopted a presumably orphaned girl named Sophia. Two of his sisters, Mary and Elizabeth, were mistresses at a small boarding school for girls. They lived on the premises and Mary's husband lived there too. Charles somehow arranged for the Bells' daughter Alice to attend the school where his sisters worked. There she learned reading and writing, French, piano and dance. Charles gave her a religious instruction book, ostensibly to encourage her to read, but probably to impress her parents and particularly her older sister Charlotte. While Alice boarded in London, Charles sent her books from time to time, inscribing them 'To Alice Gillam Bell, from her friend Charles Todd', and later, 'from her admirer, Charles Todd'. Who paid for Alice's education is a mystery, but Charles was the link to the school.[4]

In that same year, a deadly wave of cholera swept through Cambridge, killing nineteen-year-old Charlotte, just as previous cholera outbreaks had killed five of Charlotte's brothers and sisters. Her parents returned the Bible to Charles, perhaps as a memento of her.[5]

In 1851, the first World's Fair was held in London. The Great Exhibition of the Works of Industry of All Nations was claimed to be Prince Albert's idea, but it was really the brainchild of a brilliant public servant named Henry Cole. A colossal glass structure called the Crystal Palace was erected in Hyde Park and became home to a panoply of displays of science, engineering, art and artifacts of nations and cultures around the world. Cheap entry tickets and access by rail allowed the public to attend in droves.[6]

The opening ceremony in May was attended by Queen Victoria herself. By the time a choir sang Handel's 'Hallelujah' chorus at the closing ceremony in November, more than six million people had visited the Crystal Palace, including virtually all the luminaries of the age: Charles Darwin, Charles Dickens, Karl Marx, Emily and Charlotte Brontë, and others.

Afterwards, the Crystal Palace—which had become a symbol of Victorian England, the high-water mark of an empire and its culture—was dismantled and carefully reconstructed in Sydenham Hill in south-east London. When it burned to the ground in 1936, a crowd of a hundred thousand people flocked there to watch. Winston Churchill lamented, 'This is the end of an age.'

George Airy, the Royal Astronomer and Todd's former boss, attended the Great Exhibition, where there were numerous displays of scientific advances, including telegraphy. One display that piqued his interest was a system for using a telegraph wire to drop a time ball. That innovation meant that time signals could be sent instantaneously from Airy's observatory in Greenwich to other parts of the country.[7]

There were already a few time balls in England, including one above Greenwich Observatory itself. This huge black sphere was impaled on a vertical pole. Each afternoon, as one o' clock approached, the time ball would be cranked by pulley to the top of the pole, then, at 1 p.m. exactly, it would drop. Anyone with a line of sight, including nearby anchored ships, could watch for the drop to synchronise their clocks. With the invention he saw at the Crystal Palace, Airy planned a network of time balls across England that could all drop at exactly the same time: Greenwich Time.

The first step was to synchronise the Greenwich Time Ball with the timekeeping apparatus inside the observatory. This was done in 1852, allowing the public access to true 'Greenwich Time'. Next, Airy needed to synchronise the observatories, so he contacted the head of Cambridge Observatory, James Challis, to assign someone to test the system at their end of the line. Challis assigned Todd, who had lately been responsible for maintaining his timekeeping devices and also the batteries that powered them (batteries were another emerging technology). Todd performed so well that Airy poached him back from Cambridge and placed him in charge of establishing the time signal system.

The next step was to link the observatory with a time ball in Deal, a nearby harbour town. The Deal time ball commenced operation in 1855, but harsh mid-winter weather quickly put it out of action. Arriving by train to troubleshoot, Todd found the mechanism encrusted in ice. He fetched a bucket of seawater and splashed it over the battery terminals and the time ball began working again.

Meanwhile, Airy had been asked by the Colonial Office to recommend someone for the South Australian post; after a fruitless search elsewhere, he approached Todd. When Airy's message reached him, Todd was staying in Tunbridge, partway along the line, stuck there due to the ongoing bad weather and suffering a cold. The message said that he had been offered the role of Chief Telegraphist for the British Colony of South Australia; an answer was required immediately. Todd replied the next morning, asking for two days' leave, because he wanted to consult 'a valued friend at Cambridge' before responding.[8]

That 'valued friend' is sometimes claimed to have been Alice Bell, but was probably James Breen, First Assistant Astronomer at Cambridge Observatory, who had mentored Todd at both Cambridge and Greenwich. Breen and Todd were assistant astronomers, lived next to each other at the observatory, and were close friends. Whoever it was, Todd returned to Cambridge, consulted with his friend, then accepted the position.[9]

When he signed his employment contract at the Colonial Office in London on 22 February, his pending salary as Colonial Astronomer and Telegraphist was listed at a whopping £400 per year, plus free transport to Australia, plus free accommodation. It was more than six times his current salary and, for that matter, more than six times his father's income as a shopkeeper. Indeed, he would be one of the twenty highest paid officials in the colony, earning the same as the Colonial Surgeon and almost as much as the Chief of Police (although only a fraction of the Governor, whose stipend of £4000 put everyone else in the shade).[10]

He visited the Bell household. According to Bell family lore, Mrs Bell asked Todd whether he planned to marry anyone before his mid-year departure. Todd replied that he knew of no one who would be willing to accompany him to Australia. At that moment, Alice, who was now seventeen and who had been eavesdropping, appeared and said, 'I will go with you, Mr Todd.'[11]

Todd was ten years older than Alice, but he accepted her unorthodox proposal.

Hasty arrangements were made. Charles Todd and Alice Bell (henceforth Alice Todd) were married in the Cambridge Baptist church on St Andrews Street on 5 April 1855, only three months before their departure in July.[12]

George Airy fretted that Todd might not be up to the job. In a private letter, he worried whether Todd 'had the boldness and independence of character which may be required in an Australian establishment'.[13] But his worry was unfounded. Todd's charter was quite modest: all they wanted him to do, apparently, was to build a telegraph line between the city of Adelaide and its port. For him, this was simple stuff, having built a much longer line between Greenwich and Deal. He was already planning way beyond that. He wrote to

Captain Charles Sturt, retired explorer of the Australian inland, expressing a hope for an international telegraph network: 'I look forward to the time when the telegraph system will extend to join the several seats of commerce in Australia and also, it is no idle dream in the present age of wonders, where I shall be able to . . . [connect] Asia by submarine cable thence via Calcutta and London.'[14]

But Todd had not yet set foot on the Australian continent and no white man—perhaps no person at all—had ever crossed the interior from coast to coast. These visions of a grand telecommunications highway were based on nothing more than a map, on which most of the continent's interior was blank.

4

Battle Lines

Adelaide, 1855

The journey to Adelaide aboard the steamship *Irene* took three-and-a-half months. They sailed down the west coast of Africa, around the Cape of Good Hope, across the Indian Ocean to Perth and then on to Adelaide. Neither Charles nor Alice had travelled beyond England before this. Charles enjoyed taking his own navigational readings and comparing his results with those of the ship's captain.

Before leaving England, Todd had recruited an assistant named Edward Charles Cracknell, who was also aboard with his heavily pregnant wife. She gave birth during the voyage, but their newborn baby boy died before reaching Adelaide. Alice was also pregnant.

They arrived at the Port of Adelaide on Sunday, 4 November 1855. They could see the tops of the handful of taller buildings in the city, about seven miles inland, the entire distance of the proposed telegraph line Todd was supposed to build. The *Irene* was stuck offshore for five days, waiting for favourable tides to take it across the shallow water to the landing. Apparently, a channel-deepening project was in the works, but for now, the larger ships had to navigate the inlet on the whim of the tides. While the passengers and crew waited, Adelaide reporters came aboard. Todd commented later, it was 'quite a relief to see fresh faces'.

Todd's arrival caused quite a fuss. In a letter to Alice's parents, he boasted, 'I have been well received by the Governor and Heads and am, I assure you, quite an aristocrat here.'[1]

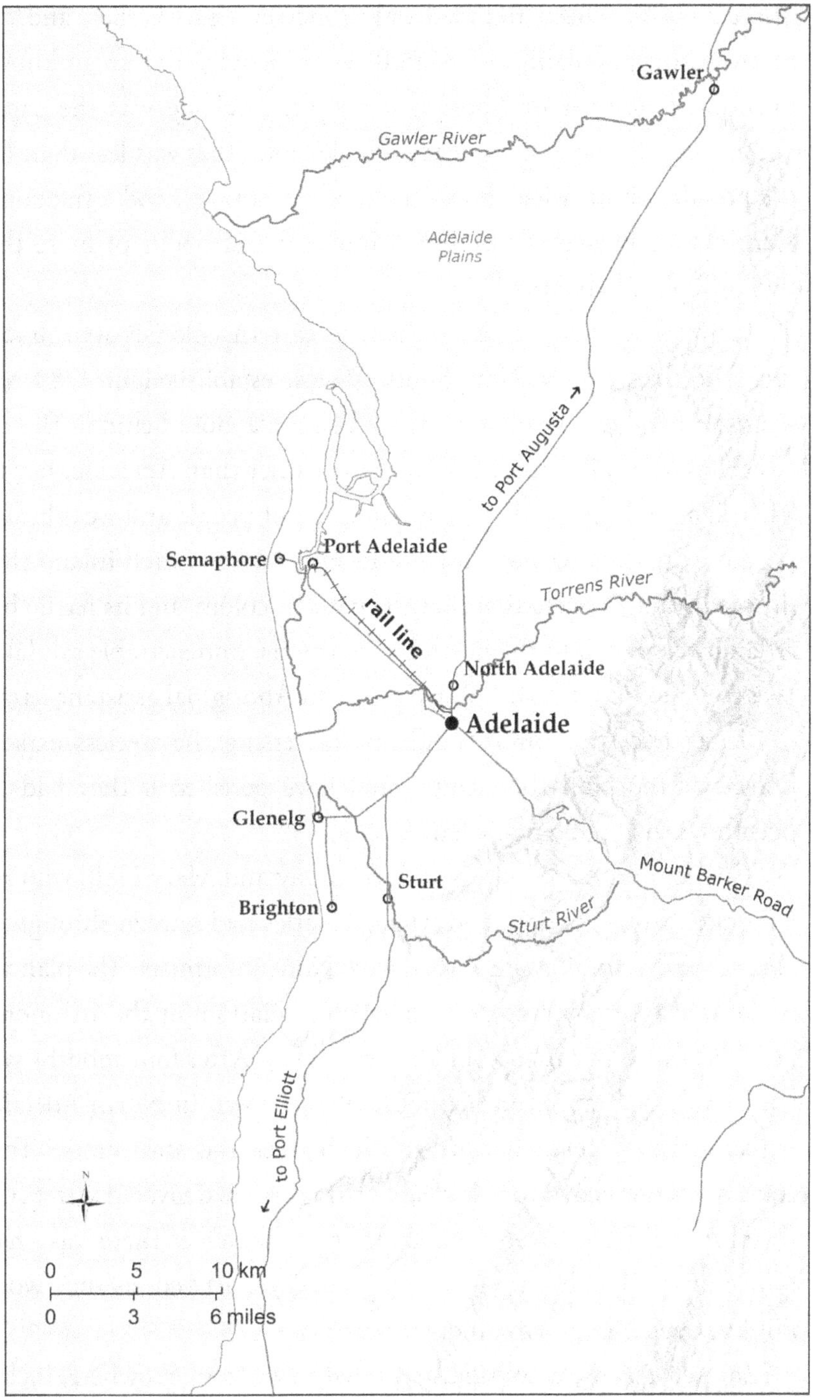

Adelaide and hinterland in 1865

The colony had been founded only nineteen years earlier, and currently had a population of 85,000 white people, and an unknown, uncounted number of Aboriginal people. Adelaide was the capital and largest city, with a population of 18,000. That was less than half the population of Alice's home town of Cambridge, and a fraction of Charles's birthplace of London, a bustling metropolis of more than two million inhabitants.[2]

Compared to South Australia, the eastern colonies were booming. The first colony, New South Wales, established in 1788, had almost a fifty-year head start, with Tasmania close behind. The city of Melbourne was founded only a year earlier than Adelaide, but the Victorian gold rush had brought an influx of people and wealth.

An early explorer named Edward Eyre had ventured inland three times, dismally concluding that the nascent colony and its fertile hinterland was ringed to the north by enormous, impenetrable salt lakes. West was no better. In 1840, Eyre and an Aboriginal assistant named Wylie set out west towards Albany, traversing the treeless expanse known as the Nullarbor, and would have perished if they had not been rescued by a French whaling ship.

Charles and Alice lodged with Anthony and Mary Hall, who had emigrated from London, and whom Charles had known through his church, and who, like the Todds, were Nonconformists. The plan was to construct an observatory with accommodation for the astronomer and his family, but that would be years away. After four months with the Halls, they moved into a house of their own in North Adelaide. It had a large yard with vines and fruit trees and ants' nests.[3] There was no town water supply. Instead, water carriers delivered water from the nearby Torrens River to Adelaide homes for a fee. There was a half-built railway line, but no locomotives had yet arrived, as they would not be needed for at least another year.[4]

In each colony, newspapers reported news from elsewhere, including from the other colonies, from newspapers they received by ship. The biggest news story was the Crimean War. In response to fears of Russian aggression, some locals had formed a volunteer regiment named the Adelaide Marksmen, to defend South Australia from Russian forces.[5] Melbourne and Sydney newspapers often ran a column titled 'South Australia'. On more than one occasion, in Melbourne's *Argus*, readers were treated to a terse summary: 'A few Adelaide newspapers to the 24th ultimo have come to hand, but the news is not very interesting.'[6]

However, something interesting *had* happened while the Todds were en route from England: a local entrepreneur had built a telegraph line from the city to the port. Its creator, an energetic 23-year-old, James MacGeorge, had cheekily opened it, with much fanfare, on the day of Todd's arrival. He had announced the project while the Todds were sailing down the coast of Africa aboard the *Irene*. MacGeorge's plan was controversial because this was what Charles Todd had been appointed to build.

One pro-MacGeorge newspaper, the *Register*, was scornful of the objections: '"The Government is going to set up a telegraph itself." Exactly so; it has been "going" to do so for the last two years. But has it done so? Where is the zeal?' If MacGeorge wants to do it, suggested the editor of the *Register*, 'what possible harm could setting up a few posts do?'

As a priority, Todd inspected MacGeorge's line and was unimpressed. The poles were mostly thin, rough saplings, still covered in bark, haphazardly stuck in the ground. The insulators were old and brown; obviously second-hand. And the line had only one wire with one rudimentary telegraph device at each end, meaning that messages could be sent in only one direction at a time. It was the bare minimum needed to rig something up and call it a telegraph line. It was almost as if it had been done in a rush, before Todd could start his own line. It was almost as if it was done to embarrass him.[7]

MacGeorge petitioned parliament to prevent Todd from constructing a line in competition with his own, but parliament went into recess over the Christmas period, so his petition was not tabled until mid-January. His cause was championed by the politician John Hart, a former whaler and staunch anti-tax conservative who believed that 'the only duties of parliament [are] to protect the country from foreign aggression or internal disorders, and provide for the administration of justice and the protection of property'. Hart despised government intervention of any kind and believed that Charles Todd should never have been appointed.[8]

Within a few weeks of arriving, Todd commenced construction of his own line. He intended to integrate his service with the city–port railway under construction, just as telegraph and rail worked hand in hand back in England, so his telegraph line followed the rail line. Poles were planted and wires strung.

One summer night, vandals cut the line and dragged the wires some distance away. The following night, a different section was sabotaged. This happened for several nights in a row, each attack occurring on a different part of the line. The attacks stopped for a while, then one night a few weeks later, wires from both Todd's line and MacGeorge's line were cut and entangled together. Nobody was ever charged.[9]

As a publicity stunt, MacGeorge hosted a chess game by telegraph, with one player at the city terminal in Green's Exchange and the other at the port.[10]

Todd engaged in some public relations of his own. A bazaar was held in the recently constructed city railway station to raise money to build a church. Todd and Cracknell set up an exhibition of a telegraph line, sending messages to each other across the room for the curious onlookers.[11]

Due to other pressing business, parliament did not consider MacGeorge's petition to stop Todd until late January. When they did, to their astonishment, they learned that the issue was moot. While they had all been lazing around on long summer holidays, Todd had been busy. His telegraph line—*their* telegraph line—was finished, and would be open for business in a fortnight. It was too late to stop him.

He had done this while working with a bureaucratic millstone. The Colonial Office had instructed him to build two sections of the line underground, encased in gutta-percha (high-quality Indian rubber). Todd said later:

> These underground wires, for which there was no necessity, added very greatly to the cost, and were very soon an endless source of trouble, as indeed were all the underground wires laid in England about this time, owing to the insulation becoming defective, and they were ultimately abandoned.[12]

A reporter noted wryly, 'During the intervening weeks the second telegraph had been erected with a promptitude most unusual in Government undertakings . . .'[13]

Todd did not mess around. Less than four months after stepping ashore, he had overseen the construction of a public telegraph line between the city and the port. It officially opened for business on 19 February 1856, with the telegraph offices based at the railway stations at each end. The first train would not run for another month, but Todd was already putting the rail line to good use. The charges were sixpence for twenty words, with additional costs for hand-delivering the message to its recipient, and further costs for boat hire if the recipient was on a ship at port.[14]

Todd had trained several fourteen-year-old boys as telegraphists; they were the same age as he had been when he entered the workforce. His instruments were Henley's magnetic system. Where the line went through sandy soil, Todd ran it through metal pipes, and closer to the port, it briefly went underwater, encased in gutta-percha, as per his instructions from London.[15]

While MacGeorge fired off outraged letters to local newspapers, Todd kept quiet. His only foray into the public debate was to highlight his assistant Edward Cracknell's contribution. He wrote to the *Adelaide Observer*, complaining about a recent article of theirs:

> . . . no mention is made of that gentleman to whose zealous and active co-operation I am so much indebted for the progress that has been made. Had it not been for his assistance in the constant superintendence of the works I could not possibly have carried them on so quickly, and at the same time trained a staff for the instruments.
>
> In making this public acknowledgement, I am but doing justice to Mr Cracknell.[16]

John Hart proposed that the colony should compensate MacGeorge for the wrong done to him by Todd's work, and that it should offer to purchase his telegraph line. The motion was defeated, on the ground that governments should not bail out private business: a sentiment that surely Hart agreed with, even if he would not admit it.[17]

The spirited MacGeorge protested to all and sundry that he loved his creation and would not part with it for all the money in the world. He declared, 'I am so well satisfied that no sum likely to be offered by the government would induce me to relinquish it.'[18]

It can't all have been a coincidence. Whatever MacGeorge's funding arrangements were, his telegraph line certainly looked like a plan to embarrass Todd or even to bring him down. Maybe Todd's opponents thought they were dealing with an effete Cambridge scholar who would wilt and buckle and return home in disgrace. If so, they guessed wrong. Todd had no intention of packing his suitcases. Here was someone who grew up watching his parents struggle for every penny; who had worked hard since the age of fourteen; for whom sixty-hour or even eighty-hour working weeks were a normal part of life; who had rest days only on Sundays; and for whom a month-long Christmas holiday break simply did not compute.

MacGeorge was charging one shilling for twenty words. Todd undercut him, charging half that rate: only sixpence for twenty words (in old British currency there were twelve pence in a shilling, and twenty shillings in a pound). MacGeorge lowered his prices to match Todd's.

MacGeorge's defenders were livid. One letter writer to the *Register* complained:

> The object of the Government *appears* to be to compel Mr MacGeorge to shut up; if so, it is a most unworthy one. Governments can seldom compete successfully with private enterprise, and I think I may add they can never do so with fairness to the community at large. Why should the revenue of a country be made to suffer to enable its government to compete with private individuals?[19]

Was this true? Was Todd bleeding the colony's coffers in a vengeful quest to bankrupt an honest businessman?

The difference between the two lines was stark. It was not just the choice of technology (MacGeorge used American systems whereas Todd employed British); the difference in quality was apparent just by looking. That was to be expected, though, because Todd's line had been generously bankrolled by the government, whereas MacGeorge had funded his line himself or with the help of unknown backers. But Todd's was better also because Todd had previous experience and knew much more about telegraphs.[20]

MacGeorge upped the stakes. He announced his intention to extend his line from the city to Gawler Town, twenty miles further north, only to learn that Charles Todd had already lodged plans with the Surveyor-General to build a line to Gawler Town and Dry Creek.

MacGeorge again aired his grievance in the media: 'I do not comment upon these circumstances, but I would ask—What is a legitimate field of enterprise for a private individual if the Government is to compete with him at every step he takes?'[21] To win hearts and minds, he opened his city office to the public in March, displaying new equipment based on 'Morse's American principle' imported from America and modified by local engineers for his rather rudimentary telegraph.[22]

The news editors were on his side. The *Observer* suggested that the real reason that Todd was extending his line was that Todd and Cracknell had been brought out from England on salaries of £400 and £225 respectively, and they needed something to do.[23]

On learning of MacGeorge's expansion plans, the *Adelaide Times* editor wrote, 'We wish him every possible success.'[24] This was on the heels of a hit piece on Todd, published in the same paper:

> **The Cheap and Nasty Telegraph**
> The Government Magnetic Telegraph, like all the Government undertakings, is earning for itself an unenviable notoriety in the way of *bungling* . . . Thank goodness that MacGeorge's Telegraph is in good working order, or we confess we should have a feeling of insecurity very much augmented in considering the probability of a Russian or American fleet taking possession of our harbour some day . . . We do not wonder at such mistakes, when we hear that a parcel of boys do the duty which should devolve upon experienced and responsible persons.[25]

Todd pressed forward with his Gawler Town plan, again following the railway line under construction. He insisted that the telegraph was needed for safe, efficient rail. And here was his biggest advantage. The simple fact was that Todd knew how rail telegraph systems worked and MacGeorge did not. There were calls to put the Gawler Line project out to tender and to make Todd sell his wire stockpile to

MacGeorge, but those calls were unrealistic. Todd was the best person for the job. He pressed his case and the government relented.

Telegram boys, already a familiar sight in places like Paris, London, and New York, appeared for the first time on the streets of Adelaide. These messengers, usually teenaged boys, would deliver incoming telegraph messages (known as telegrams) to their recipients on foot. The service was later combined with the regular post for standard, non-urgent telegrams, but telegram boys were a feature of the city for decades to come.

The rivalry ended not with a bang, but with a whimper. The two lines operated in parallel for a year, then in February 1857, MacGeorge folded. He terminated his city office lease and sold his line to James Allen Jr, proprietor of the *Adelaide Times*. Allen's private line meant that he could get news faster and more efficiently from port than the other news editors.[26] But after nine months, Allen in turn put the line up for auction. Todd bought it for £80, then dismantled it, salvaging the wire, batteries and apparatus.[27]

James MacGeorge turned to architecture and civil engineering, where he prospered. Having emigrated from England with his family at the age of seven, he returned sixty years later to live out a long retirement in Kent.[28]

5

The Intercolonial Link

Adelaide and Melbourne, 1856

In Melbourne, Samuel McGowan was excited by Todd's arrival in the colonies and his early successes. He and Todd corresponded by mail, their letters travelling by mail steamer. They discussed the possibility for an intercolonial network that linked Adelaide, Melbourne and Sydney, starting with a link between their two homes of Melbourne and Adelaide.

Todd asked parliament for permission to visit McGowan in an official capacity so as to flesh out the plan, and was surprised by how resistant the politicians were. One politician suggested that surely there was no need to actually go and meet McGowan; couldn't Todd just write him a letter proposing a line, and see if the Victorians said yes?

Another asked, amid laughter, 'What need is there to send Mr Todd to Melbourne? Except to show what a *lion* we got, and what a *clever* man we have imported!'[1]

They mockingly suggested that, if they let him go, his brilliance would be seen by all; he would be poached and would never return. Another member of parliament lamented, 'It would a pity if, on arriving at Melbourne, our lion should be caged!'

Todd had also requested, via the Surveyor-General's Department, that £500 be allocated to survey a possible route between Adelaide and the town of Penola near the Victorian border. He was refused. What was the point, they asked, of outlaying all that money before the Victorians had even agreed to their end of the bargain? And what about funding the roads instead? Many roads in the colony became unusable after heavy rain; surely, they were a higher priority.

The politicians made him a counteroffer. They allocated him only £100 for the surveying and said that, if he wanted the route surveyed, he could do it himself. There was much scepticism that he was up to it. One politician said that Todd's very 'scientific' brain would not understand the bush. 'A scientific man might be in the vicinity of a tree, and never see it. In little hollows there might be found gum trees, etc., which a strictly scientific man, in a passing journey, would never see.'

Another said, 'There are plenty in the colony who can give him better information than his own eyes would.' That caused much chuckling, because they all knew that Todd wore spectacles.

Another said, 'It's spending money to show Mr Todd the way to Penola! It reminds me of the celebrated expedition of Mr Rawnsley!' More laughter.

The Rawnsley reference cut to the heart of the issue. Because, to be fair, the colonists of South Australia had suffered a string of bad appointments: incompetent yet well-connected men sent from London on bloated salaries, who did nothing, achieved nothing, and hated being here. Henry C. Rawnsley had been the worst. He had arrived from London in 1848 as the new Colonial Engineer, though he had no qualifications or experience in engineering. Nobody in Adelaide knew he was coming; his appointment was announced in the mailbag that was brought ashore from the same ship that brought him. Rawnsley was disdainful and sneering towards everyone and was such a bad boss that, when he called for tenders for public works, nobody applied. He got it into his head that he wanted to be an explorer, so he took a large survey expedition north.

The interior is a harsh and unforgiving place, where many have perished, but Rawnsley's expedition was in no danger. His party rode 150 miles through settled countryside to Mount Remarkable, known to be a difficult climb. Rawnsley and his entire expedition climbed the mountain—the high point of his career, both literally and metaphorically. He climbed the mountain so he could fix its latitude and longitude, even though this had previously been done by the explorer Edward Frome.

The view must indeed have been 'remarkable' on Mount Remarkable, because Rawnsley camped on the pinnacle. There he stayed for almost a month, while his staff clambered up and down, fetching water and provisions as he kept trying to calculate the latitude and longitude. Even if the coordinates were not already known (and they were), calculating them was something that a skilled surveyor could have achieved in a single afternoon.[2]

After four weeks, Rawnsley descended from the mount then roamed the countryside, camping with his retinue in safely explored locations, doing surveys and calculations that were of no use to anyone. Meanwhile, farmers needed surveying work to comply with regulations. They resorted to paying for private surveyors out of their own pockets. Pointed questions were asked. What, exactly, was Rawnsley doing out there? Nobody knew and, when he finally returned, he had no satisfactory answers. His famous expedition was such an appalling waste of time and money that there were calls to shut down the engineering department entirely.[3]

Yes, the older colonists had seen a few Rawnsleys in their time; in their eyes, Charles Todd was just one more of them. And how did he get the job, they wondered. Oh, so he was personally recommended by the Royal Astronomer? Well, lah-de-dah. Isn't it nice to have connections. John Hart complained that even a hundred pounds for Todd's survey scheme was too much. He protested:

> But it will do no good to send Mr Todd across the country, who has probably never travelled ten miles in the colony! Let the Government advertise for tenders for constructing the line, stating the points along the route through which the line must pass. Mr MacGeorge's Port line didn't cost £50 a mile, and he will doubtless be ready to contract to carry one to Penola for that sum.

But in the end, the parliament agreed to Todd's Victorian trip and allotted him £100 for a survey, which was not nearly enough.

Todd sailed from Port Adelaide on 9 July aboard the steamer *Burra Burra*, arriving in Melbourne three days later. But he could not simply meet with Samuel McGowan; there were protocols that were inflicted on him. First, he had to introduce himself to the Colonial Secretary of Victoria and present a sealed letter from the Governor of South Australia delegating to him the Governor's authority. The Colonial Secretary had then to introduce him to the trade minister, who in turn introduced him to McGowan, who had similarly been delegated to act on behalf of the Governor of Victoria. The two could then enter official discussions with each other.

They became instant friends and remained friends for life.

McGowan gave Todd a tour of the Melbourne telegraph office and then, over the following days, gave him a tour of Victoria's burgeoning network. They visited McGowan's first triumph, the short line that curled around the port to Williamstown, as well as a new line, even shorter, to the Melbourne docklands. They travelled along the line to Geelong and then to Queenscliff near the entrance of Port Phillip Bay. They visited other lines under construction, radiating from Melbourne into the regions like crooked spokes on a wheel, to the goldfield towns of Ballarat and Bendigo, with other lines planned to the north and west, in anticipation of links with Sydney and Adelaide.

McGowan showed Todd the latest American equipment and encouraged him to switch from the British Cooke–Wheatstone system to the Morse way. After all, if they were going to link their networks, they would need to use the same protocol, so someone had to change. Todd was persuaded and, on his return, transitioned his own network to Morse. McGowan also showed him an exciting new machine, developed in Germany, that could transmit messages in opposite directions along the same wire at the same time, halving the number of wires needed.

Through McGowan, Todd met a wire and insulation sales representative named Joseph Oppenheimer, with whom he struck up a friendship. The connection would prove useful, because Oppenheimer later became a major manufacturer of metal telegraph poles (known as 'Oppenheimer poles').[4] During Todd's stay, a Tasmanian official also visited McGowan to negotiate the laying of an undersea cable, connecting Tasmania to the mainland.

Over six weeks, the two friends designed an intercolonial network that connected Adelaide, Melbourne and Sydney. They still needed to convince politicians to provide money, of course.

On that, Victoria was no obstacle. McGowan was the darling of the political establishment and, besides, because Melbourne would be the hub of the network, Victoria would be a clear winner. Todd thought he probably could persuade his colonial masters, although it was far from certain. New South Wales might be a stumbling block, but they were not strictly needed: if necessary, Victoria and South Australia could link together without them.

Todd and McGowan wrote a joint report, urging their colonies to build this line. They concluded their report by expressing the hope that one day a telegraph line would connect Australia with the world. Their project, they hoped, was just the beginning: '[It is] a step in the direction of our ultimate telegraph communications, via India, with England, a scheme vast and difficult as it may appear, and really will, we doubt not, at no very distant date be carried out.'[5]

It was time for Todd to return to Adelaide. He explained to McGowan that he would not be returning by ship. Instead, he planned to sail only as far as Portland, then travel overland from there on horseback, to survey the proposed telegraph route. The South Australian police had provided a trooper, John Ewens, who would meet him there and accompany him to Adelaide.

Ewens discovered that Todd could not actually ride, so they spent two days at Portland, while Ewens gave Todd riding lessons on the beach. From there, it was a two-day ride to Mount Gambier, a small town across the border in South Australia, where they stayed for several days. During that time, Todd visited Penola to the north. Despite having been mocked that he 'needed to be shown the way to Penola', Todd believed that the inland road via Penola was unsuitable for the telegraph and his trip there confirmed his opinion. Instead, the Victorian line would connect at Mount Gambier and, from there, would lope along the coastline to a fishing village called Robe and then to Adelaide.[6]

There were three options for getting the line from Mount Gambier to Robe. First, there was an almost perfectly straight ridge along the coast; second, there was a horse-and-buggy track inland and parallel to the ridge; and third, a wide plain dotted with forests. Todd and Ewens investigated all three.

Todd chose the plain. The limestone ridge was too hard for sinking poles, and the horse-and-buggy track passed through gullies and rough forests. Admittedly, the plain was prone to flooding, but he believed that was less problematic than it seemed. He wrote in his report:

> A great part of the flat—I may say all—is underwater during the winter, and was so when I rode over it; but it is good holding ground, and seldom boggy. Beneath the surface, about two feet, there is a thin crust of limestone, and below that black sandy soil. There would be very little clearing required, and that principally consisting of short honeysuckles, whilst an abundant supply of posts—more than sufficient for the line to the Bay—could be readily obtained from the Mount Burr Ranges.[7]

On a single day during his explorations around Mount Gambier, Todd surveyed three mountains and a lake, achieving more in that one day than the incompetent Rawnsley had achieved in six months.

When they reached Robe, the horses were tired and Ewens was sick, so they were waylaid for a while.

After they resumed their journey, they crossed grassy plains and swamps, battled through thick scrub and climbed a ridge that gave them spectacular views of a string of coastal lakes. They tried to cross one lake by boat, but rain and gales forced them to go around it. Through all of this, Todd was measuring, noting and mapping where his telegraph line would run. The ideal terrain for a line was flat land. It needed to be easy to sink poles in, to have good timber nearby for cutting and making poles, and not require too much clearance of scrub. When they encountered unsuitable terrain, they would go on meandering detours, looking for better alternatives. Sometimes they would find a hidden valley thick with tall gums or a long, flat plain of good soil. They did this despite the warnings that Todd's 'scientific' brain would miss such things.

Sunburnt and dirty, Todd and Ewens rode into Adelaide on 2 October 1856, having covered more than a thousand miles since leaving Melbourne. Todd carried a set of survey maps he had created himself, of the south-eastern corner of the colony, with a proposed telegraph route marked on them. Before construction could start, the government would have to pony up for a proper, professional survey, as he had previously requested. They had given him a hundred pounds and had told him to do it himself, which he had, to the best of his ability. They could not refuse him now.

That crusty old sailor, John Hart, began to change his opinion of young Charles Todd: Hart recognised and respected a fighter. In years to come, he would become one of Todd's staunchest supporters.

6

Todd's Progress

South Australia, 1858

After Todd's impressive horseback survey of the route between Melbourne and Adelaide, £500 was provided for a detailed survey, plus £20,000 to build the South Australian section of the line. Morse equipment was ordered from America and timber from Tasmania.

In April 1857, Todd travelled with the survey team, pegging out the line to the border while, under Ed Cracknell's eye, construction from Adelaide began. In the same month, the Gawler railway station opened, fully integrating the telegraph into its operation.[1]

The line was optimistically predicted to be finished by Christmas, but Christmas came and went, and Todd was struggling with construction. His line traversed rough, unsettled terrain with few good roads and sparse villages. He was dealing with flood-prone plains, gnarly ridges and sections requiring underwater cables. The official opening had been gazetted for May 1858, but that had to be cancelled because the line was still incomplete. By June, construction was finished but the line was still not operational; test messages were occasionally transmitted with success, but failed more often than not.

Impatience was brewing. The *Register* informed its readers: 'The idea of an intermittent telegraph is, we believe, quite a novelty in electric communication, and will no doubt be duly appreciated wherever the marvel is stated.'[2]

Todd, at the fishing town of Robe on Guichen Bay, wrote a long apologetic explanation to the *Register*:

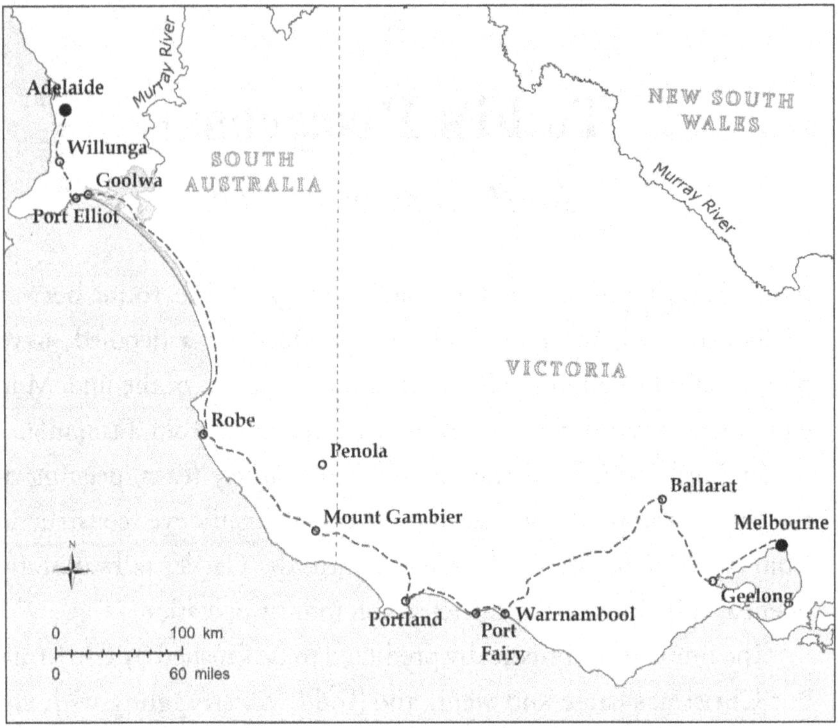

The Adelaide to Melbourne telegraph line, completed in 1858

> I am not at all surprised that either you or your readers should have become impatient at the—to you and them—inexplicable delay in the opening of the line, for which I am sure you will give me credit for regretting as much as yourself.
>
> I must, however, request you to suspend your judgment for a few days . . .
>
> Since I have been here the weather has been most unfavourable for telegraphic operations; high gales of wind, heavy rains, and strong currents of atmospheric electricity have frequently defeated all my plans, spoiled my tests, and rendered useless the hard labour of days . . .[3]

He was also bewildered by the faltering battery signals. The line was possibly being earthed somewhere, draining the voltage, but, if so, he did not know where.

The editor of the *Register* doubled down, castigating Todd's tardiness and mocking his excuses:

> Almost every journal we receive wonders what is the matter, and even the Governor of Victoria rates us for our slowness. Now, however, the mystery is out. On our side of the border we succumb to no vulgar obstacles like fallen posts or severed wires—the mysterious forces of nature alone can appal and overcome us. Mr Todd is the sport of the elements. Storms assail him, rains labour to extinguish him, currents of atmospheric electricity purposely thwart his purposes.[4]

Todd installed a repeating station at Mount Gambier to try to solve the weak signal problem and tested the line voltage at various points, particularly the terminals of the underwater cables.[5]

Dissatisfied with Todd's efforts, the government sent a telegraphist, Mr Towler, to investigate the problems, with instructions to report to the Commissioner of Public Works, bypassing Todd. Towler discovered a fault in the cable under the mouth of the Murray River at Goolwa. There were breaks in the gutta-percha, letting seawater in. That was the cause of the mysterious earthing.[6]

After troublesome repairs at Goolwa, and after a Melbourne telegraphist was despatched to operate the Mount Gambier station, the line was operational.

Melbourne's *Argus* reported the first telegraphic despatch from Adelaide on 19 July 1858. It was a big one: the explorer Augustus Gregory had arrived at Mount Hopeless in the Flinders Ranges, 360 miles north of Adelaide, having forged a path across the interior. There was an official opening ceremony at noon that Wednesday, with the Governor, Sir Richard MacDonnell, doing the honours.

The line operated perfectly all afternoon after the opening, but failed that evening. It was up and running again by 11 am the next day.

Four months later, a telegraph line joining Melbourne to Sydney was completed. Planning was underway for a cable across the Bass Strait to Tasmania (laid the following year), and an overland line from Sydney to Brisbane (completed three years later). Adelaide was linked to the eastern colonies.

There were more intermittent failures on the Adelaide-to-Melbourne line. In mid-December 1858, the cable between Hindmarsh Island and Mundoo Island, in the Coorong Lakes at the mouth of the Murray River, was swept down Holmes' Channel, causing a stoppage of several days. But after a shaky start, the line ran smoothly and became in indispensable asset.[7]

Several years later, Todd used the line to find the colony's eastern border. When South Australia was founded, planners in London defined the colony's borders with lines drawn on their maps with rulers. They decided that the eastern border, adjoining New South Wales and Victoria, should be the line of longitude at 141 degrees. Such a line is easy to point to on a globe, or on a map, but finding the physical place in the bush, and declaring it to be a point on an imaginary line, was harder.

Todd relied on his years of study and experience in astronomy. His technique could be roughly summarised this way: the position of certain objects in the sky was measured from two locations at the same time, one location being the border. He could then use slight differences in the measured angles to work out the exact distance between the two locations.

Surveyors had long before pegged out where they believed the border was, but Todd proved them wrong. The true border was about six-and-a-half miles east of where it had been marked.[8]

The monthly mail steamer from London came via Galle in Ceylon (now Sri Lanka), stopping at King George's Sound in Western Australia (near the town of Albany), then steaming across to Melbourne, bypassing South Australia. Previously there was a compromise arrangement:

the mail ship would visit Kangaroo Island on its way to Melbourne, where a courier ship would collect mailbags for Adelaide, but that system had ended in 1856 when London revised the arrangement, under pressure from Victoria. Melbourne was now the first colonial city to get the mail—and the news from the outside world—while Adelaide waited several more days for the delivery from Melbourne.

South Australia contracted a fast branch steamer to wait at King George's Sound, where it would collect mail and courier it directly to Adelaide, cutting the need for the roundabout Melbourne circuit. This gazumped the Victorians: Adelaide now got the news first, about 30 hours ahead of Melbourne. And because of the intercolonial telegraph, it could sell that news to the other colonies at a premium. Journalists from major east-coast papers such as the *Sydney Morning Herald* and the Melbourne *Argus* were posted to Adelaide, their job being to meet the branch steamer, scour the incoming news, then send stories eastwards as fast as they could.

The monthly arrival of the branch steamer was a commotion. The first Sydney or Melbourne paper to break a major story would clean up that day, so the pressure was on journalists to get the story first. They rented boats to intercept the branch steamer while it was still in harbour, begging the captain to give them their mailbag before anyone else. Journalists would devour letters and overseas newspapers as quickly as they could, then send them east from the telegraph station. Sometimes, in order to thwart their rivals, a journalist would block the line by telegraphing chunks of text from the Bible while they composed a story.

Adelaide the backwater had become Adelaide the colonial news hub.

7

The Race to Cable the World

1858–1862

The world-wide growth of the telegraph was phenomenal. It did not exist before 1837, but within twenty years, thousands of miles of cable criss-crossed the planet. The wires zigzagged above city streets, snaked along valleys, conquered mountain ranges, and dived along ocean floors. In Australia, the twin empires of Todd and McGowan spanned out, linking hands. A cable connecting Tasmania to Victoria was laid, then broke, was laid again, broke again, then laid again. Nascent networks edged forth from Sydney and Brisbane.

Parallel to this, the invention of the steam train was having a similar impact and the railways were growing at a similar rate. Telegraph and railroad marched outwards, connecting far-flung cities and towns and countries, making the world smaller.

It was only natural that, in Australia, people would want these technologies to conquer what later came to be called 'the tyranny of distance'. But there were unique challenges. The interior was unexplored and was uninhabited by white people. The fact that non-white people already lived there, and had done so for a very long time, was not considered to be a factor either way, unless those people proved hostile.

And the interior was, and is, harsh. The Aboriginal people there knew that surviving it required wit, tenacity, and millennia of tough lessons. White people had some lessons yet to learn.

In 1858, British entrepreneur Lionel Gisborne proposed a plan to connect Australia to Asia by undersea cable and thus to the world. In his pitch to the British Government, he described three sections.

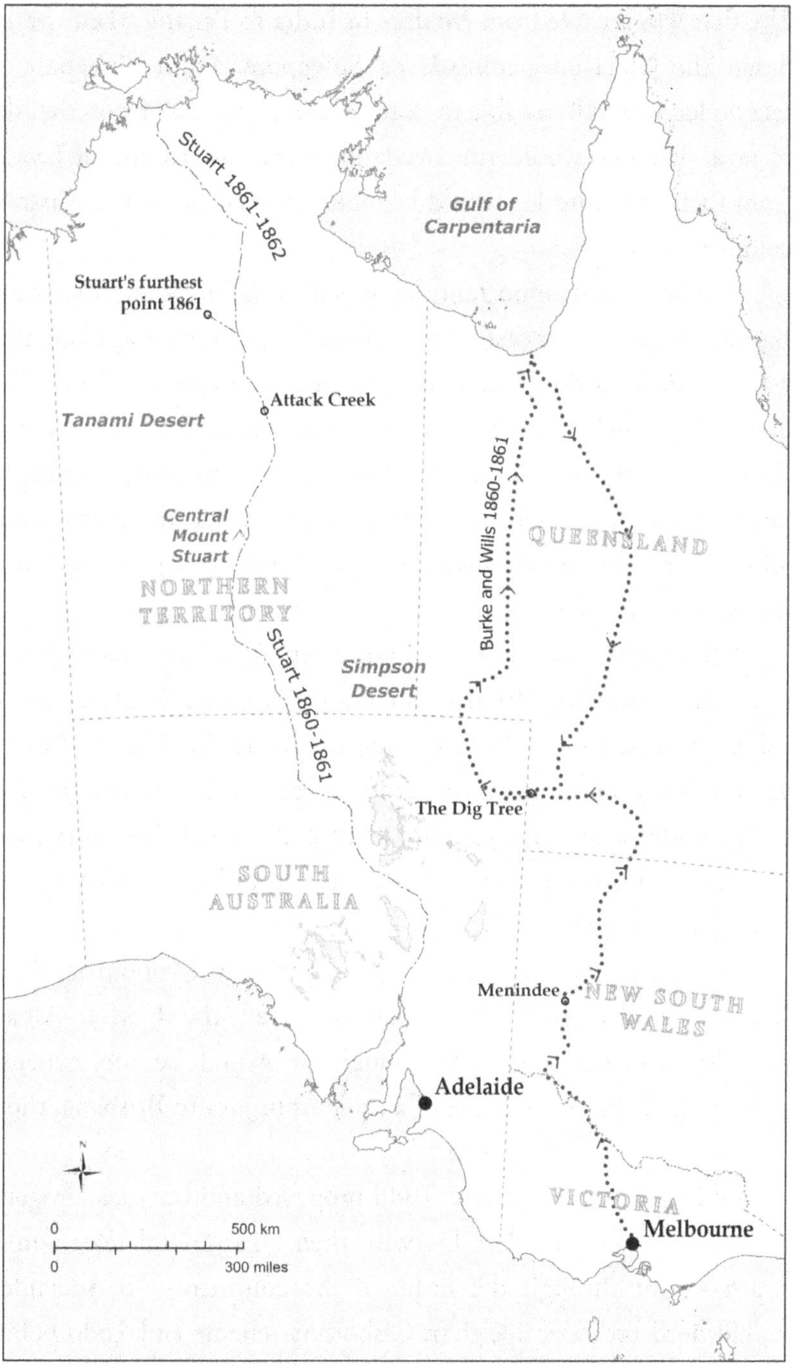

Routes taken by the expeditions of John McDouall Stuart and of Burke and Wills across the continent between 1860 and 1862

The first was a cable from Madras in India to Penang, then overland down the Malayan peninsula to Singapore. From Singapore, the second leg would be a cable to Batavia, the Dutch colony on the island of Java. The line would run overland to the eastern end of Java and from there the third leg would be an undersea cable to the Australian colonies.

This last, most important, leg was also the most ambitious: from Banjoewangie, on the eastern tip of Java, Gisborne envisaged an underwater cable into the Timor Sea, running through the Torres Strait down Australia's eastern coastline to Moreton Bay near Brisbane. Running for almost 3500 miles, it would cost a fortune, but Gisborne saw no obstacle in that, because he presumed that the cost would be jointly borne by private investors, the Dutch colony of Batavia and the Australian colonies.[1]

A rival consortium came to light. Brett and Carmichael, the team that had connected Britain and France with an English Channel cable, proposed a link from Ceylon to Albany in Western Australia via the Keeling Islands, and from there a cable across the Bight to Adelaide; a revival of a plan they had floated five years earlier. A variant on this idea was to lay a cable from Java to Albany, rather than from Ceylon.[2]

On this topic, Todd and his good friend in Melbourne, Samuel McGowan, disagreed. McGowan preferred the Ceylon–Albany–Adelaide scheme, but Todd thought it would be too expensive, preferring Gisborne's scheme of a cable from Java to Brisbane, though he had a proposal of his own.[3]

Adding to these options, Todd proposed another idea altogether: a cable from Java to Port Darwin, then an overland telegraph line south—right through the heart of the continent—to Adelaide. It would need far less cable than Gisborne's scheme and Todd believed it would be a quarter of the cost; moreover, the line might, in time, become a trade route for exporting horses to India.

If it had been proposed even two years earlier, Todd's plan would have sounded suicidal, due to Eyre's discovery of a ring of salt lakes to the north of Adelaide. Since then, there had been a number of miserable expeditions, the most striking by Captain Sturt, who was so confident he would find an inland sea that his expedition took a boat. Instead, he and his party became stranded for months in an arid wasteland and were lucky to return alive.

But recent expeditions had shed new light on the interior. The explorers Babbage, Warburton, Gregory and Stuart had all, in 1858, charted passages beyond the salt plains, finding waterholes along the way, and had found pockets of fertility far inland. Some of these were watered by springs fed by the Great Artesian Basin, a vast reservoir that had formed over millions of years under the Australian continent, accumulating water from the mountain ranges on the Queensland coast far to the east.

The most significant of these explorers was John McDouall Stuart, who had been a surveyor in Captain Sturt's dismal 1844 expedition. Stuart was a small, wiry, wizened Scottish orphan with a penchant for the bottle. After gaining a surveying qualification, he had emigrated to South Australia, where he lived in remote huts and drank to excess, until his talent for surveying and exploration was discovered by two Adelaide businessmen.[4]

Some claim that Stuart was the greatest of all Australian explorers, and perhaps he was. His methods were radical. He did not take large retinues of assistants or wagons, or even tents. Sometimes he had just one travelling companion, and they would sleep under the stars or clouds or rain. When leaving for a journey of several months, he would pack enough food for only a few weeks, and hunt along the way. His journals were similarly sparse and were merely an adjunct to his excellent mapmaking.

In pushing for an overland route, Todd cited these discoveries, and particularly those of Stuart, as reason for hope:

> [An overland telegraph] has naturally enough obtained advocates in South Australia, where our hopes have been raised by the discovery of valuable country by messrs Stuart, Babbage and Warburton; and the confident tone assumed by those explorers of its extension northwards; but nowhere else am I aware of its being regarded with similar favour—perhaps, owing to the generally prevailing belief of the desert character of the whole interior.
>
> Having had occasional conversations with the three gentlemen I have just named, I do think it probable that an overland route will ultimately be found practicable; and while I am writing, Mr Stuart's return to Adelaide, after having crossed (as I hear) our northern boundary, and found available country still stretching to the north, confirms my opinion in this respect; and I would recommend that Mr Gisborne should immediately be placed in possession of the results of Mr Stuart's explorations.[5]

It was a strong pitch. He reassured doubters that more exploration would have to happen first and a viable pathway found:

> I do not wish it to be understood that I am advocating a line across a desert; it is only on its being shown to traverse country available for settlement that I recommend its adoption.

Governor MacDonnell urged parliament to fund an expedition to send Stuart north, so that he could find a track through the interior. New South Wales and Victoria were approached to co-sponsor the expedition, but they declined, and the project was shelved for the time being.[6]

In November 1858, a meeting was held in Melbourne for concerned citizens who wanted to support exploration that could lead to an overland railway and telegraph across Australia. This push would soon lead to the disastrous Burke and Wills expedition.

A correspondent to *The Argus* urged the building of both an inland rail and a telegraph line, to bring harmony and cooperation:

> Lay down a tram line, and by its side, three feet below the surface, green glass pipes, cut in two lengthwise, into the lower half of which the cable could be laid, the upper half then being laid thereupon, and pinned by green glass bolts, the soil then covering it up, and the telegraph cable would be completely insulated and uninjurable.[7]

The South Australians tried a new tactic. Instead of bankrolling an expedition directly, in July 1859, they offered reward money for any explorer who could chart a track between Australia's north and south coasts. A proviso was that the winning track had to cross 'through the country lately discovered by Mr Stuart'. Stuart's track, of course, led back to Adelaide so, by insisting that any explorer claiming the prize had to cross his track, the government guaranteed that any discoveries would benefit South Australia. It would unlock the north for the colony.[8]

Stuart's backers, William Finke and James Chambers, eager to win the prize, financed him to go on an expedition to discover a track north.

Stuart departed his base camp at Chambers Creek on 2 March 1860, riding north. He was accompanied by his trusty companion, William Kekwick and a third man, Benjamin Head, plus thirteen horses. They crossed the invisible boundary between South Australia and the Northern Territory, becoming the first white people to do so. British colonists had drawn that line on the map many years earlier—it is completely straight because it was drawn with a ruler and a pencil—but none of them had actually been there. Until Stuart, Kekwick and Head rode across it, the border existed only as a concept, a thing unseen by the Aboriginal inhabitants of the area.

Stuart's party trudged across the vast, desolate interior, the landscape changing through the days and weeks under their horses' hooves. They encountered deserts, oases, grassy plains, dry riverbeds, and strange geological formations. They beheld a striking pillar of rock arising out of a flat plain. Stuart named it Chambers' Pillar after his benefactor and financier.

They came to a long, gnarly mountain range running east–west; Stuart reckoned it would be an obstacle to constructing a telegraph line. He named it the MacDonnell Ranges, after the Governor. He and his companions crossed over it without too much trouble, but they were lightly equipped and on horseback. It would be a different story for construction parties with bullock teams carting heavy loads.

Further north, Stuart arrived at what he calculated as the centre of the continent: this he defined as being the middle of the shortest line from north to south, intersected by a line between the easternmost and westernmost reaches.

From time to time, they encountered Aboriginal people. The responses they elicited varied: curiosity; astonishment; friendliness; timidity; fear. A primary source of fear often seemed to be the horses. For most of the journey, these interactions were peaceful and without incident.

But on 26 June 1860, about 320 miles north of the MacDonnell Ranges, they had a violent encounter with the Warumungu people. Stuart marked the location of the encounter with the name 'Attack Creek'. He gave up and returned south.

Six months later, Stuart's expedition arrived at an outlying settlement in the Flinders Ranges, where they were greeted with relief and excitement; until then, nobody had been sure if they were still alive. He sent a letter to James Chambers in advance of his arrival in Adelaide. Despite his failure to reach the northern coastline, he was now sure that a way through could be found and that a telegraph line was viable:

> I arrived here on the 17th inst. from a terrible journey in a very exhausted state, I am sorry to say that I have been unable to make the North West Coast. The difficulties have been more than I was able to overcome. After arriving at the Centre I was visited by that dreadful disease the Scurvey which completely prostrated me, and rendered me quite helpless, still I persevered and endeavoured to reach the mouth of the Victoria River on the North West Coast, but was beat back twice from want of water, the country into which I got on the first course was an immense plain of red light soil covered with nothing but spinifex and large Gum trees, not a blade of grass on it . . . I met with no desert but with three or four Mulga scrubs the broadest a little more than 60 miles, the ranges not higher than the Flinders range and many not near so high . . . The Telgraph could be laid down, there is no obstacal but what can be overcome as far as I have gone.[9]

In Stuart's absence, the Victorians had launched a rival expedition. A former police officer named Robert O'Hara Burke had departed from Melbourne with a large, well-funded expedition in August, bent on finding a track to the north coast.

The Victorians had introduced what they believed to be a game-changing innovation: camels. These had been imported by Burke's second-in-command, George Landells. Melburnians viewed them almost as a secret weapon in the race across the continent.

Burke was a colourful, larger-than-life personality, with plenty of experience of the Victorian bushlands, but he had never been an explorer. His backers believed that his brains and leadership ability would be sufficient to see him through. Unfortunately, the second of these was soon found wanting: in October, in the town of Menindee in New South Wales, he had a falling out with Landells, who quit and returned to Melbourne. To fill the vacancy, Burke promoted surveyor and scientist William Wills to be his new second-in-command.

The South Australians were alarmed, but they believed that they could still win. In March 1861, only six weeks after his return and with his health still not recovered, Stuart was again despatched north, with a bigger, better-funded expedition than he had ever had. This time, instead of two companions, he had a dozen men. They journeyed to Attack Creek and beyond uneventfully, but were thwarted by the endless scrublands and lack of water. They encountered more hostility from Aboriginal people near a place they named Newcastle Waters.

When they arrived back in outlying settlements in August, Stuart learned that Burke and Wills were missing.

Before long, news arrived that they were dead.

John McDouall Stuart might be the best of the Australian explorers, but Burke and Wills are the best known, for the opposite reason. They reached the northern coastline; or at least some wide marshy, mangrove swamps that adjoin the Gulf of Carpentaria. They did not see the sea, but they did taste salt water and knew that they had succeeded.

The problem was their return. They took longer than expected, which led the base camp to believe they had perished, so the base camp packed up and left.

Before doing so, the base camp buried some provisions in a trunk near a tree, and carved the word 'Dig' into the tree. This was a common trick for outback surveyors, as buried goods lasted longer and were hidden from Aboriginal visitors.

Burke and Wills, and their companion, John King, arrived at the depot on the same day that the base team departed. The two parties missed each other by a matter of hours. Burke and Wills found the Dig Tree, retrieved the supplies, then carefully reburied the trunk, despairing at having been abandoned. They were too weak to catch up with the retreating base team, so Burke made the foolish, fatal decision to strike south-west, hoping to reach Adelaide.

Several days later, members of the base team returned to the depot to check whether Burke and Wills had arrived after all. The ground near the Dig Tree appeared undisturbed, so they concluded that nobody had come. Days later, Wills returned to the depot alone, but there was no evidence that anyone had been there. Burke and Wills both perished on Cooper Creek. Their companion John King survived, living with the Yandruwandha people for several months.

History has not been kind to Burke and Wills. They have become the embodiment of effete, bumbling colonists, going where they didn't belong and suffering the consequences. British gents with an inflated view of their abilities, fatally out of their depth. But this historical judgement is too harsh. Yes, it's true that they departed Melbourne with grandiose pomp and they had a ludicrously over-provisioned expedition. And it is true that Burke made serious mistakes. But they learned and improved as they went, and they did actually reach the northern coastline. And furthermore, they beat to the punch that drunken magician of the outback, John McDouall Stuart. Moreover, after reaching the coast, they even made it back to their base camp.

The mix-up with the Dig Tree was tragicomical. If, instead of missing each other by hours, the two parties had found each other, the Burke and Wills story would be celebrated as a triumph over adversity.[10]

Stuart set forth on his final expedition on 23 October 1861. He and his party rode onto a beach in the Northern Territory at the mouth of the Mary River, not far from present-day Darwin, on 24 July 1862. Around the Roper River and further north to the coast they found running rivers and fertile land. Stuart was sick from scurvy, so sick that, for the last part of the journey home, the others carried him by a stretcher slung between two of the horses. They returned to much acclaim.

Stuart was partially blind from years of desert glare and his mind was wasted from years of drink. He returned to England, where he retired on a stipend generated from the reward money, and lived with a sister until his death in 1866.

8

Alice

Adelaide, 1858–1868

Charles's job had brought Alice into contact with the upper echelon of Adelaide society. Every May, the governor held a ball to celebrate the Queen's birthday, and Charles and Alice were always on the invitation list. Charles had a quirky, disarming sense of humour. Raising a cup of tea to his lips, he would quip, 'Without my tea (T), I would indeed be ODD.'[1]

But Alice, with her humble origins, felt out of place amid all the pomp. She was homesick. She wrote to her older sister, Sarah, admitting that she missed 'the dear quiet life of Cambridge'.

She complained to her sister that the Adelaide elite were 'stuck up . . . they think of nothing but dress and going out and giving parties . . . I much prefer being at home than going to the grand affairs at Government House.'[2] She preferred sitting in the garden with a book or picking fruit from the fruit trees. She and Charles had befriended Captain Bruce, skipper of the *Irene*, who had brought them to Adelaide, and they joined him aboard the *Irene* on occasion when it was in port.[3]

She was not a social butterfly. She had a few close friends, and the family home was the centre of her world.

She had given birth to their first child on 12 March 1856, a mere four months after disembarking from the *Irene*. This was Charlotte Elizabeth, who would be known as Elizabeth or Lizzie. Alice fell pregnant again the following year. She stumbled while picking almonds one day and was scared she would lose the baby, but Charles Edward Todd was born hale and hearty on 7 April 1858. There is a family story that one time when Elizabeth was minding her baby brother, she left him on an ant hill and was unperturbed by the swarm of insects crawling over his body. The little boy's screams of pain summoned Caroline, Alice's servant and friend, to the rescue.[4]

The terror of ants' nests aside, Adelaide was a safe and pleasant place to raise children. After having had five siblings die young in England, Alice could take comfort in the colony's universal vaccination program, which held the demons of disease at bay.[5]

Charles was away for long stretches. For three months, when he visited Melbourne and rode back, then long trips south to survey the intercontinental line, then build it, then troubleshoot it. It was a lonely existence, but not so bad: Alice had small children to keep her occupied, but she also had servants.

The family moved into the newly built observatory residence on West Terrace in May 1860, although construction of the observatory itself was still a work in progress. Two months later, she gave birth at home to their third child, Hedley.

She longed to see her family again. In 1862, she and Lizzie visited England, sailing there and back on the *Irene* with their friend, Captain Bruce. The two little boys stayed in Adelaide in the care of the nanny.

During their absence, Charles received a letter from Alice's sister Sarah:

> Dear Mr Todd,
>
> A few nights a go at 12 of the clock I heard the post chaise coming down the street and soon there was a knock at the door. Hardly waiting to put a wrap over his night-shirt, dear Papa hurried down, while Mama and I waited anxiously on the landing. 'Mama,' cried Papa. 'It is dear Alice and little Elizabeth!' 'No!' said Mama. 'Yes,' said Papa.[6]

Alice also caught up with Charles's family; she was close to his sisters, whom she had lived with and learned from at boarding school. Their older brother Griffith had died the previous year in Calcutta and his orphaned twelve-year-old daughter Frances had returned to

England. Alice decided to adopt her and bring her to Australia. There were no rules for adoption—and certainly no laws—but there were conventions, and the convention was that adopted children were, at least nominally, considered 'servants' rather than family members. That was the case for Frances. While this may gall modern sensibilities, it was a far better outcome for Frances than staying in Dickensian England, where orphans crowded the streets and died by the thousands. Frances's older brother, Griffith junior, followed her to Australia a few years later, to also live under the Todds' roof.

Alice's father died in 1866 and her sister, Sarah Squires, who had been living with their parents, died two years later. Sarah's husband had abandoned her, for reasons unknown, but he became a pauper and eked out his life in charity houses. Alice's older brother Edward was an up-and-coming businessman who had no interest in supporting his parents or other relatives. The upshot of all of this was that Alice's mother found herself the sole guardian of Sarah's boy William (Alice's nephew).[7] Unable to support herself and William, Mrs Bell packed their belongings, and she and her grandson boarded a ship to Adelaide.

In addition to their own large and growing family, the Todds were now supporting three orphans (Frances, Griffith and William), Alice's elderly, ailing mother, and Caroline the maid. The family was also seduced by the beaches and by the local custom of long summer holidays in nearby beach towns. Alice and the children and the maids would pass the long, languid summers in Port Elliot, a little seaside town about fifty miles south of Adelaide.[8]

The Todds had a strange sort of life. Charles's salary was substantial. They lived in a mansion, with servants and assistants; their children went to good schools; they attended all the very best functions of high society; they were public figures and expected to dress the part. Yet Alice fretted about the costs involved, because their income was consumed by mouths to feed and appearances to keep.[9]

Sunday church was a major weekly event. She wrote to her sister: 'Every Sunday morning we get up early and I help Caroline as much as possible . . . we all get off to chapel by 10 o'clock. Caroline enjoys going to a chapel near us as the Ministers are good plain men and she seems to understand everything they say.'[10]

'Chapel' meant the Congregational Church near the city post office, about a mile away. As they walked there on Sunday mornings, they would pass other families, also dressed in their Sunday bests, walking to their own churches. The little Congregational church suited her more than others. The strident, pious Adelaide Baptists left her cold, and she disliked the pomp and ritual of the Anglican high church, confiding to Charles, 'There is a great deal too much of that nowadays.'[11]

She felt at home there. She wrote (in a letter to Charles while he was away), 'They are such good nice people and I like them so much.'[12] The church itself—the 'chapel'—was modest, but they were fundraising to build a bigger one (which would be named the Stow Memorial Church, and is now known as the Pilgrim Uniting Church). She helped with fundraising activities, attended Bible studies, and helped with the church's charities for the poor. Between church and the children, there was quite enough to fill her days.

Charles did not rest after completing the overland line to Melbourne. He built a line to Kangaroo Island. He collaborated with his former assistant Ed Cracknell, now the head of the New South Wales telegraph, to construct an Adelaide-to-Sydney line, completed in 1866. In his role as chief astronomer, he studied the stars and planets . . . and also the weather. And on quiet evenings, he worked on plans for the big one: the international link. The connection to England.

But as distracted as he was, working and travelling and chasing wild ambitions, it is clear from their letters that he loved her, and that she loved him. She preferred having him home.

9

Escape Cliffs

Northern Territory, 1863–1866

John McDouall Stuart's maps, linking the coast of South Australia to the continent's northern edge by the Timor Sea, excited the people of Adelaide. They believed that the maps could free them from the chains of the salt-lake prison around them, allowing the colony to prosper.

In London, the colony's agents lobbied for control of the Northern Territory in order to exploit Stuart's discoveries. The lobbying paid off—the Territory was then held by New South Wales, which considered it of little value and was happy to let it go. The Northern Territory was transferred to South Australia's custodianship on 6 July 1863.

Sensing a chance for profit, the government moved fast. Within weeks of the Northern Territory acquisition, a plan was in motion to sell half-a-million acres of 'country land' and 1500 'town lots' to investors. Never mind that there were no roads, cities or towns there yet.[1]

The first batch of land lots were put up for sale simultaneously in Adelaide and London in March 1864, available during a four-week period. A pamphlet was circulated, publicising the benefits of the Northern Territory, containing extracts of a book titled *A handbook for colonists in Northern Australia*.

Most of the Adelaide offerings sold, but the response from London, when it arrived by mail steamer two months later, was disappointing. Only about half of the London-allocated lots had been sold.[2] But even the lacklustre sales raked in more than £70,000. For the first time in its short history, the colony's coffers overflowed with cash. The sale of every country acre and every town lot was pure gain; the land had cost nothing to acquire, other than a bit of political manoeuvring.

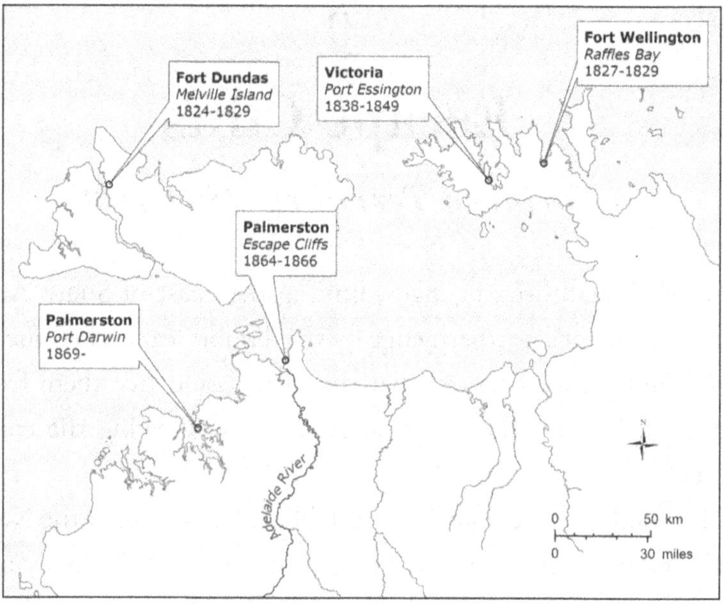

The five attempts by Britain to establish a colony on the Northern Territory coast

The land parcels were not even for specific blocks or lots; nobody yet knew where the towns and roads would be. These things would all be determined in due course.

But the bonanza could only go on for so long. Investors had paid good money, so the government needed to deliver.

A large team of surveyors was quickly assembled, loaded onto a ship and sent to the Northern Territory to peg out all the country land and town lots. Their first job would be to decide where the city and port would be. They departed on 23 April 1864, only days after the land sales reports arrived from London. An army man was put in charge of the expedition, with instructions to take charge of the Northern Territory on behalf of Queen Victoria. That man was, unfortunately, Colonel Boyle Travers Finniss.

The British had tried three times previously to colonise the Northern Territory, each attempt a failure.

The first had been on Melville Island in 1824, where a garrison named Fort Dundas was built with convict and soldier labour. It predated by several years the settlements of Perth, Melbourne and Adelaide. The goals were to pre-empt any Dutch claim on the territory and to establish a trading route with Singapore.

It had started optimistically enough. There were friendly first interactions with the local Tiwi people, the soil was fertile, and construction was quick. But they landed on the island in September, in favourable conditions, near the end of the dry season. The wet season came, and with it came mosquitoes and disease. Malaria claimed many lives and so did spears. Despite the early smiles of the locals on the beach, the colonists learned that, if they ventured too far into the island's interior, they would meet lethal resistance. Compounding these troubles, the hoped-for trading routes with Singapore and elsewhere did not eventuate.

Three years later, a second garrison named Fort Wellington was established on the nearby mainland at Raffles Bay. This attempt suffered deaths at the hands of the Iwaidja people and the health of those living there deteriorated quickly as they had insufficient lime juice to ward off scurvy. The fort's surgeon himself died of scurvy, leaving a colony riven by disease and with no medicine and no medical expertise.

Fort Dundas and Fort Wellington were abandoned in 1829. Fort Dundas had lasted five years; Fort Wellington just two.[3]

Nine years later, a British sailing ship had brought 38 marines, some wives and children, and an assortment of other workers, to Port Essington. This small garrison lasted from 1838 to 1849. Unlike the two earlier colonies, Port Essington did not experience conflict with the Iwaidja; quite the opposite. This was driven in part by the colonists' fascination with Aboriginal culture.

Professor Mark McKenna of the University of Sydney explained recently how the journals kept by the colonists show their evolution.[4]

> They are starting to perceive the intricacy, the knowledge, the craft, the skill of those Aboriginal people.
>
> That experience at close quarters caused them to start asking questions about their own culture and its alleged superiority.
>
> Because as they could see, Aboriginal people were living in this environment effortlessly, and they were learning from them how to live.

They had such friendly relations (and possibly more) that when the last settlers packed up and left, Iwaidja women wept. However, while they had neither brought nor elicited violence, they had brought disease.

Port Essington was beset by cyclones, wild weather, and disease; but, most of all, by a lack of purpose. Like its predecessor colonies, there was no trade, no confrontation with the Dutch, no settlement, or established agriculture. In short, there was nothing to do.

Those three colonies had come and gone years before, leaving only remnants of buildings behind. If there were lessons from those past endeavours to be learned, Colonel Boyle Travers Finniss did not heed them.

Colonel Finniss was a British officer of the traditional stripe, trained at England's Royal Military Academy at Sandhurst. The surveying work itself was not his business—Chief Surveyor J.T. Manton was in charge of that—but Finniss *was* responsible for choosing the site for the first settlement. In this, his very first decision, he chose poorly.

He chose a place called Escape Cliffs, on a hill near the mouth of the Adelaide River, about thirty miles north-east of present-day Darwin, and he named it Palmerston. (I should clarify that today's Palmerston, a satellite city of Darwin, is not the same place).

To be fair, they arrived during the dry season, when the river plains were inviting, so it must have looked quite idyllic, but when the wet season came, the plains flooded, morphing into a mosquito-infested swamp. It did not take long for the surveyors to discover a better location nearby at present-day Darwin, which was less flood-prone and swampy. They advised and suggested—and ultimately implored—Finniss to allow them to relocate there, but Finniss had made his decision and, by God, he intended to stick with it.

A steamer arrived from Adelaide in December, bringing fresh supplies of food, horses, and more workers. Also on board were 38 settlers, people who had bought some of those parcels of land and who had arrived to take possession. It was pouring with rain when they landed. The settlement was just a campsite on a hill, surrounded by water in all directions. The air was humid and alive with mosquitoes.

The steamer had already gone, chugging its way back to Adelaide, by the time the settlers decided they did not want to stay. Then another ship visited port; it was not heading for Adelaide, but it did have a longboat on board. Some of the settlers purchased the longboat, christened it the *Forlorn Hope*, threw their belongings into it, and sailed west.

Theirs was an unsung, epic journey. They sailed more than 1600 miles in that tiny vessel around the coast of Western Australia, finally reaching Geraldton. There, they left the *Forlorn Hope* behind, found passage to Perth, then returned to Adelaide by steamship.

Their arrival in Adelaide—and their terrible tales of the state of things up north—caused uproar and a political crisis. The government had no choice but to recall Finniss, placing Manton the surveyor in charge in his absence. A steamship was despatched to bring Finniss back.

When the steamship returned with the shamefaced Finniss, the captain brought with him a letter from Manton, revealing how bad things were in the territory. It confirmed everyone's worst fears:

> A greater scene of desolation and waste could not be pictured. The whole improvements on the settlement would be much

> overestimated at 200 pounds, exclusive of the wooden houses forwarded here from Adelaide. As a seaport and city this place is worthless. The land up the Adelaide I have visited where the survey parties have been employed, and not one individual landholder out of every hundred could make a selection upon which he could erect his homestead without the almost positive certainty of being washed off by floods that must of a certainty occur nearly every season.[5]

Manton's missive was the last straw. The government had no choice but to call the whole thing off.

Another ship was despatched, carrying with it instructions for Manton to abandon the settlement, pack up, and bring everyone home. That ship arrived at Escape Cliffs on 22 December 1866, collected every white person in the Northern Territory and took them back to Adelaide.

10

The Cable Cometh

South Australia, 1868

The east and west coasts of the United States were linked by telegraph on 24 October 1861. Since Morse's line from Washington to Baltimore, two coastal networks had grown separately. The Western Union Company linked east and west, with a line that was more than 1200 miles long, crossing the western prairies through Nebraska, Utah and Nevada, and clambering over the Rocky Mountains.

Months later, when this news reached colonial shores, Australians were inspired. If America could do it, then surely so could they. But there were additional barriers. The American transcontinental line traversed existing wagon trails, through mostly settled country. By contrast, an Australian overland line would be longer and would have to cross terrain with no towns, no settlements, no wagon trails. In places, the land was punishingly arid.

The dream of an overland line hit a snag when Lionel Gisborne, the English entrepreneur who had championed the idea, died suddenly that same year. But his dream did not die with him: his younger brother, Francis, continued to espouse the cause.

Francis had been involved in Lionel's previous schemes. In fact, Lionel had sent him to Australia in 1859 to drum up support for his latest idea. So, a year after Lionel's death, Francis founded his own company with the same goals as his brother's now defunct company.

Meanwhile, Sir Richard MacDonnell's stint as Governor of South Australia had come to an end. Francis Gisborne seized the chance to gather some inside information. Soon after MacDonnell returned to England, Gisborne visited him, probing him about the social and political state of play regarding the telegraph. MacDonnell informed

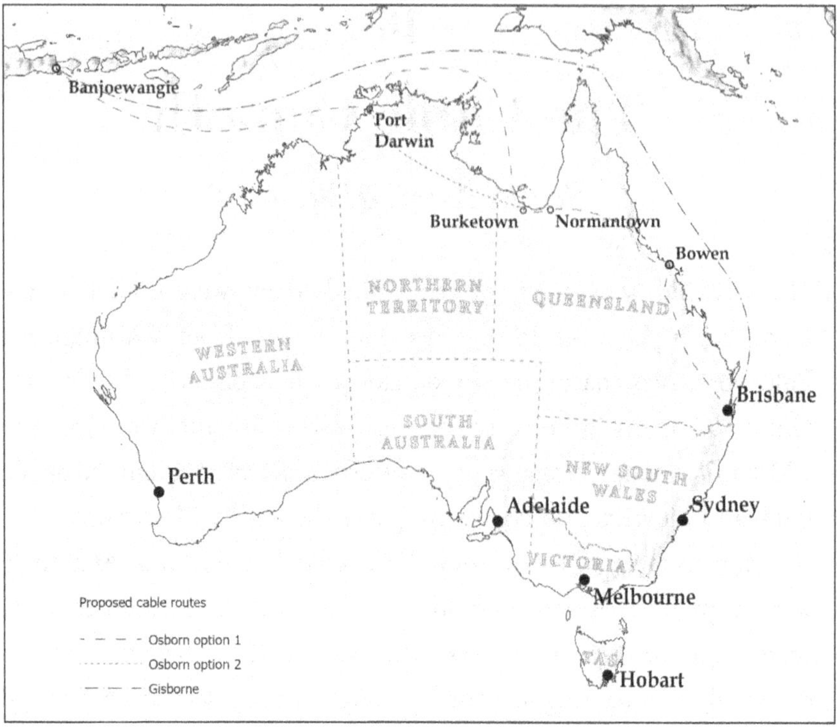

The proposed telegraph cable routes to Australia in 1869

him that South Australia—and perhaps he made particular mention of Charles Todd—hoped for an overland line from Adelaide to northern Australia.

That was not Gisborne's preferred option, but he was encouraged to learn that the colonies were keen to get a telegraph connection one way or another. He issued a new prospectus, seeking funds to build a cable through the Gulf of Carpentaria to Burketown on the Queensland coast. From there, it would run east to Normanton, then run to the east coast, where it would connect with the colonial networks.[1]

But Gisborne knew from MacDonnell that Charles Todd would not like this plan and he might cause trouble. So, to pre-empt any objections that the line should run overland to Adelaide, he offered an alternative: he would join the cable to a South Australian line, but only if the South Australians built their overland line first and did so within the next two years. If they could achieve that then, by all means, Gisborne would move heaven and earth to connect them with an undersea cable. He proposed Cambridge Gulf as the connection point, a remote place in Western Australia beyond thousands of miles of harsh, uncharted land.

Gisborne's prospectus almost sounded as if he was taunting Todd, mocking his foolish notion:

> I have lately conferred with Sir Richard MacDonnell on this subject (terminus of cable), and have no desire to adopt any terminus other than Cambridge Gulf, if South Australia will extend its telegraph system to that point by the end of 1864.
>
> I do not believe that any of the colonies will assist South Australia in carrying out such a work, nor do I believe it to be practicable to carry it out within that time.
>
> I might add that I do not believe that such a line of Telegraph will be maintained in permanent working order, until the white population becomes considerable and continuous throughout the intervening country.[2]

The South Australians had maps of a route to Port Darwin, but not to Cambridge Gulf. It couldn't be done. Gisborne shrugged; he had given Todd a chance. His undersea cable to Queensland was now the only plan on the table.

Todd's offsider, Ed Cracknell, had left Adelaide in 1857 to take charge of telegraphy in New South Wales. Two years after Cracknell took that job, Queensland was split from New South Wales and made into a separate colony. When the new colony cast around for a chief telegraphist of its own, Cracknell recommended his younger brother, William, who was given the Queensland job.

At 31, William Cracknell had energy and ambition. He commenced a rapid program of expansion of his nascent eight-station network and harboured hopes that Queensland could be the colony that joined Australia to the world.

With Cracknell's encouragement, the Queenslanders were keen on Gisborne's plan, but Gisborne failed to find enough big investors and the enterprise folded.

While Australia languished in isolation, the global reach of telegraph spread. India, with its own burgeoning network, was connected to London in 1865 by a route through Europe, Turkey and Persia. But the London–Karachi route passed through many countries, so it was insecure for the purposes of government and commerce, and was vulnerable to war and unrest. Even as the first message was sent, there was talk of duplicating the line with underwater cables.[3] That was because underwater cables—also known as 'submarine cables'—were emerging as a game-changing innovation. The first transatlantic cable from Ireland to Newfoundland had been laid in 1858. It soon broke, and so did its replacement, but the third cable across the Atlantic floor, laid in July 1866, was sound.

Submarine cables presented new challenges: a wire the thickness of a hand, traversing hundreds of miles of sea floor, weighed many tons. Huge ships crawled across the seas, uncoiling cables behind them that dropped into the black depths. Repairs were often impossible: if a section was damaged—by rocks or coral or imperfections—the entire line was lost. The industry was dominated by British companies. For investors, it was a gambler's den. Fortunes were lost when the cable broke; fortunes were made when the cable held.

British entrepreneurs had discovered that gutta-percha was the perfect underwater insulator. The Indian rubber was a versatile, malleable, durable substance, already widely used in manufacturing. Every submarine cable was coated in gutta-percha.

Planning began in 1866 for an undersea cable from Suez to Bombay, to link India and Britain.[4]

Francis Gisborne burst back onto the scene that same year with a new company and a new prospectus, again proposing a cable linking Australia to the world. As before, he was pushing to build a cable to Queensland. His plan was to lay a cable from Rangoon to Australia via Singapore and Java. But when he could not raise enough capital from private investors, he pitched it to the British Government.

The total cost would have been an enormous two-and-a-half million pounds. Even given the wealth of the British Empire, that was too much, and it was rejected.

In 1868 there was yet another attempt to colonise the Northern Territory and this time it was a success. Planning for a telegraph terminus was a factor, but the main reason was financial: the colony had sold half-a-million acres of Territory land in 1864 and the five-year period to survey those lots was approaching. The government had to either complete the surveys or give refunds, which would have broken the colony's finances. Hence, the new Premier of South Australia, Henry Bull Templar Strangways, made one last push for a settlement.

Strangways decided that the settlement should be at Port Darwin and the person he chose to implement it was George Goyder, his colony's Surveyor-General. Both were good calls. It also helped that Goyder's expedition arrived in February 1869, at the start of the dry season. Goyder named the city Palmerston, the same name that Finniss had given his ill-fated settlement further east at the mouth of the Adelaide River. However, from the start, it was referred to as Port Darwin and later just Darwin.[5]

With the success of the Goyder expedition, Todd was now convinced that Port Darwin was the appropriate place for a submarine cable terminus.[6] In July 1869, he wrote a widely published report for the government on the various options that had been floated. None of the London speculators was proposing an overland route from Darwin to Adelaide: the options were a connection to Western Australia (either from Sri Lanka or Java), with a connection to Darwin and then overland to Queensland; or a cable from Java to the Queensland coast. Of these, Todd preferred the Western Australian option, partly because South Australia would benefit from being closer to the cable terminus.[7]

Six months later, at the start of 1870, the government merged Todd's Telegraph Department with the postal service, placing him in charge of both. On top of his other roles, he was now also South Australia's Postmaster General. The surprise move was criticised for being too hasty, to which the Premier replied that the merge of the two departments had been planned for 'months'. There were hints that the former Postmaster had been taking kickbacks from contractors, and in particular, the transport company Cobb & Co. But whatever the reason, Todd was now in charge of both the telegraph and the post: the new and the old.[8]

In 1870, submarine cables linked India with London. The cables passed entirely through British Empire territories, except for one land station in Portugal, a British ally. The cables of this proudly 'Empire-only' telegraph stretched across the floor of the Indian Ocean between Egypt and Bombay; other cables snaked west across the Mediterranean sea floor and around the Iberian Peninsula to London. The cables east of India, travelling from Madras to Penang and then on to Singapore, were in place by the end of 1870.[9]

In 1868, the imperturbable Gisborne announced yet another prospectus, with the same goals as previously but at a lower cost. However, he had a new competitor.

A navy officer, Captain Sherard Osborn had been one of the driving forces behind the Suez–Bombay line and, as chairman of the newly formed British Australian Telegraph Company, he announced his intention to build an India–Australia telegraph line. Like Gisborne, he planned a cable to Queensland; but, unlike Gisborne, he was open to other proposals. Critically, he was considering the possibility of running an underwater cable at Port Darwin.

Captain Osborn sent his younger brother, Commander Noel Osborn, to Australia to negotiate with the colonies involved, and to finalise a deal. Charles Todd sensed an opportunity.

Part II
The Deal

11

The Captain's Company

Adelaide, 1870

Commander Noel Osborn arrived at Port Adelaide on Monday, 11 April 1870, on the steamer *Alexandra*.[1] He was a mid-thirties, overweight Englishman and an officer of the Royal Navy.[2] He was also the representative of the British Australian Telegraph Company, of which his brother Sherard was the managing director. Commander Osborn had travelled halfway around the world to negotiate the construction of a telegraph line from Singapore to the Australian colonies, connecting that far-flung continent to the rest of the world.

The company planned to lay an undersea cable from Singapore to Java and from Java to Port Darwin on Australia's north coast. It would then connect to an overland line to Burketown in Queensland and to the telegraph network across eastern and southern Australia.[3]

The company needed permission from nobody to drop cables into the sea, but bringing them ashore was another matter. From Port Darwin, the line would run through the lush mountains and flood-prone plains of Australia's Northern Territory before crossing the border into the Colony of Queensland. As the Northern Territory was a possession of the colony of South Australia, the South Australian Government had to give consent.

Adelaide was the first business stop in Osborn's colonial tour; from there he planned to circuit around the south and east coasts, initially to Melbourne, then Sydney and finally Brisbane, before heading home. He was there to negotiate with the colonial governments about the specifics of building the telegraph line and had two objectives. The first was to secure permission and cooperation to undertake the work. This should not have been hard because the colonies were desperate to access the new communications technology that was transforming international commerce. His second goal was to reduce costs for the corporation, primarily by getting the various colonies involved to pay for as much of the project as possible. They would, after all, benefit greatly from the telegraph.

Soon after Commander Osborn stepped ashore in South Australia, a man approached him and introduced himself as Charles Todd, the colony's Chief Telegraphist. They travelled by coach from the port to Adelaide city. Osborn booked into the York Hotel, and were soon discussing business.[4]

Todd later recalled:

> I took the first opportunity of discussing with him my old project of a landline directly across the continent and pointed out the great advantages that such a line would possess over one which kept, as theirs and that of Queensland would, over so great a distance in the tropics and flooded country of the Northern Territory and lowlands round the gulf of Carpentaria. I also showed that our line would be much shorter, and that Queensland could easily tap it by an extension from Normanton.[5]

Todd told him at the outset that South Australia would contribute, even if the line went to Queensland. But he proposed an alternative: how about, after the line connects to Port Darwin, instead of running an overland line east, why not run it south, all the way down to Adelaide? Or specifically, almost all the way down, because Port Augusta, two hundred miles up the coast, was already connected to Adelaide by telegraph. The line could run two thousand miles north–south. No need to deal with the Queenslanders at all. Todd reassured him that South Australia would invest heavily in such a plan.

Osborn found Todd persuasive, perhaps in part because he was ignorant of Australian geography: the overland plan came with a whole new set of challenges, which Todd breezed over.

But this conversation was merely an informal chat. After talking with Todd, the commander met Premier Strangways, who instructed him to liaise with Charles Todd. Osborn and Todd resumed their discussion some days later, with Todd now able to negotiate as the colony's official. He chaperoned Osborn around town, taking him on a tour of Adelaide's Botanic Gardens, a surprising jewel in the city's crown, thanks to the dedication and vision of the chief botanist, Dr Richard Schomburgk.[6]

Meanwhile, Todd managed his political masters, lobbying the Premier hard for the overland telegraph plan, just as he lobbied Osborn.

Osborn played hard to get. He had not yet been to Queensland; maybe they would persuade him back to the original plan. Todd offered a sweetener: South Australia would build and pay for the entire overland telegraph line itself. The company would be responsible only for the cable to Port Darwin.

A week after Osborn's arrival, Todd delivered a report to parliament about the feasibility of an overland line. He reckoned it would cost about £120,000 and that it would take a year and a half to complete. It was expensive, but Todd explained the benefits: there would be revenue from telegrams, plus indirect benefits from the boost to trade and business.[7]

Todd wrote, 'It is some 11 or 12 years since I first drew the attention of government to the practicability of erecting a land line from Port Augusta to the Northern Coast, and every addition to our knowledge of the interior since acquired has confirmed the view I then advanced.'

The deal needed to be made quickly, before Osborn went to Queensland and got a better offer. A bill to approve and fund the line was steamrolled through parliament in two days. It was the most expensive outlay in the colony's short history, and the lack of debate rankled some.

Opponents dismissed the plan as a crackpot idea. How could the line be built through unexplored country? Todd responded that the explorer John McDouall Stuart had travelled to the north coast and back in 1862, and had provided maps of his journey. These maps would be used to construct the telegraph following Stuart's track.

And what about timber, the naysayers asked. According to Stuart, swathes of the interior were deserts and treeless plains. Where would the workers harvest timber to make the poles? Todd responded that there were abundant supplies of wood along much of the track, or near to it. For the treeless sections, they could build poles from stone cairns, transport logs long distances on bullock drays or even import steel poles. Todd had factored all those things into the cost, he said.

Premier Strangways drafted an official proposal and presented it to Commander Osborn on 23 April, in which the Colony of South Australia offered to build an overland telegraph line at its own expense and would be able to do so within an eighteen-month period.[8] Osborn accepted, with the caveat that it was just a handshake agreement until London signed off on it. But that was a mere formality; Osborn reassured them that the deal was on.

A copy of the proposal was sent to London on 25 April. Naturally, Osborn's brother would not receive it for three weeks, because a physical copy of the message had to be delivered by ship to Ceylon, from where it would be transmitted by telegraph. A reply—hopefully an enthusiastic endorsement—would be forthcoming some weeks after that by return mail.[9]

While they waited for confirmation, the colony's London representative, Francis Stacker Dutton, sent a confidential memo on 9 May, which arrived in early June. While Todd was negotiating with Commander Osborn in Adelaide, Dutton had been conducting parallel negotiations with Captain Sherard Osborn in London.

Dutton revealed that the company was willing to drop the Queensland plan and had paused negotiations with Queensland, but to clinch the deal, South Australia needed to officially promise to pay for everything and to complete it by the start of 1872, and needed to send a formal and binding offer by June.[10]

Todd wrote to his Queensland counterpart, William Cracknell, updating him on developments, and, in an attempt to cool down any intercolonial jealousy, reassured him that if the north–south line went ahead, Queensland would be permitted to run a connecting line to it.[11]

Cracknell was unmollified. He urged Todd to give up the north–south overland telegraph scheme and let Queensland build its line to Port Darwin. The Queensland line would be much shorter and was already under construction. Cracknell pointed out the folly of Todd's plan:

> The description given by Stuart in his journal of a journey across the continent during 1861 and 1862 would seem to show that the route proposed offers few facilities for the construction of a line, the country, for the most part, being described as intensely hot, devoid of necessary timber, and, owing to its sandy nature, permanent water is exceedingly scarce. Under these circumstances, it is not at all improbable that the work would cost considerably more than the amount estimated . . .[12]

Cracknell observed that the company's plan had been to bring the submarine cable to Port Darwin, then from there, take it overland to Burketown. Cracknell hoped to persuade the company to extend the submarine cable all the way to the Queensland coast (perhaps with financial inducement); Charles Todd, by lobbying for an unrealistic alternative, was only going to delay construction of any telegraph line and his motivation seemed to be to deprive Queensland of telegraph revenue.

Sherard Osborn's reply arrived on 4 June. It was an acceptance, with a catch. The company promised to lay an undersea cable to Port Darwin, but only if South Australia could absolutely guarantee that a landline between Adelaide and Port Darwin would be completed by New Year's Day, 1872. That was a time frame of just over eighteen months.[13]

There was heated debate when the bill came up in parliament. One member decried the plan as 'an egregious piece of insanity', and declared that the way it was being rammed through parliament was 'a monstrous piece of absurdity'. Another accused the government of pushing the bill through with 'brute force', a slanderous accusation that the member was forced to withdraw. He said it was wrong that the government 'prostrate its privileges as the feet of a mere company' and drew parliament's attention to Commander Osborn watching the debate from a seat in the gallery, musing cynically how pleased the captain must be to see parliament doing his bidding.[14]

One member, Mr Duffield, complained about the haste with which the bill was pushed through and the lack of debate. He said he had never known a bill to be pushed forward with so little information: 'The childish game of opening your mouth and shutting your eyes has been carried to its fullest extent in this matter. One member referred to this as a white elephant, and the Northern Territory is a white elephant; so that if we go on in this way, we will soon have a whole breed of white elephants . . .'[15]

The critics were sceptical of Todd's estimates and feared that it would cost far more. They pleaded for a select committee to look into the matter. All their objections were in vain. The bill was passed.[16]

A formal and binding offer was sent to London. Funds were immediately released for Todd to spend. Commander Osborn packed his bags and boarded a steamer, bound for Melbourne and then Sydney.[17]

It's easy to laugh now at Todd's detractors and sceptics because he succeeded. But they were right, not just about the projected costs and time frames, but about the very decision to build the line.

It *was* insanity. Sure, one exploration party had crossed the continent and returned alive eight years earlier, but nobody had done it since. John McDouall Stuart's maps were insufficient for the task, because he had travelled light, on horseback, and the track he took could not be taken by wagons and bullock teams. There were, as the critics said, expanses of desert. There were deserts of sand, deserts of glassy stones, deserts of clay, as well as salt plains, mulga plains, grass plains. There were mountain ranges and twisting gorges. Further north were swamps and bogs, and rivers that broke their banks and flooded every year in the wet season. There were also Aboriginal people, who varied greatly in their attitudes to strangers and interlopers who used their waterholes and invaded their traditional hunting grounds.

Todd's plan was a gamble. It is a wonder that he is now lauded as a visionary and not derided as a fool.

12

To Port Darwin, and Quickly

Northern Territory, June–August 1870

The Osborn plan caught the South Australians off guard. After years of bungling, indecision and inaction, they had finally made progress towards colonising Port Darwin. But the project was still half-baked: surveyor-in-charge George Goyder was back in Adelaide, while a small crew of surveyors and some troopers remained there to keep surveying, with no sense of urgency.

Every British colony had a governor—a representative of the monarch, Queen Victoria—or, in the case of a territory under the control of another, a government resident could be appointed; a sort of second-order governor. There was currently a physician named Dr J.S. Millner living in Port Darwin, who was currently the acting government resident, who would step down once the official appointment was made.

When the news of Commander Noel Osborn's forthcoming visit reached Adelaide, a search for a suitable person was made. By the time Osborn stepped ashore into Todd's welcoming handshake, an individual had been selected, sworn in as government resident and despatched by ship to Port Darwin.

They appointed William Bloomfield Douglas, a British naval officer, to the role; Dr Millner would step down and assume the dual roles of Government Physician and Protector of Aborigines.[1] A provisional constitution for the Northern Territory was hastily drafted and approved.

One of the priorities in the constitution was the 'treatment of Aborigines'. The general principle was that the British Empire was taking control, but they wanted to do it nicely. They wanted to minimise conflict and the transmission of disease, and to win the hearts and minds of the locals. For example, here is a warning to Dr Millner, the 'Protector of Aborigines' to be careful visiting vulnerable island communities:[2]

> As it is possible that contagious diseases may be introduced by intercourse with the inhabitants of the approval of the neighbouring islands, you will, with the approval of the Government Resident, adopt such measures as may effectually prevent the spread of such diseases among the members of the expedition, or the Aboriginal inhabitants of the territory.

Millner also received instructions that they were to be treated well, have legal protection, and there should be an overall policy of winning them over. He was told to learn their languages, provide them with medical care, and recognise their social structures. He was also told to encourage them to enter the employment of white settlers.[3]

Douglas was under instructions to establish an experimental plant nursery, in order to learn what crops would grow in the Port Darwin climate. The plan was the brainchild of Dr Richard Schomburgk, director of Adelaide's botanic gardens.[4]

Douglas, with his wife, seven children, and a nursemaid, departed Port Adelaide aboard the government-owned steamer *Gulnare* on 28 April 1870, three days after an in-principle deal had been reached between Todd and Osborn. In the cargo, they had a range of plants for cultivation, including arrowroot, yams, sweet potato, papaya, Norfolk Island pines, indigo, tobacco, several varieties of cotton, banana trees, various other fruit, vegetables, and herbs, and a thousand cuttings of sugar cane.[5]

While the Douglas family packed their bags, parliament was in turmoil. Premier Strangways had a loud, abrasive personality, and a pushy leadership style that earned him widespread enmity. He called an election in response to a no-confidence vote, but following the election, even former colleagues had abandoned him. After two weeks of futile manoeuvring, he stepped down. John Hart humbly stepped forward to replace him.

In all the confusion, nobody seems to have briefed the Government Resident on the latest developments or updated his instructions. He was left unaware that the prospect of a Darwin-to-Adelaide overland line was looking increasingly likely. As Port Adelaide disappeared behind him, Douglas's brief was to prepare Port Darwin for the landing of a submarine cable and for the construction of an overland telegraph from there to Burketown in Queensland. He thought that several months would pass, at least, before work began.

The *Gulnare* took the Douglas family around the east coast of Australia ('eastabout') to Port Darwin, but was delayed in Brisbane for three weeks for repairs before continuing. They arrived at Port Darwin on 24 June. During their journey, legislation was passed to complete an overland telegraph from coast to coast by the end of the following year.[6]

William Bloomfield Douglas was a respected gentleman from the English upper class with an excellent resume and pedigree. He had joined the British Navy in his youth as a junior officer, and in the 1850s had earned plaudits for his role in fighting Malay pirates. Since arriving in Adelaide in 1858 he had served as harbourmaster, collector of customs, and president of the Marine Board. He also surveyed Kangaroo Island, the Murray River Mouth, and other areas. But despite his impressive resume, Douglas was not particularly talented. His achievements were due in part to his uncle James Brooke, First Rajah of Sarawak. Douglas was a ladder-climber who loved the trappings of class.[7]

Northern Territory land investors were excited by these developments. They might finally get their money's worth after all. A month after Douglas's departure, a second ship, the *Bengal*, left Adelaide for Port Darwin, taking a group of selectors there. Rumours of gold in the north only increased their anticipation. If there was to be another gold rush, they would get in early.

The *Bengal* took the settlers westabout, via Perth. Meanwhile, the *Gulnare* had taken such a long time sailing eastabout around the continent that the two ships arrived in Port Darwin on the same day, within an hour of each other. As the ships anchored, a cannon shot boomed from the shore. It was a salute to welcome the Government Resident.[8]

There was no wharf. There was a small jetty, but it was suitable only for dinghies or for sitting on with a fishing line. Both ships' passengers came ashore in the ships' boats, while a collection of men formed a welcoming party on the beach. The settlement's white population consisted of a few dozen surveyors and some guards. Dr Millner, the port's physician and acting Government Resident, introduced himself.

The settlement itself consisted of a scattering of wooden buildings up the slope from the waterline. There was a fence around the perimeter. The huts, though rudimentary, were comfortable, because the Larrakeeyah people had supplied them with bark.

The Larrakeeyah lived on the other side of the perimeter fence. Their numbers fluctuated; sometimes as few as thirty were living in the Larrakeeyah settlement; at other times, there were more than a hundred. They had friendly relations with the whites in Port Darwin; some of the Larrakeeyah even worked in the white settlement and were paid with food rations.[9]

Three weeks before the ships arrived, the Larrakeeyah had a deadly clash with the Woolner people. Some Larrakeeyah men had come to Dr Millner to warn him that the Woolner people were coming and were planning to attack the white settlement. Sure enough, that same evening, more than a hundred members of the Woolner people armed with spears and adorned with war paint camped nearby. Millner ordered the perimeter to be guarded around the clock.

Two days later, at dawn, some Larrakeeyah called for help at the perimeter fence. Millner hurried over. The Larrakeeyah said that the Woolners had attacked them, that some members of the community were wounded.

Millner hurried to their camp, where he found three wounded people. The most serious case was a young man, Orunga, who had been speared in the back, where it was still lodged. Millner could hear blood gurgling in his lungs. They took Orunga to the white settlement and placed him in a spare tent, where Millner tried to save him, but he could not be saved. He died in the tent surrounded by his father and brothers, who then wrapped him in grass and paperbark and carried him back to their own camp.

Millner also returned to the Larrakeeyah camp, where he treated a man and a woman with less serious injuries. One man told him that they had been attacked as punishment for warning the whites about the Woolners' plans.

The whites were perplexed by the 'love–hate relationship' between the Larrakeeyah and Woolner tribes, swinging from friendship to warfare then back again.[10]

Government Resident Douglas found no buildings in Port Darwin suitable for a man of his status, but some of the surveyors had built for themselves a sturdy log cabin with ocean views. Douglas evicted them and moved in with his family. He ordered the surveyors to commence construction of a proper governor's residence, built from stone.

Douglas had been issued with various instructions from Adelaide. An urgent priority was surveying an overland route from Port Darwin to the Roper River suitable for a telegraph line. When those instructions were written, the prevailing belief had still been that a British company would lay a submarine cable to Port Darwin and would then construct an overland line from there to Queensland. Douglas sent Port Darwin's chief surveyor, George Galbraith McLachlan, on a surveying expedition to the south-east.

In nineteenth-century Australia, surveyors wore two hats. Sometimes they were bookish bureaucrats, while at other times, they were intrepid explorers. McLachlan was asked to ride forth into the wilderness, chart a road through hundreds of miles of wild terrain, then return with appropriate maps. He chose some assistants to accompany him, prepared the horses, packed rations and sleeping gear, and rode away.

In the annals of Australian exploration, McLachlan does not rank highly. He and his party were gone for three months, far longer than expected.

Meanwhile, the selectors who had arrived on the *Bengal* began some exploration of their own. They claimed to be looking for arable land, but were actually looking for gold. After prospecting for weeks, they found a few meagre grains in a creek bed. Most of them returned to Adelaide on the next available ship.[11]

13
Double Deals
Melbourne, July 1870

An intercolonial conference opened in Melbourne on 5 July 1870. This was the occasion for delegates from Australian colonies to discuss important matters. Telegraph was one of those matters. Queensland, for some reason, did not send a delegate.[1]

The South Australian Premier John Hart arrived in Port Melbourne by steamship, accompanied by Charles Todd. Hart announced the deal and, although it was just a handshake agreement, he had evidence: the colony's London agent, Francis Dutton, had written a letter stating that he had been told South Australia was 'the company's preferred partner'. Hart tabled that letter.

But Hart received a nasty surprise. The New South Wales Premier, Charles Cowper, dramatically tabled a similar memo from *their* London agent, revealing that an identical promise had been made to Queensland! And to rub salt in, the Queensland deal involved a submarine cable from Port Darwin to the Queensland coast: in their scheme, there would be no overland component in the Northern Territory at all. The Osborn brothers had played the colonies against each other.[2]

This was embarrassing. Todd had been allocated all funds required to build the overland line and he had already started spending the money. He had ordered large shipments of telegraph equipment from Britain, had called for tenders to undertake various parts of the work, and had commissioned an explorer.

Todd sent Queensland an offer: if Todd's overland line was built, Queensland could build a branch line connecting to it, sharing the revenue. But the Queenslanders were having none of that. They wanted submarine cables all the way to the Queensland coast and peremptorily rejected any deal that involved South Australia at all. They refused to even agree to a plan that used Port Darwin as a staging post for cables to Queensland.[3]

Revenue was the sticking point. Building a telegraph line was expensive and the only way to recoup that money was revenue, and lots of it. As far as each colony was concerned, monopoly was the only viable business model.

Commander Osborn may not have intentionally misled Todd. He was an agent of the British Australian Telegraph Company, but that was just a subsidiary of manufacturing giant the Telegraph Construction and Maintenance Company, which lurked in the background, ready to sell shiploads of equipment once a deal was sealed. For the people Osborn represented, that was where the real money was going to be made. The upshot was that one company made verbal promises to South Australia, while the other made verbal promises to Queensland, and there were no paper trails for any of it.

Both colonies were outraged. Questions were asked about the whereabouts of Commander Osborn, who had some explaining to do. He seemed hard to find.[4]

Commander Osborn left the Australian colonies for New Zealand at the end of July, briefly visited Queensland, then set up residence in Sydney. By the time he showed his face again in Adelaide the following year, his part in the duplicity was forgotten. He dined with the Governor and other dignitaries. He was welcomed as an old friend; as the man who had believed in South Australia.[5]

No doubt, a decision about which plan to accept—Queensland's or South Australia's—was being made in London. Perhaps the decision had already been made. The delegates had to wait for the next mail steamer from Ceylon and for the news it carried. Meanwhile, Todd pressed ahead as if the deal was already his. If he waited, there was no way the line would be built by January 1872 and the game would be over, regardless of the company's decision.

14

First Contracts

Adelaide, July 1870

The telegraph line needed three things: wire, stations, and people.[1]

Todd needed enough wire to run, end to end, between Port Augusta and Darwin. If the wire touched the ground or a tree or a body of water, it would 'earth': the voltage would drain into the ground and the message would be lost. The wire needed to be strung from poles, suspended in the air. To prevent the current earthing on the poles, the wire needed to be separated from them by insulator pins. A battery in a station would put voltage in the wire so that a Morse message could be sent to the other end.

But the distance was two thousand miles. The voltage would dissipate (or 'attenuate', to use the technical term) to nothing before it reached a fraction of that distance. Todd needed several relay stations along the line—'signal boosters'. Each station would pick up the weak signal from the station before it and transmit it to the next section with its own battery. These repeater stations needed to be spaced about 180 miles apart at most, with extra stations in already-populated regions. He already knew where he would place the first three: Beltana, Strangways Springs, and The Peake. They would be able to serve as telegraph offices in their own right, but their primary role was to boost the signal so that messages could travel between Adelaide and Port Darwin. As for where to put the other repeater stations . . . well, he would have to wait and see.

Most importantly, the line needed people. It needed a telegraphist at each end to send and receive Morse messages. Staff would be needed at the repeater stations to work as telegraphists, and maintain the batteries and repair the line when needed. Those staff would be living in the remotest places imaginable, but they would be in touch, via the line, with the rest of the world.

Almost as soon as he had waved Commander Osborn bon voyage, Todd announced a call for tenders for the construction of the line, which was divided into two parts, with one tender sought to build the southern part of the line and another to build the north.[2] The southern contract was given to well-connected timber and transport merchant and former politician John Rounsevell. The tender for the northern part was awarded to a partnership of two businessmen, Joseph Darwent and William Trevett Dalwood. Both tenders were doomed to fail: the first quickly, the second one slowly.[3]

Rounsevell was trouble from the start. When he was shown the contract, he complained that it contained clauses not mentioned in the call for tenders. Negotiations over the wording dragged on for two weeks, until the government issued him with an ultimatum to sign by midday of 22 July. Midday came and went. Still playing games, Rounsevell swanned in an hour after the deadline, ready to sign. John Hart, who was Treasurer, told Rounsevell that the offer of contract had been revoked. Then Hart informed Todd that he would have to build the southern part of the line himself.[4]

Todd protested. He could not possibly oversee the construction of part of the project while also managing the entire project, and running the telegraph and postal systems. Hart compromised: Todd could divide the southern part into two halves, manage one half himself and issue a new tender for the other half. He was given permission to find a private contractor for the southernmost part, which was mostly through settled districts with roads, but Hart could give no further concession than that. He insisted Todd manage the central section himself: the remotest, driest, harshest section of line, through unknown terrain.

There were now three sections of line: Southern, Central, and Northern. The Southern Section would be relatively easy, and

Todd had no trouble finding a new tenderer. The job was given to E.M. Bagot, who was later revealed to be a proxy agent for Rounsevell. Bagot proved to be a competent manager, and over the next year and a half, he built his allotted portion on budget and on time. When Todd called for tenders to run a mail and delivery service along the line, Rounsevell bid again and was awarded that contract. This time, he did not argue about the terms and conditions.

Part III
The Great Work

15

Explorers for Hire

Adelaide, July–August 1870

Charles Todd had confidently assured everyone that John McDouall Stuart's maps would be enough, that they proved that the continent could be traversed and that, in Stuart's own words, 'The Telgraph could be laid down.' But he knew that those maps were insufficient.

Stuart's charts snaked across the vast, blank unknown of the interior like a museum tour by lamplight—the lands beyond those narrow slivers of illumination were a mystery. Furthermore, Stuart himself had warned that crossing the MacDonnell Ranges would be a problem; although the ranges were not high, they were rugged and rough, and he had found no passage suitable for wagon roads. And it was not even clear how to reach the ranges, because, unlike the wily Stuart, Todd's construction teams would be moving slowly and would need campsites with access to water.[1]

Todd commissioned a station manager, John Ross, to lead an exploration party ahead of the construction crews. Ross's brief was to find a suitable route for the line beyond the MacDonnell Ranges; horses, bullock drays and wagons would need to traverse that route, and there needed to be timber nearby that could be harvested for poles.[2]

Ross recruited a team of four. His second-in-command was William Harvey, a surveyor, who had signed on with Todd to manage a construction crew on a remote stretch of the line. Harvey's team, travelling with loaded wagons and bullock drays, would take several months to reach their worksite, so it was agreed he could explore with Ross, then ride north to take charge of his team when they had finished exploring.

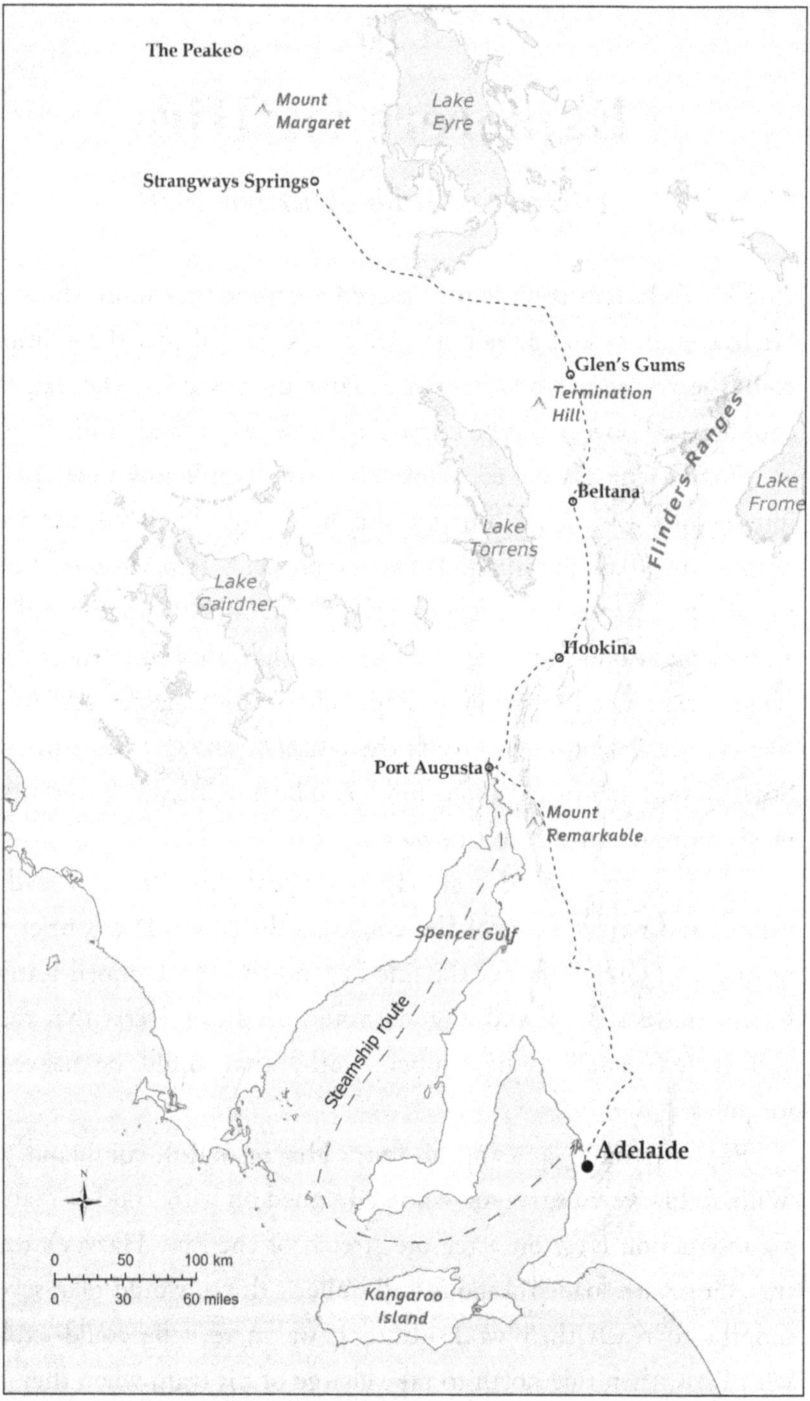

The route from Port Augusta to the Peake

Another member of the team was Alfred Giles, aged 24. Throughout their travels, Giles kept detailed records, which he published 56 years later, at the age of 80, in his memoir, *Exploring in the seventies and the construction of the Overland Telegraph Line.*[3]

Ross, Harvey, Giles, and the others rode from Adelaide to Beltana, a cattle station at the foot of the Flinders Ranges. Only weeks earlier, copper had been found in the hills to the east, a discovery that for decades would lure mining companies and sole prospectors with wheelbarrows, wanting to try their luck. Across the horizon to the west lay the dry salt plain known by the misleading name of Lake Torrens, and north of that, a larger salt plain known as Lake Eyre.[4]

The station's owner, Thomas Elder, had his eyes to the future. Four years earlier, his agent John Stuckey had bought a herd of 134 camels in Kandahar and Kabul, and employed 31 Afghan cameleers to accompany them to Australia, to breed and train camels at Beltana and another station he owned. Already there were reports of feral camels roaming the countryside.[5]

Camels would, in time, become a standard feature of Australian exploration, but that time had not yet come. Ross had no interest, because the animals had a poor track record. There had been much palaver about Burke and Wills's camels, but Burke and Wills perished. The feted crosser of the continent, John McDouall Stuart, had shunned them. Any explorer worth their salt would rather be like Stuart (perhaps minus the drinking) than like Burke and Wills, so Ross's reluctance to use these strange animals was understandable. Furthermore, using camels would mean employing one or more cameleers, adding to the size and cost of the expedition.

Todd did not share Ross's misgivings and had already arranged for the camels and several Afghan cameleers to run a delivery service along the telegraph line.

The team spent a few days preparing at Beltana, shoeing horses, oiling gear, making flourbags, and studying their maps, and so on, then left on 28 July, riding north. A week later they turned west, through the sliver of habitable land between the two great salt plains, Torrens and Eyre. They glimpsed Lake Eyre off to their right; its bright, deadly expanse glistening on the horizon.[6]

They camped without tents, as Stuart had done and as Aboriginal people did. Giles wrote, 'Blazing sun or soaking rain always found us in the open. Nor do I think we felt the worse for it. We were brazened and browned, but hardened and hale.'[7]

West of Lake Eyre, they camped at Mount Margaret Station on 10 August 1870. They were on the outer reaches of white settlement. The only road beyond here was a north-west track to a remote property called The Peake. Ross penned a letter to Todd, informing him that there were grasslands all the way from Beltana to Mount Margaret, which meant that horse and bullock teams could travel the route. This would hardly be news to Todd, but Ross intended to prove his worth early on. He also wrote that construction teams would be met with generous hospitality all along the route, 'speaking from experience'. The bad news was the lack of trees. Locals had talked of a pine forest ten miles off the track near Lake Torrens, but he had not seen it himself, so he could not be sure it existed.[8]

John Ross did not follow the lonely track to The Peake. Instead, on 14 August, he rode directly north, hewing closely to the fringes of Lake Eyre. He was following in the tracks of John McDouall Stuart, destined for the MacDonnell Ranges.

His party crossed Sturt's stony desert, which Alfred Giles described vividly:

> . . . it is a mass of loose stones, red and flinty looking, and one would think that all the loose stones in the universe had been scattered over these plains. Not an inch of soil can be seen. Most of the stones are flat and quite level. One would think an immense roller had passed over them. The country is also destitute of

> timber, giving a rather dismal appearance; yet, strange to say, plenty of grass peeps up between the stones, showing that the soil below must be good, and, somehow, forbids one calling it a desert.[9]

Ross made camp at a waterhole on the Truer River. The river flow was barely a stream, dotted with waterholes. They followed it north-west, upstream. To their right, beyond the north-east bank, was a sandy desert. To their left, on the other bank, a stony tableland. They rode along the almost-dry river for five days, until they reached the far edge of the sandy desert, then they struck due north, where they found a forest of good timber for telegraph poles.[10]

North of the Truer River, they encountered people for the first time on their journey: a group of ten, who hid in the bushes. The party dismounted and Ross hurried after the Aboriginal group, returning with a boy who could speak a bit of English. Soon afterwards, a man boldly marched into their campsite. He was completely naked; his hair was tied in long ringlets behind his head. It was clear he had also encountered white people before: he made signs indicating that he wanted tobacco, which they gave him. The others soon emerged and there was a somewhat awkward but friendly interaction between the two groups, each finding the other strange. Ross's explorers gave the group a mirror and other trinkets.

That night, they heard movement around the campsite, and believed that perhaps the black people had returned, but the intruders were dingoes, investigating the camp until chased away.[11]

As the party rode north, they sometimes saw smoke from campfires, and on two occasions entered campsites that had been abandoned quickly, presumably out of fear of them and their horses. They found cooked food—which they did not eat—and warm embers.[12]

They eventually met other Aboriginal groups. Ross's instructions were to make a good impression with them and to act peaceably at all times. His fellow explorers carried guns, but they were only allowed to use them in self-defence. Ross gave Aboriginal people he met presents, such as shirts, a bucket and a tomahawk. On one occasion, they discovered a small water supply which the local people relied on. Giles wrote, 'Their only water was a muddy claypan, and they had most ingeniously made the water to filter through sand by digging holes on the upper side of the claypan.' Ross dismounted to drink, but a group of men approached him, waving their spears and waddies, and gesturing for him to leave. Realising that the water supply was precious to them, he left immediately.[13]

Todd's written instructions to Ross gave no guidance on dealing with Aboriginal people, but his verbal instructions probably echoed those to his managers: make peace. The fact that Ross took small mirrors and other items that could be traded or gifted reveals that making peace was the strategy from the very start. While laudable, it was also pragmatic: hostile Aboriginal communities would make trouble for the overland telegraph.

16
The Plan
Adelaide, August 1870

The city of Adelaide and nearby towns moved to the beat of Todd's timetable. Blacksmiths pulled countless horseshoes from furnaces; saddlers made saddles, harnesses and straps; steel mills made coils of wire. A timber yard at Port Adelaide made 30,000 insulator pins from ironbark. The main saddlery in Adelaide's Gawler Place was busy each day from sunrise until midnight, the owner promising his staff generous bonuses for their efforts.[1]

Acting against advice to use Melbourne-made wagons, Todd gave a blueprint to a local manufacturer to make lighter wagons that he believed would be more suitable. It is unknown who designed Todd's wagon, but it was probably Todd himself.

Tinned meat was produced by J.V. Hughes, the owner of Booyoolie Station. The product would be known as Booyoolie Beef and later 'bully beef'.

The August London mail steamer brought welcome news: the British Australian Telegraph Company had decided to lay a telegraph cable from Java to Port Darwin. The cable would be open for business at the start of the year 1872, provided that South Australia started construction of the overland line in the meantime. The decision to take the cable to Port Darwin rather than Burketown showed that Queensland's all-or-nothing gambit had backfired, partly because of the Queenslanders' reluctance to contribute capital for cable-laying. Even so, the company encouraged the two colonies to sort out their differences and cooperate.[2]

But there was still no official agreement, and the company had another small request. Charles Todd's promise to the Osborn brothers that he would finish the line by 1872 was not enough; they wanted proof that the colony's parliament had authorised the construction of the landline. Once that was received, the company would commit. That was easy to provide and was sent on the next outgoing mail steamer to London.

The contractors for the northern end were moving swiftly. Darwent and Dalwood had recruited 75 men and chartered the steamship *Omeo* to transport them to Port Darwin, and a second steamship, *St Magnus*, to take equipment and livestock.

They purchased working horses, bullocks, bullock drays, food rations, pots, shovels, axes. Large coils of telegraph wire, provided to them by Todd on the government's tab, arrived at the dock to be hauled into the *Omeo*'s hold. They knew the rations would be insufficient, so they arranged for a herd of cattle from Queensland and a herd of sheep from western New South Wales to be brought overland to supply meat. There were, as yet, no roads between those colonies and Port Darwin, and much of the terrain was either desert or mangrove swamp, so the plan was wildly optimistic. Neither the cattle nor the sheep ever arrived.[3]

They had insufficient food and the wrong kind of horses (their heavy workhorses were poorly suited to the hot, muggy tropical climate). But most critically, they did not comprehend the perils of the wet season.

The ships left on 20 August. Crowds thronged to Port Adelaide to see them go. The atmosphere was electric. In a speech to the workers and onlookers, Darwent announced that if they finished the contract on time, a thousand pounds would be distributed to everyone as a bonus. A cheer rose up. One man, getting cold feet, muttered that his wife had taken ill and asked to stay behind. His place was eagerly taken by another man who had missed out.

Joseph Darwent, the elder business partner, remained behind, although his nephew, also named Joseph, went aboard as a team leader. Dalwood went aboard with his wife; they planned to see the commencement of work in Port Darwin before returning.

Todd boarded the *Omeo* and stayed on board as far as the heads, then he wished them all bon voyage, then returned by boat to shore.[4]

Todd had his own section of the line, the Central Section, to build and he acted with speed and efficiency borne from years of planning. He, too, recruited men and purchased equipment, animals and rations. There was no ship for Todd's construction teams: they were going inland to the heart of Australia and would go by foot.

He produced, as if out of thin air, a thorough, finely crafted and well-researched rulebook for his managers, which he titled 'Instructions for Overseers'. A lot of it covered record-keeping and other basics, but also dispensed advice on animal welfare, 'morals', and interactions with Aboriginal people.[5]

He encouraged the work crews to be kind to their animals:

> Horses or bullocks not to be ill-treated. No horse is on any account struck on the head or legs, nor punished severely except for positive vice. Teamsters and others must remember that more is to be done by kindness, and by humouring horses than by blows, and that the safety of the party may depend upon keeping the horses in good working order, they must, therefore, be very particular in looking after them, and keeping them in good condition. The same remarks apply to bullocks, and similar precautions are to be observed, care taken with them as the horses.

In the scorching desert, the rulebook advised to travel in the 'cool of the day' or by moonlight. There was to be no gambling, swearing, or quarrelling, and in place of these, the manager was encouraged to promote 'rational amusements'. Explorations for water should be made before making camp.

With water, Todd relied on Stuart's expertise:

> Stuart says that water may often be obtained by digging in the beds of creeks, and this should therefore be tried. All bright green places should be visited as being likely spots in which drainage water has collected. Mound springs may sometimes be discovered by a fringe of rushes or reeds upon an apparent sand hill. Reeds are almost always a good sign of permanent water; rushes often only indicate where water may be found during the wet season; they are, however, not a bad indication for shallow sinking.

He had advice for when someone got lost, which sounded, at times, rather obvious, but worth documenting regardless. First, he insisted: 'Men lost must be searched for', and the search must be conducted systematically. The direction the lost person had gone should be ascertained and tracks sought. Light fire signals; leave marks pointing in the direction of the camp; and, when searching, make your tracks as conspicuous as possible. Todd added, 'Cunningham, the naturalist to one of Sir Thomas Mitchell's expeditions, who lost himself, would have been probably saved had such precaution been taken.'

Todd's policy regarding Aboriginal people can be summed up as 'be nice, but leave them alone and encourage them to leave us alone'. He was wary of sexual relations between the white men working for him and black women, believing it risked tension and conflict.[6]

> **Treatment of Natives.** Should any natives be met with, they must be treated kindly but firmly. No native must be allowed to come within 100 yards of the Camp without permission

from the officer in charge, and then not more than three at any one time.

Not to visit Native Camp without leave. No one is allowed to visit the natives' camp without special permission; and, in all cases, previous intimation is to be given to the natives.

No Communication with Native Women. The officer in charge is especially cautioned to allow no communication between any of his party and the native women, or any conduct likely to create jealousy on the part of the natives. This is not to apply to any women engaged by him, in the absence of a man, as guides to point out the situation of water.

Property of Natives not to be touched. If a native camp, or burial ground, is met with, the property of the natives, it is to be left untouched. If any natives are seen, they must be warned by cooeying of the approach of a white man, as their first impulse of terror at the unaccustomed sight often leads them to throw their spears at him.

Mode of Attack by Natives. When natives attack a party, they generally do it by setting fire to the grass, and approaching under cover of the flames and smoke; it is therefore desirable, when deciding upon a camping place where there are signs of the presence of natives, to bear this in mind, and either choose a place where the grass is scanty, or burn a piece round the intended camp. Under these circumstances it would be well to choose a good position commanding the surrounding country, and where, say 100 yards around, there is no shelter for a black to creep unseen towards the camp.

Not to Fire upon Natives except in cases of necessity. Statement of affray to be drawn up. It is most strictly forbidden to fire upon the natives except in the last extremity, when it may become necessary for the safety of the party; and in such a case the statement is to be drawn up by the

> officer in charge, detailing all the circumstances which led to this action, together with all subsequent occurrences, and this statement must be supplemented by the written evidence of such men as were present at the time, duly signed by them.

He produced equipment lists that were actuarial in their precision. Each man was allocated a weekly ration of flour, tinned meat, salt, mustard, pepper, biscuits, tea, sugar, tobacco, pipes and matches. There was also a weekly lime juice quotient of four ounces, to ward off scurvy.

The conquest of scurvy had been, when first discovered, one of Britain's secret weapons; medicine can be an instrument of conquest as powerful as guns. The advent of Europe's maritime age brought very long sea voyages, on which fresh food could be unavailable for months. Ships' crews suffered deficiency in vitamin C, which manifests as scurvy. Britain was the first to solve this problem, enabling their warships to blockade French and German ports for months, while delivery vessels provided the sailors with fresh lemons. For economic and supply reasons, the British Navy switched from lemon to lime juice, although lemon has a higher vitamin C content.

Quinine, which suppresses the symptoms of malaria, was arranged for workers in the Northern Section.

Todd had been preparing for this moment for years. The ships had sailed. Wagons and drays were amassing at the stockyards. The city hummed with activity, fuelled by a fire that he had lit.

17

Go North, Young Man

Adelaide, 29 August 1870

At first light on 29 August 1870, seventy men gathered at the Adelaide stockyards. They were the members of three of Todd's five construction crews. Each crew included labourers, bullock teamsters, cook, blacksmith, wheelwright, foreman, cadet surveyor, sub-inspector, and an inspector (the crew manager).[1]

After a roll was called, Todd read a brief summary of the regulations, then addressed them. He explained that they had a long journey ahead: they would follow the road to The Peake cattle station near Lake Eyre, about a 600-mile walk, which would take about six weeks. Todd said he would meet them there. Beyond The Peake there were no roads, but they would be guided by Stuart's maps and by the discoveries of Todd's explorer, John Ross. He told them that, although they would undergo many hardships, he knew that they were all 'men of the right stamp'. Someone shouted a question about bonuses. Todd reassured them that all would get bonuses, but only if the line was completed on time.[2]

He assured them that they would have ample entertainment, because the Governor's wife, Lady Edith Fergusson, had generously donated five whole boxes of books to the expedition. Someone called for three cheers for Todd and three cheers for Lady Edith.

The delivery of the books was delayed, but they were sent and were apparently well curated, because the workers' diaries reveal that the books were, in fact, read and enjoyed. They were light reads, mostly forgotten today, including sensation novels by Mary Elizabeth Braddon such as *Eleanor's Victory* and *Captain of the Vulture*; *Holmby House*, a historical romance-mystery by Whyte Melville; and a comedy, *The world in light and shade* by A.W. Cole.

The crews headed out of the stockyards in a slow procession north. Crowds gathered along the streets to watch them go by. Each crew had thirty horses, three wagons, two drays, and one express wagon. Todd accompanied the supervisors to the northern edge of the city, where he wished them Godspeed and they parted ways.[3]

A week later, the last two of his Central Section crews departed in the same manner: they assembled at the stockyards, heard a motivational speech from Todd, then began the long walk north.

The crews trudged forward, camping by the road each night. It rained heavily for part of the journey, but they were in good spirits. It was the start of an adventure and they felt important.[4] The first of them arrived in Port Augusta, 191 miles north, in mid-September, setting up camp on the outskirts of town.[5] Port Augusta's population was a mere 450 residents, but, as the northernmost port, it played an outsized role in the colony. The same day that Todd had stood in the Adelaide stockyards reading out regulations, the steamer *Kangaroo* had arrived at the Port Augusta wharf; its hold was crammed with supplies including tools, wire, water tanks, and three months' supply of food per worker, packed in tins.[6] The cargo was piled into makeshift stores on the wharf.

Herds of bullocks and horses arrived from outlying stations and were distributed to the crews. Last-minute orders were placed with the town's blacksmiths for horseshoes, wagon parts, and other sundry items. The blacksmiths had never been so busy. They worked late into the evenings to fulfil the extraordinary demand. Afghan camel drivers arrived with a hundred camels, setting up a camel camp nearby.[7]

The townsfolk threw a party for the visitors. The next morning, the men, horses, wagons, bullocks, and camel teams commenced the journey further north, leaving at intervals in mid- to late September.[8]

Meanwhile, the crews for the Southern Section—that part of the line through settled districts that had been subcontracted to Mr Bagot—began leaving Adelaide on their shorter journey north, also via Port Augusta.

18
A Surprise for Port Darwin
August 1870

Government Resident William Bloomfield Douglas got the shock of his life on 9 September 1870, when the *Omeo* and *St Magnus* steamed into Port Darwin. He had, until that moment, believed that the international telegraph link was still in the planning stage and that when it happened, it would probably connect to Queensland. He had been told to make preparations, but there seemed to be no sense of urgency about it, so work had proceeded slowly.

Up to now, the surveying teams had passed the time drinking, gambling, playing the concertina, and beachcombing. They had become so enthralled with the beautiful seashells on the beaches that collecting them had become an obsession. The Larrakeeyah took full advantage of this, selling shells to the white men in exchange for food and clothes. The ships' arrival spelled a sudden end to the surveyors' languor, and curtailed the Larrakeeyah's brisk trade.[1]

There was no wharf. Douglas had been told to have one built, but it had been sidelined because he decided that the building of his residence was more important. To be fair, he had with him a wife, seven children, and a maid, all living together in a little log cabin. Even so, the wharf should have been built.

The horses on the ships were loosely tethered and pushed into the water. They swam behind a boat, two at a time, to the shore. The next day, the bullocks came ashore in similar fashion. At the same time, other boats ferried between the ships and the shore, bringing equipment and stores.[2]

Work began right away. A ceremony was organised for the planting of the first pole near the shore. Survey pins in the grass indicated

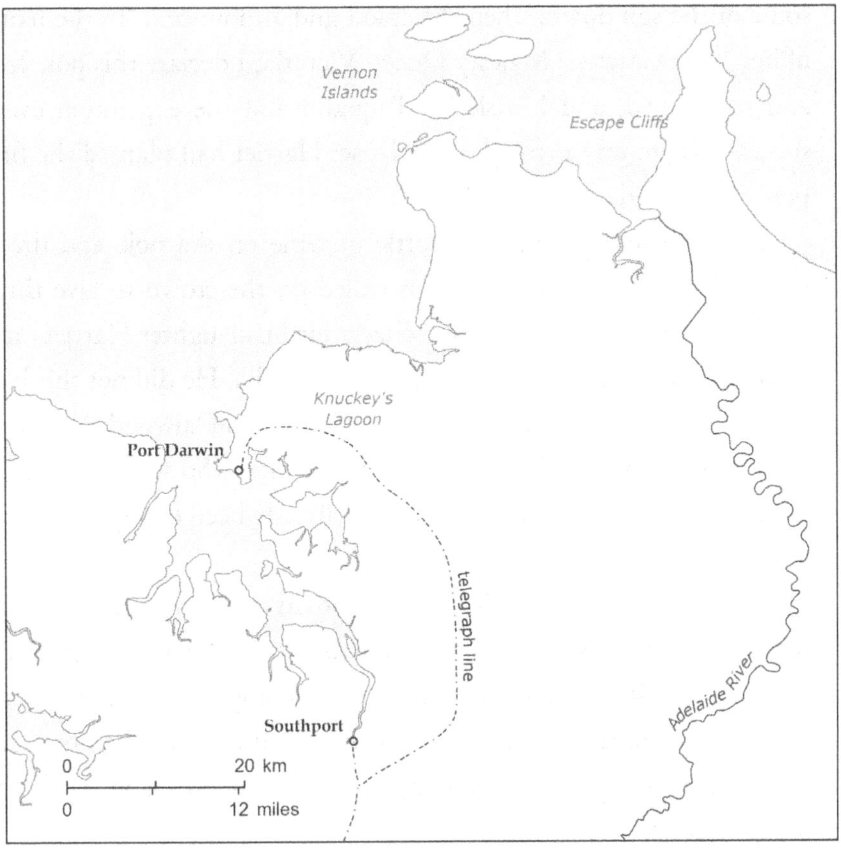

Port Darwin, 1870, showing the route of the telegraph line to be constructed

that the spot was on the corner of two gazetted streets, Bennett and Mitchell. Douglas issued a warning that only invited guests were welcome to this special event and that everyone else should stay away. The surveyors, construction workers, and the Larrakeeyah ignored his edict, and gathered to watch.

The Government Resident's daughter Harriet was chosen for the honour of planting the first pole. She had some help. A team of workers dug a hole and hauled a post next to it. Then, when everyone had arrived, they lifted the post and dropped it in the hole, then shovelled dirt around its base. Finally, Harriet was invited to come forward. She was handed a little wooden tamp and she bent and firmly pressed some of the soil down. Then she stood and announced, 'In the name of her Most Gracious Majesty Queen Victoria, I declare this pole well and truly fixed, and I wish Mr Paqualin and the expedition every success.' There was a round of applause: Harriet had planted the first pole of the overland telegraph!

Mrs Dalwood smashed a bottle of wine on the pole and drove in the first insulator pin. Douglas called on the crowd to give three cheers for Queen Victoria, three cheers for his daughter Harriet, and three cheers for the Governor of South Australia. He did not think to call for three cheers for the contractor's wife, Mrs Dalwood. Nor were any cheers deemed necessary for the many men who would sweat for months in building the line. There had already been enough cheering for one day.

After all the cheering, the cannon aboard the *Omeo* fired a 21-gun salute. Samuel Sweet, captain of the *Gulnare*, had recently given up the seafaring life to start a new career as a photographer, but had been persuaded to return to the seas for this special task. He had brought his camera, so after the ceremony, he took a photograph of all the official guests.[3]

The ceremony was not just for show: it really did mark the commencement of work, and when it was all done and Douglas's daughter had been proudly led back to her log-cabin mansion, the teams dug more holes and planted more poles, a line that led away from the water and into the bush.

To the Larrakeeyah, it must have seemed absurd: all that fuss about sticking a tree trunk in a hole. But that little event was, in a way, more significant to them than the settlement itself, which so far had had minimal impact on their lives. While the settlement brought some downsides for Aboriginal people, there had also been benefits, including gullible white men who were actually willing to pay for seashells. But, for the most part, traditional life had so far continued as before. The telegraph would be the event that changed everything for them.

Two days later, the *Omeo* chugged out of port on its return voyage to Adelaide. The Dalwoods left with the *Omeo*, leaving their manager, William Paqualin, to run things. And thus, with Darwent and Dalwood both in Adelaide, a rivalry began between the two people who held the delegated power. One was Paqualin, with a laissez-faire, 'she'll be right' mindset. The other was the government overseer, William McMinn, acting as Todd's eyes and ears.

During his brief stay, Dalwood had realised that there was not enough heavy transportation power so, after he returned to Adelaide, he purchased 69 more bullocks, to be delivered to Port Darwin aboard the *St Magnus* in October.[4]

Meantime, the scrub was thick and needed to be cleared before poles could be erected. Teams of woodcutters (or 'axemen') cut a track, then the polers would come and plant the poles. Behind the polers came the wire-riggers, installing the telegraph wire. After the wire was rigged, a Canadian telegraphist named James Thomas Stapleton would test the wire. Their campsites were temporary; they would pack and move as the line progressed.

Paqualin divided the workers into two teams. One group commenced at the settlement at Port Darwin, continuing the line of poles that started at the opening ceremony. A second group took a boat across the harbour to the southern reaches, then walked four miles further inland to a place called Tumbling Waters and started planting poles there.[5] The first group camped at a place known as Knuckey's Lagoon, where they found towering termite mounds more than ten feet high. It was nice there. The cool evening air was filled with the sounds of birdsong and croaking frogs. But before long, they left that arcadia, relocating to a clearing infested with sandflies and mosquitoes.

The explorer McLachlan, who was supposed to advise on the best route south, had not yet returned. But work needed to start, so the government overseer McMinn consulted Goyder's survey maps and plotted a suitable route as far as the Adelaide River, about ninety miles to the south-east. He hoped that by the time they reached the river, McLachlan would be back and could advise on the route beyond.

19

From Port to Peake

September–November 1870

In the last weekend of September, the mail steamer delivered a letter that sent Adelaide into a spin. The letter was from the colony's agent in London, Francis Dutton, about arrangements with the telegraph cable company. The good news—for South Australia, at least—was that Queensland's bid had collapsed. The company had demanded heavy payments to take a cable to the Queensland coast; the Queenslanders had rejected the deal, countering with an offer of their own, but their terms were unacceptable and the deal was off. There would be no underwater cable to Queensland. Port Darwin would be the terminus.

But the Port Darwin deal was also at risk of falling through. The company had taken a dim view of Charles Todd's promise to finish the line by 1872, which, in their eyes, was merely a 'moral obligation', not binding, and therefore put them at risk of the colony changing its mind. They had therefore asked for a written guarantee, but none had arrived in time for the company's meeting. This was unfair, because the premier *had* sent them a written assurance, but the mail steamer to London had broken down and it had not arrived.[1]

The company took a hard line. Its chairman, Lord Monck, stipulated that the Colony of South Australia must pass a bill, stating that if the overland telegraph line was not complete by 1 January 1870, then the colony would pay a fine of £70 per day, every day, until the line was completed. Those were the terms and if South Australia did not agree, then the deal was off.

But the deal could not be called off, because money had been spent, explorers despatched, and hundreds of construction workers were travelling inland, already halfway to the border. Todd had even contacted his German friend, Joseph Oppenheimer, to place an order for high-quality iron telegraph poles, known as Oppenheimer poles. If South Australia was to pass the law demanded by the company, they had less than two weeks to do it, because the return mail steamer to London was leaving on 11 October and they would need to send their response on that ship.

It was an outrageous act of political blackmail. Those who had opposed the project were justifiably livid, and they held up proceedings with long speeches about how aggrieved they were and how unfair the deal was. One politician said that they should not pass such a bill. The *Register* reported, 'He admitted that they had gone so far with a bad job that they must carry out the land line, but they were not compelled to jump down the mouths of the Company, and accept its terms.' Another politician said that no deal should be made unless the company likewise promised to pay a fine if its work is finished late. The recently deposed Premier, Henry Strangways, opposed the bill, claiming to have insider information that the company would start the work even with no guarantee.[2]

On and on it went, into the night, and then the next day. It was passed on the afternoon of 11 October, rushed to the Governor, signed into law, sealed, delivered to the harbour and taken aboard the waiting mail steamer, which had delayed its departure by an hour.[3]

Charles Todd was not in Adelaide to witness this high drama. He had stepped onto the Port Augusta wharf a week earlier, on 4 October, having arrived on the *Kangaroo* on its weekly run from Adelaide, accompanied by one of his managers, Ben Babbage. The campsites and temporary stables around Port Augusta were mostly empty, but two horses had been prepared and were waiting for them at the makeshift depot. While in town, Todd received the heartening news that the first telegraph pole had been planted in the Northern Territory three weeks before.[4]

The first pole of the Southern Section had been planted at the little town of Stirling, about five miles east of Port Augusta, on 1 October. The foreman had given everyone a glass of beer, and several workers inscribed their names on the pole before resuming work.[5]

On Sunday, 9 October, a telegram arrived for Todd with good news: the overland telegraph bill was on track to pass in time to be sent aboard the London mail steamer. Todd and Babbage saddled up and rode out: their destination, The Peake.[6] After four days' ride they reached Beltana, where several others were waiting to join them on their journey.

On the second day out from Beltana, at a camping spot called Glen's Gums, Todd expressed his annoyance at the indirectness of the route. It would take them north to Marree, then west along the isthmus between the salt lakes. He questioned why they could not just ride north-west from there and bypass Marree. The others explained that was no diagonal shortcut, no track except for the one through Marree.

Todd suggested that they try to find a shortcut, but his men preferred to stick to the track. Todd chose Babbage and two others to accompany him, then wished his men good luck, promising to meet them further north. He and his little exploration party struck out to search for a north-west route.[7]

The land was flat and dry and mostly featureless, but they had a map and compass. There appeared to be water in the distance, near the horizon. They thought it was a lake, but it was a mirage. They passed a bump named Mount Nor-West and another called Termination Hill. Todd's party crossed, in his words, 'desolate, waterless places'.[8]

After five days they found the east–west track, and then a campsite with a hundred camels and their drivers, as well as the remainder of their band of travellers. Todd maintained the north-west track they had taken could be used as an alternate travel route, but it never was.

Some days later they overtook some construction crews and on 24 October arrived at the settlement of Strangways Springs, on the western side of Lake Eyre. This was where Todd had arranged to meet explorer John Ross. Within hours of their arrival, Ross arrived from the north with his surveyor William Harvey. They had left the rest of their group camped at The Peake and had ridden down to report.[9]

Ross's report was disappointing. He had mapped a route quite a long way north—as far as the Hugh River—and the route he had found was flat, easy travelling, dotted with waterholes for campsites. He recommended that the construction crews follow that route, then camp at the junction of the Hugh and Finke rivers, about 270 miles north of The Peake, beyond the Northern Territory border.[10] But Ross had not solved the biggest problem: he had failed to find a way across the MacDonnell Ranges. In fact, he had not even reached the ranges. His party had approached from the south, but had had to cross a wide mulga plain with no water to be found anywhere. Their water ran very low they and their horses were at risk of dying of thirst, so they had retreated.

That would not do. Todd told Ross to try again. Todd was headed to The Peake himself and would deliver specific instructions in a few days.

Nothing remains of Peake Station today, other than some crumbling walls; however, in its heyday, it was a bustling little outpost with a cluster of eight or nine buildings. The nearby creek ran intermittently, and behind the station was a range of rocky, sandy hills. It was owned by Philip Levi, who also owned the larger Mount Margaret Station.[11] Todd had contracted with Levi to use the place as a depot and campsite, and planned to build a telegraph station there. He had placed a man named Blood in charge of the depot. When he arrived on 4 November, some of the crews had already arrived and set up camp.[12]

Based on Ross's advice, Todd decided to build a second depot about two hundred miles north, at the junction of the Hugh and

Finke rivers. He contracted a man named Harley Bacon to run that second depot.[13]

Ross and Harvey arrived the next day.

Todd reiterated his instruction to Ross to find a passage across the MacDonnell Ranges, and to explore the terrain between the MacDonnell Ranges and the Fergusson Ranges beyond it, then to rendezvous with the construction crews to instruct them how to get across the ranges. The crews would wait for them at the junction of the Hugh and Finke rivers. Until Ross had found a way to the ranges and across them, the crews would not be able to go any further. The entire project was relying on the success of his exploration.[14]

Todd told Ross that if, on his way north, he changed his opinion of the route he had mapped, or if he wanted to amend it, to leave a message for those coming behind: 'You had better leave a note in some conspicuous place where Mr Woods will be likely to camp on the way up.'[15]

Once he had explored the ranges, found a route to the lands beyond, and conveyed that information to the crews, Ross was not then to return home but should continue into the Northern Territory—using Stuart's maps to find the way—to report to the crews working south from Port Darwin. Todd said that his government overseer, William McMinn, would meet Ross at the Roper River and would provide signals to guide them there:

> To assist you in finding the place indicated, he has been directed (vide enclosed printed directions) to cut down timber for some distance in several lines running south from the river, marking on some trees the bearing and distance of the camp. He will also light three fires making good smoke every day at noon precisely, the fires being nearly equidistant, ranging nearly east and west—the fires to be kept burning for two or three hours.[16]

Ross's men prepared for their next venture, fixing worn equipment, setting horseshoes, and jerking beef from freshly killed bullocks. Jerked beef is made by cutting the meat into thin strips, with all the fat removed, then hanging the strips in the sun. After a day or so, the meat dries out, shrivels and curls up. It is preserved by smoking or salting, then packed in bags. It was ideal for explorers because it lasted for months without going rancid. The explorers called it 'bootlaces' because it was as fun as eating bootlaces for breakfast.[17]

As more crews arrived, the paddocks around The Peake became a tent city, populated entirely by young men in dirt-stained working clothes. Horses, bullocks, and camels grazed in nearby paddocks. Drovers arrived, driving a flock of 2000 sheep, a self-propelled supply of meat.[18] And in another paddock lay piles of logs to be used as telegraph poles.

Beyond The Peake there were no roads, nor fences, nor houses. Numerous little delays and problems accrued. As Todd put it: 'it takes a long time to shod and cue so many horses and bullocks'. He decided to stay longer than he'd planned, to oversee the preparations and ensure that they went smoothly. Depending on their profession, some men were busy while others were idle. Todd assigned the idle workers the task of building a stone storehouse for Mr Blood.[19]

On Sundays, Todd held a brief church service in the station manager's house. Sunday services were in his rulebook: Todd stipulated that workers should not be made to work on Sunday; that managers should read a short service; and that attendance was voluntary.[20]

One of the overseers, James Beckwith, was afflicted with severe headaches and swelling around the eyes, with one eye almost completely closed. He had tried to read a Bible passage at a Sunday service, but could not see the page. Todd sent him back to Adelaide, appointing an assistant overseer, Whitfield Mills, in his place. Beckwith's replacement was the man who would find and name Alice Springs.

Ross and his explorers left on 16 November. The crews and bullock teams left the next day at a slower pace.[21]

At the end of November, after watching his explorers and workers amble off into the wilderness, Charles Todd returned to Adelaide.

20

Poles in the Jungle

November 1870

Poles went up rapidly in the Northern Territory. By the start of November, the two crews had linked their sections into a single line of poles ninety miles from Port Darwin, through the woodlands and down to Southport. Here, they encountered frill-necked lizards, flying foxes, dingoes, and native bees that thankfully did not sting.[1]

The crews had positive interactions so far with the Aboriginal people they encountered. Todd had issued them with revolvers, only to be used 'in the last extremity' if they were under attack. With such friendly and interesting local communities, the last extremity seemed unlikely to ever occur. In a hard day's work, a revolver was a needless encumbrance, so the workers stopped carrying them. Occasionally they used them for hunting. The weapons were neither powerful nor accurate, having been retrieved from long storage at the Adelaide garrison.[2]

One worker, Sidney Herbert, who kept a diary of his life on the line, recalled a striking conversation with an Aboriginal man. The man told him that fifty years earlier, the population had been much bigger, but that Indonesian traders had brought a smallpox epidemic, which devastated the local communities. It is certainly true that traders had been visiting long before the white people came, and so it is entirely possible that those traders brought smallpox to Australia. But is also possible that smallpox arrived with the ill-fated British colonies of Fort Dundas and Fort Wellington, which, perhaps tellingly, had both been abandoned about fifty years earlier.[3]

The Aboriginal people boiled and ate the leaves of a tall tree that the workers, copying them, called a 'cabbage tree'. The Aboriginal people also assured them that flying foxes were edible, but the white men would not try them.[4] They ate snakes and occasionally the white men killed and ate snake; but if it was offered to the Aboriginal people they would refuse. They had seen how carelessly the white men killed snakes and worried that they might have allowed the dying snake to bite itself, poisoning its own flesh, thus poisoning whoever ate it.[5]

Flies pestered the crews incessantly. In the sweltering heat, the woodcutters clearing the way complained that their woollen shirts were getting flyblown. If the problem was not remedied at once, as one worker put it, 'live objects would soon make their appearance'.[6] The incessant flies caused sickness, vomiting, and an eye infection known as 'bung-eyes'.[7] The humidity gave them heat rash, which they called 'prickly heat'.

The woodcutters were harassed by wasps and green ants, which nested in trees and high bushes. Occasionally, when an axe hit a tree trunk, a shower of ants would fall onto the axe wielder's head.[8]

There were also mosquitoes, and with mosquitoes came malaria. Todd had sent them with large quantities of quinine, which did not prevent malaria, but warded off the symptoms. At first, every worker made a daily visit to the doctor's tent for a dose of quinine. But Darwent and Dalwood's manager, Paqualin, grew irritated with the system, deeming it disruptive and inconvenient, so he discontinued it. The impact of that decision was not immediately apparent, but in the months that followed, malaria ran rampant. The workers called it 'intermittent fever' or 'ague'.[9]

The food was basic, but bearable. According to Sidney Herbert:

> For provisions we had tinned meats, prepared by the Booyoolie Meat Preserving Works in South Australia; preserved potatoes, dried in rough particles about the size of half a pea, not unlike tapioca, but yellow in colour; dried vegetables in small cakes, well pressed; flour, in small bags; and biscuits for occasional use.

> Mention may be made of some of the cook's dishes. 'Hash-me gandie', made by putting dried potatoes into half a bucket of boiling water, adding eight pounds of tinned meats, and stirring well with a ladle. As an alternative, this stew may be put into tins and baked. 'Lobscouse' is about the same as the foregoing, with this difference: that preserved vegetables are added, and the baking takes longer. Once a week were supposed to have a plum pudding (usually called plum duff) but later on and much against our desire, it was often replaced by boiled rice with too few currants thrown in. Occasionally a cake decorated our tarpaulin (used in lieu of a tablecloth). Tinned butter was supplied for a few weeks only, the hot climate was against its use; jams, and dried apples were other items of our menu.[10]

Despite all this, despite the heat and flies and ants and wasps and malaria, they made progress, although slower than hoped. But the man Todd had sent to supervise on his behalf, William McMinn, was worried. To him, Paqualin's management seemed slipshod and cavalier. He was particularly worried about supply lines. The further the crews got from Port Darwin, the harder they would be to supply. They were traversing rivers, mountains, swamps, and jungles where the supply wagons and bullock drays carved tracks, creating haphazard roads with no planning or forethought. McMinn urged Paqualin to build proper roads, but Paqualin replied that he had no spare workers, since, as he saw it, the bullock tracks were becoming roads of a sort, there was no need.

There was nobody for McMinn to consult: Paqualin's bosses, Darwent and Dalwood, were four weeks by ship away in Adelaide, and so was his boss, Charles Todd. He quietly approached Dalwood's nephew Joseph Dalwood, a construction crew leader, to encourage him to fire Paqualin on behalf of his uncle, promising to back his decision if he did. But Joseph Dalwood declined, so Paqualin stayed in charge, and the show went on, careening towards disaster.[11]

McMinn came up with another idea. To the south, the Roper River cut east–west across the Northern Territory. From its mouth in the Gulf of Carpentaria, the river cut deep inland and was possibly wide enough to navigate by ship. Perhaps, instead of carting supplies along hundreds of miles of boggy bullock tracks, cargo could be taken up that river to be deposited inland.

The Territory's official explorer, G.G. McLachlan, had returned from an expedition to the Roper River by land.[12] McMinn sent him out to explore the Roper River a second time, this time by sea, to find out if it could be navigated by ships. The Territory also had its own schooner, the *Gulnare*, laying idle in Darwin harbour between shopping trips to the Dutch settlement on Timor for the Government Resident. McMinn instructed its skipper, Captain Sweet, to take McLachlan and a party of explorers to the Roper River and back. McLachlan's team left Port Darwin aboard the *Gulnare* on 5 November.[13] The wet season was approaching; the sooner they returned, the better. Unfortunately for McMinn—and for everyone involved—they took much longer to return than anticipated.

Meanwhile, McMinn went investigating. Todd had instructed him to explore ahead of the crews when necessary, in order to find the best route and to check that the planned route was not susceptible to flooding. McLachlan's most recent foray had been almost useless. He had followed Stuart's maps for safety and failed to find a suitable telegraph route to extend the work being done, leaving the poling crews without practical guidance beyond the Adelaide River; Stuart's maps were more important as a proof of concept rather than the basis for a plan. McMinn set out for the Katherine River, about two hundred miles away. The early miles were easy, because the surveyors had been surveying the land nearby, but after about a hundred miles, far from the survey maps and west of Stuart's maps, he was in completely uncharted territory.

About halfway to the Katherine River, McMinn found unmistakable wheel and horse tracks near a creek. A horse-and-dray had been there. There were similar tracks, appearing to be less than two years old, at various other places. No white person had ever reached Port Darwin by land, so presumably whoever had made these tracks had perished.

Near Yam Creek, McMinn met a group of Aboriginal people who were in possession of a blue blanket, a new billy can, and a nail tin. He could not learn from them whether they had discovered and taken these possessions from the vanished travellers, or whether they had killed them or had acquired the items some other way. At any rate, the identity of the person or persons who had made the wheel tracks was never determined. One theory was that it was a Queenslander named Cameron, said to have set out for Port Darwin two years earlier. Another theory was that it was a man named Whitting, who had attempted to drove some sheep from the Barrier Ranges and who was not heard of again.[14]

McMinn discovered a large river, which he named the Fergusson, and two tributary rivers flowing into it, which were named the Edith and the Cullen. The Edith River was particularly beautiful, with a series of waterfalls and a lake edged by sandstone cliffs, and with large fish and turtles swimming in its crystal-clear water.[15]

On his return, McMinn provided Paqualin with a suitable telegraph route from the Adelaide River to the Katherine River. The *Gulnare* and McLachlan's expedition had not yet returned.

The first thunderstorm of the wet season came on 16 November. By then, the crews had crossed the Adelaide River. The terrain became boggy and progress slowed but, for now at least, they continued.

21

Number Two Depot

December 1870

On the sandstone tableland south of the Adelaide River, a hole-sinking team found gold at a place they called Pine Creek.[1] Paqualin decided to set up a depot at nearby Yam Creek, which he called 'Number Two Depot' (Number One Depot being a storehouse much closer to Port Darwin). He announced that from now on, Number Two Depot would be his operational headquarters. William McMinn did not like the idea, but Paqualin was immune to his carping.

McMinn believed that the current depot—now 'Number One Depot'—should be kept as the main depot and the base of operations. The place that Paqualin had chosen had no obvious advantages at all. It was too remote, connected to the port by a long string of treacherous tracks, and even a river—the Adelaide River. They argued about it, but McMinn had no power—he was merely Todd's observer, after all—so Paqualin had his way and Number Two Depot was established.[2]

They celebrated Christmas at Pine Creek. A working bullock was slaughtered and cooked and a concert held, which mainly consisted of people singing songs. Sidney Herbert described the proceedings:

> On Christmas morning a race track was prepared, and sports were indulged in consisting of foot races, jumping, putting the stone, grinning through a horse collar, and bobbing at the duff. The latter took place in the afternoon on the bank of a lily pond in the creek.
>
> The duff, covered with sticky sauce, was suspended by a string to the branch of a tree, and competitors were invited to take a bite of the pudding at the risk of falling into the pond.

> All prizes were then distributed, and to my surprise being a teetotaller I was presented with a bottle of Jamaica Rum. This was a joke by Mr Paqualin, as Tommy R., our champion step dancer, who was not a teetotaller, received a bottle of lime juice for his exhibition of skill. Needless to say Tommy soon interviewed me with a view to exchanging prizes; but as I held the trump card in the deal he had to 'ante-up' some tobacco as well.[3]

More thunderstorms came, the ground got boggy, and the work got slower, but still they poled, the line of poles edging further into the wilderness. Some of the workers were intrigued to find a cave that served as a burial ground, and on rocks near the caves they found artwork in red and white ochre, depicting people and various animals such as snakes, emus, and turtles.[4]

Here, south of the Adelaide River, there were fewer interactions with local people, who, unlike the Larrakeeyah, were not used to seeing white people or horses or bullocks. Sometimes they would watch or follow, only to disappear into the undergrowth when noticed. On one occasion, twenty Aboriginal people appeared out of high grass and interacted with the workers. They were invited to share some damper, but refused until they saw the white men eat it first. The visit ended on a sour note, as Sidney Herbert described:

> As their fear grew less they began to feel us over, but not liking the familiarity we made signs for them to move off. This they did, slapping their buttocks as they went, whether in token of friendship or defiance none of us knew. As night was falling and their movements slow, we fired our guns over their heads to hasten them away.[5]

22

Doubters

Adelaide, December 1870

In the foothills of the Flinders Ranges on the approach to Port Augusta, Todd encountered a poling team, under the management of the subcontractor Bagot, who had already planted a line of poles a hundred miles from the port. This was rapid progress! Wiring had commenced and was proceeding well.

Todd's journey home by horseback at walking pace took several weeks and was lengthened further because he stopped at all the post offices and telegraph offices on the way to 'inspect' them and to meet with his employees at those far-flung offices. He arrived home on 20 December, just in time for Christmas, having been gone for almost three months. He learned that James Beckwith, suffering from swollen eyes, had arrived in Adelaide, but was still suffering. Beckwith would never recover, dying a year and a half later, his death attributed to 'sunstroke' from working on the overland telegraph line.[1]

Christmas was a big deal at the Observatory. Charles and Alice now had five children of their own: Charlotte, aged fourteen; Charles Junior, aged twelve; Hedley, ten; Alice Junior, five; and Gwendoline—sometimes called 'Gwenny' and other times 'Nina'—who was only one year old (they were to have one more child, Laura, born in 1875). There was also Charles's orphaned niece, Frances (now aged eighteen, still living with them, nominally working as a servant); his orphaned nephew, Griffith Todd; and Alice's orphaned nephew, William (about fifteen). On Christmas morning, the children dressed in their 'bests', walked to church to participate in a packed service then returned home in time for lunch.

Charles's well-earned festive cheer was somewhat shaken on New Year's Eve. The *Australian and New Zealand Gazette*, a London newspaper specialising in colonial news, had published a scathing report about his overland telegraph: 'We are afraid that there is a very serious possibility of a total breakdown of the arrangements or a competition which, in our opinion, will be almost as fatal, unless some compromise is arrived at between the governments of South Australia and Queensland.'[2]

The *Gazette* lamented that Queensland's far more sensible plan had been ignored. It derided Port Darwin as a 'white elephant' and cast doubt on whether the line could be built at all, passing through '1600 miles of utterly uninhabited country'. This was not true, but, of course, the *Gazette* was referring to habitation by white people. As for the weather, the paper noted: '. . . all travellers agree that it may be at one season a waterless desert of sand and scrub, and at another a succession of swamps and floods equally dangerous and impenetrable'.

The *Gazette* predicted that, even if the overland line was completed (which they felt was by no means certain), it would never be built for the sum that Charles Todd claimed it could. Unfortunately, they were right.

Part IV
The Sunburned Country

23

The Sweeping Plains

The border of South Australia and the Northern Territory, January 1871

At the peak of summer, Richard Knuckey—known to all as Dick—was camped with his crew on a sandy, mulga-dotted plain north of The Peake. Knuckey was responsible for building Central Section A, the first stretch of the middle part of the line. He had heard another manager, Alf Woods, express a theory that there was water to the east of the track around here, so, leaving thirsty workers and animals at their camp, Knuckey and two others investigated.

They discovered a chain of lakes with drinkable water stretching for at least thirty miles; in some parts the water was almost as clear as rainwater. Convinced that the lakes were springs, he named them Dalhousie Springs, 'Dalhousie' being Lady Edith Fergusson's maiden name.

Explorers named landscape features as they found and mapped them. A practical reason was that names are handy reference points for direction giving, comparing notes and generally making sense of an otherwise bewildering mess of scribbles on parchment. They were building a language of the land, although languages of the land already existed around them in many forms.

Knuckey met and spoke to some Aboriginal people, who told him that, further east, the waters flowed into the Finke River. They also told him that the name of this chain of lakes was Quitchera. He renamed it anyway, but included the traditional name in his official report.[1]

As Knuckey rightly concluded, the lakes were fed by permanent springs from the Great Artesian Basin. Beneath the dry desert rocks, water flowed deep underground from faraway tropics and east coast highlands, percolating to the surface here, at the edge of the desert.

Since Knuckey was in charge of this part the line, he rerouted it to pass closer to Dalhousie Springs, so that travellers would have a refreshing place to rest. While his poling crew began planting poles, Knuckey went ahead with some others to survey his part of the line.

The party was camped beyond the Territory border on 10 January 1871 on a hard, treeless gibber plain. It was another searing hot day and they were again short of water. Knuckey noticed some bronze-tailed pigeons overhead, flying east, perhaps an indicator of water nearby. He saddled up and rode east, following the birds. A shimmering lake appeared before him, which he suspected was a mirage, but was real. Camping by the lake that night, the party made johnny cakes in the campfire coals from flour, water, and salt, a bush recipe called 'beggars on coals'. Knuckey was so pleased with the lake that, as the group watched the embers, he made up a simple, happy rhyme.[2]

The greatest enjoyment under the sun
Is to sit by the fire till the beggars are done.

Knuckey did not learn the Aboriginal name for the lake. He named it Charlotte Waters, after the mother of storekeeper Harley Bacon. He decided that it would be the site of his main camp, and where he would construct a telegraph station.

Knuckey had twelve months to finish this part of the line. With Charlotte Waters and Dalhousie Springs on the line, he was certain it could be done. Those discoveries would help the crews further north, too, by providing water to the supply teams up and down the line.

Charlotte Bacon had been something of a celebrity in Adelaide since her arrival six years earlier. She was born into minor aristocracy in 1801, the second child of the Earl of Oxford. Her mother,

Lady Jane Harley, had a stormy affair with the poet Lord Byron when Charlotte was eleven. The affair ended when Charlotte's parents travelled abroad, inducing the heart-stung Byron to spitefully give presents Jane had given him to Charlotte. He dedicated his famous poem, *Childe Harold's Pilgrimage,* to 'Ianthe', which was said to be his pet name, not for Jane, but for Charlotte, only thirteen when the poem was published. A female friend of Byron's claimed that he said of Charlotte, 'I shall probably marry [her] when she is old enough and bad enough to be made into a modern wife.'[3]

Whether or not he was serious, Byron was beaten to the punch by an army officer, Captain Anthony Bacon (later major, then general). Charlotte's husband became a war hero at the battle of Waterloo, squandered his wealth, then was thrown into debtor's prison, plunging Charlotte and her three children into poverty. On his release from prison, Bacon proposed a wild plan to revive his fortunes. He lobbied the British Colonial Office to found a new Australian colony on the Spencer Gulf, and to appoint him the Governor of that colony. He did not succeed, but his persistence did push London policymakers to look into such as colony, and although Bacon did not benefit, he was a driving force behind the decision to settle Adelaide and to found the colony of South Australia. After failing to raise money to take a ship of settlers to Spencer Gulf, Bacon resumed his military career, serving in the Crimean War.[4]

After General Bacon's death in 1864, his three children and his wife, Charlotte, moved to Adelaide, to live in the land he once dreamed of ruling, but never saw.

24

The Flooding Rains

Northern Territory, January 1871

The wet season was in full force by January. Furious clouds threw torrents; the tracks turned to muddy slaloms. The supply wagons and drays ran late: there had been no delivery to Number Two Depot since mid-December. Food ran low.

The wiring teams had wired the poles to Number Two Depot before the onslaught of the rain and the northern line's chief telegraphist, James Stapleton, had constructed a log cabin telegraph office just outside the Port Darwin settlement. This was one ray of sunshine: Number Two Depot was in direct communication with the Port Darwin office.

Paqualin left the advance work camp to find out from Stapleton why no deliveries had come, accompanied by Aboriginal tracker Billy Weaver. His questions, relayed back to port, were partly answered: an expected supply ship from Adelaide had not arrived, leaving Number One Depot, close to the port, empty and unused. But as for the delivery teams that had already gone down the track, Stapleton had no answers. Presumably they were bogged or stuck somewhere between the port and Number Two Depot. Also, there was no sign in port of the *Gulnare* or the McLachlan explorers, who had gone to explore the Roper River by boat.[1]

With no fresh supplies, they had to make do. Here, jerked beef was known as stringybark.

Water penetrated everything. The flour became infested with weevils, which swelled and burst in the oven, causing the bread to resemble raisin cake. They ate it, despite the offensive look and smell. The rice was worse. It was full of tiny grubs which could only be

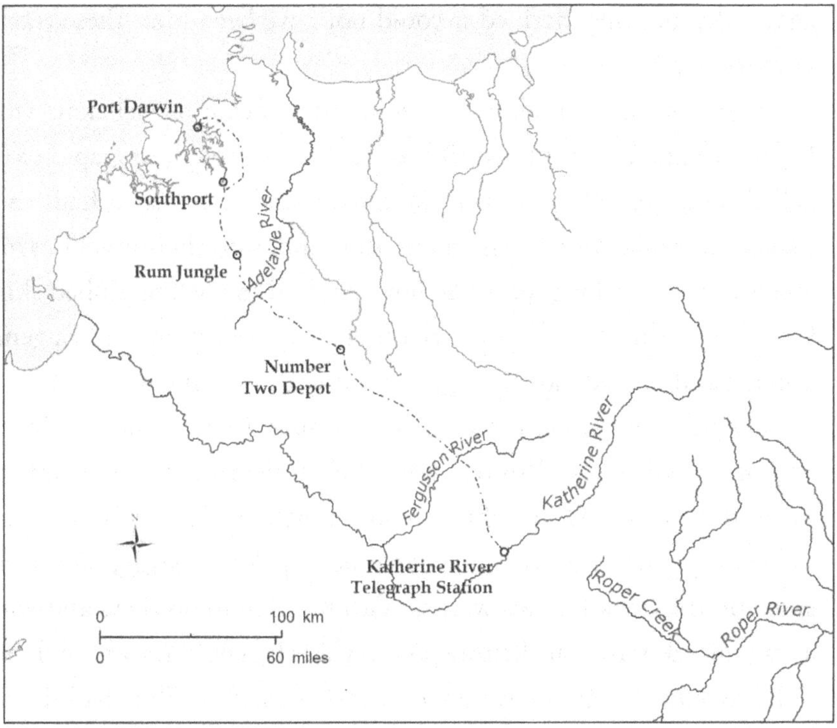

The route from Port Darwin to the Katherine River

distinguished by their brown heads. At that, a line was drawn. Nobody ate the rice.[2]

And yet still they progressed.

By the end of the January, they had poled all the way to the Katherine River. A thick undergrowth of palms covered the ground, under a dense, high canopy. The Katherine was a roiling, angry, wide torrent, seemingly impassable. They set up camp on the north bank, to wait for an opportunity to cross.

A mile downstream, someone discovered the wheel tracks and hoof marks previously found by McMinn, evidence of the passing of a horse-drawn cart or dray. They speculated who could have left those tracks. Perhaps Leichhardt, the explorer who left Queensland in 1846 intending to cross the continent east to west, and who was never seen again. But no, they decided it could not have been him: these tracks were too fresh.[3]

There was an abundance of wild fruit, including delicious wild fig, native grapes (or at least, they were similar enough to grapes to be called that), something rather like a plum and an unusual fruit they named 'Eugenia', which was an almost round, soft, slightly acidic fruit about two inches long, partly hollow, encased in a white, ribbed skin. One day, as they looked at the river's rushing waters, myriad Eugenia bobbed and floated past them, like thousands of white bubbles.[4]

Further back along the track at Number Two Depot, a delivery wagon arrived at last. This one was much anticipated because, among other things, it was bringing a consignment of rum. The delivery drivers explained that they had become hopelessly bogged and were stuck on the track for two weeks. With nothing to do there and with a wagonload of rum at their disposal, what else could they have done? What would any man have done in their situation? They had drunk all the rum.[5]

Tempers ran high at Number Two Depot that day.

The place where the delivery wagon got stuck was henceforth known as 'Rum Jungle', a name it retains today.[6]

25

The Ragged Mountain Ranges

Central Australia,
1 February–19 March 1871

Again, John Ross failed to find a route across the McDonnell Ranges.

The MacDonnell Ranges stretch for more than 200 miles east–west across the continent's heart. Far to the west, at the tip of the range, lies the Great Sandy Desert. The eastern end of the ranges joins the Fergusson Ranges, which run further east until they peter out in the Simpson Desert. There was no going around them. They had to be crossed, but their bizarre geology formed a formidable barrier.

There are no alpine slopes or cloud-cloaked lofty peaks that compare to the great mountains of the world, or even to other ranges, in Australia. There are certainly some spectacular peaks, the highest rising a kilometre above the nearby plains, but much the ranges look more like rough hills in long lines, receding beyond the horizon to infinity.

Approaching from the south across the dry, red-soiled, mulga-dotted plain, a ridge looms like an endless desert wall. Behind that ridge is a valley, and behind that valley is another ridge, then another valley, then another ridge. In some places, there is just one ridge; in other places, as many as seven. It is almost as if, at the dawn of time, long waves crashed along a gigantic inland sea, but the sea was turned to rock and the waves became a mountain range. The Arrernte people of the area had a legend that the ranges were formed by colossal warring caterpillars, frozen forever into the shapes of the ridges. Finding one gap was not enough, if that gap breached only the first ridge line. To get through, a gap needed to be found that passed through all the ridges.

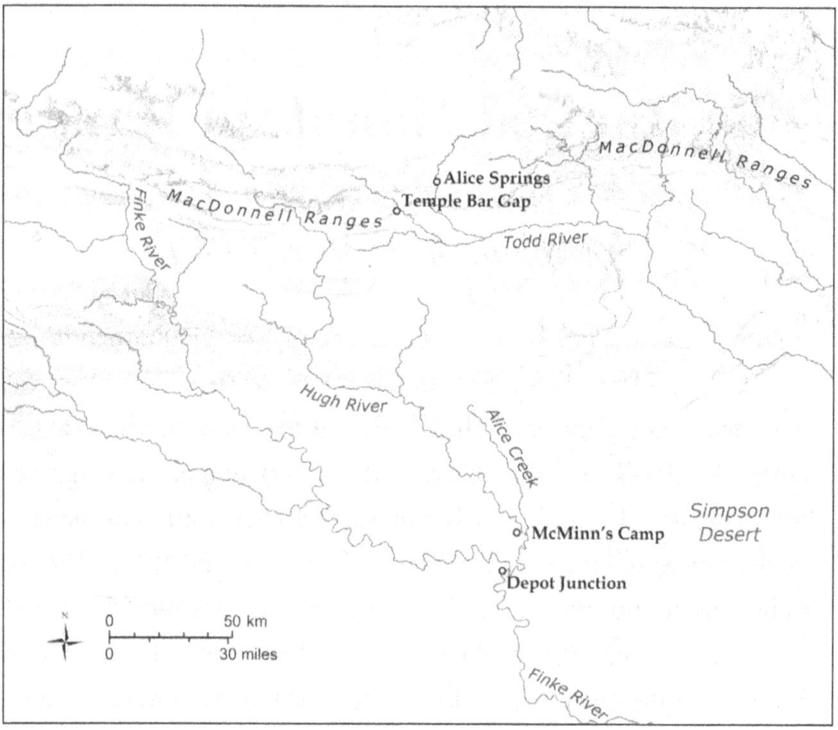

The MacDonnell Ranges

John Ross found no such gap.

By specifically instructing Ross to explore the plains on the other side, Todd had given him no option this time but to cross the ranges. Yet even given that very specific mandate, Ross went far to the east, going over the Fergusson Ranges, where the telegraph would not pass. He did so on horseback, pushing through canyons and clambering steep inclines, on a route that would be unsuitable for wagons, bullocks, and telegraph crews.

Ross's party went as far north as Central Mount Stuart—the small mountain designated by Stuart as the centre of Australia, because the distances to the east and west coastlines were the same, as were the distances to the north and south coast. Here, Ross proudly retrieved the message in a bottle left by Stuart eleven years earlier.

They meandered around the featureless mulga plain that borders the MacDonnell Ranges. In thick scrub, Ross lost his maps—his invaluable copies of John McDouall Stuart's maps—so they retraced their steps for two days, anxiously scanning the ground until they found them. They probed the MacDonnell Ranges without success. Ross's surveyor Harvey got lost in the baffling gullies, causing them another two days' delay. They ran out of water more than once, ran low on food and briefly became lost again, finally crossing to the south side of the ranges at a place called Brinkley's Bluff. Here, the mountains were high and craggy, unsuitable for wagons or telegraph lines. Ross admitted as much in his diary, writing, 'it is not possible to bring the line through this mass of precipitous mountains'.

Out of the ranges, they crossed the south mulga plain to the junction of the Hugh and Finke rivers, where they set up camp. They and their horses were tired and hungry. They had run out of flour more than a week earlier, and had run out of meat long before. There was a small, almost dry waterhole in the river bed, barely enough to satisfy their thirst.

The Hugh and Finke rivers are ephemeral desert rivers. They had no running water; their beds were dry sand. They were a string of waterholes and sand beds along a winding, dry, river-shaped canal. Gumtrees lined the dry river courses, marking for thirsty travellers a chance to find a muddy pool.

Once in a while the Finke and the Hugh, and Australia's other ephemeral rivers, do run. Once in a while, inland storms rage across the desert plains, blasting them with spectacular lightning shows and downpours, drenching the parched earth and turning those dry riverbeds into torrents. But even then, they do not flow to the ocean, but drain into that great salt plain, Lake Eyre, which in turn fills with water, teems briefly with life, then sinks back into its salty, desolate slumber.

Ross and his party of explorers would soon experience that rare event.

A day after they made camp, the first of the crews arrived at the junction, setting up their camps across from them on the Finke's south bank, where they dug a well. Two of the five central crews, designated A and B by Todd, had reached their starting points along the way, but the three others needed to continue across the long, dry plain beyond the Finke and beyond that plain, the ranges. Harley Bacon, the storekeeper, set up his storehouse and named it 'Alice Well' in honour of Charles Todd's wife, Alice, but the name did not stick. The crews simply called the place 'Depot Junction'. As with previous campsites, the place bloomed into a city of canvas tents, hammocks, and stores.[1]

Some days later, Alfred Woods, the leader of one of the central construction crews, arrived. He had also been assigned the role of explorer and was the person to whom Ross was supposed to report.

Woods had left The Peake in November with a small group, tasked with scouting the route ahead. As Ross cut long arcs across Sturt's Stony Desert and the eastern ranges, Woods made short, quick forays, seeking campsites that had access to water, then returning to report his findings to the trudging crews. He was already annoyed with Ross, because the route to the Finke was hard and treacherous and poorly suited for laden packhorses. Ross had claimed there were ample waterholes along the way, but Woods had struggled to find water, and the waterholes he did find were meagre, muddy puddles that were barely sufficient.

Most annoying of all was that Ross had not gone to the assigned meeting place. Charles Todd had told them to meet on the Hugh River, at the junction of a creek known as Alice Creek (also named after Todd's wife), a short ride north of the junction of the Hugh and the Finke. When he heard that Ross was camped at there, Woods rode down to meet him.

Woods was appalled. Ross had nothing of value, except for the memento he had collected from Central Mount Stuart, which nobody had told him to collect. He had obeyed Todd's instructions in letter but not in spirit, paying scant attention to the urgent need to find a crossing.[2]

Harvey had drawn a map of the ranges, which he unfolded and laid on the ground. As the three of them—Ross, Harvey and Woods—kneeled around the map, Ross suggested that there was probably a gap at the eastern end, between the MacDonnell and Fergusson Ranges, because the ranges appeared to decline in that direction. He could not advise on how the crews could reach there, because he did not know of waterholes along the way. Indeed, on his previous expedition to the ranges, Ross himself had been forced to turn around due to lack of water.

This suggestion of a possible gap did nothing to improve Woods's estimation of Ross; if Ross thought there was a gap, it was baffling why he had not looked for it. Anyway, Woods was sceptical about the existence of such a gap, because John McDouall Stuart, who had made all this possible, believed that the MacDonnell and Fergusson Ranges were one continuous range. Stuart's words were not God's, but when stuck in the middle of Australia they were the next best thing and they certainly counted for a lot more than the words of John Ross.

In a private report to Todd, Woods wrote, 'This entails much delay and extra work on us; and all their hardships, of which they have had not a few, and misdirected exertions, have been undergone *for nothing* [his emphasis].'[3]

Back at his camp, Woods held a crisis meeting with the other two crew leaders, Gilbert McMinn and Whitfield Mills. They had no route forward and had lost all confidence in Ross to find one. They needed to explore the ranges themselves.

More workers arrived and set up camp at Depot Junction. More bullock teams, pulling drays laden with equipment, more horses and wagons, more dogs and sheep. A hundred camels arrived on 4 February, with mail and much-needed provisions.

It was time to leave for the Roper River. Ross wrote a report for Todd, took it across the river and delivered it to Harley Bacon, who had established a makeshift post office. Ross showed his surveyor William Harvey an inventory list he had written out. Harvey lost his temper, complaining that it was insufficient, and that they would be woefully underequipped for the long journey ahead.

They argued about the list. Then they argued about other things. Ross accused Harvey of getting them lost. Harvey resigned or Ross fired him—maybe both. Regardless, Harvey left the camp and Ross no longer had a surveyor.

Alfred Giles, also in Ross's party, happened to have a brother who was a surveyor, working with construction teams further south at Charlotte Waters, so Ross sent Giles to fetch his brother and hire him as Harvey's replacement.

Giles was gone for three weeks and in the meantime, it started to rain. A trickle of water ran down the gully of the riverbed; the trickle became a stream; the stream became a rushing torrent. The river became a true river. It kept raining.

Alfred Giles's brother declined the offer to join Ross's expedition, and wrote a letter to that effect for Alfred to take back. Giles had travelled across hard, dry terrain on his way to Charlotte Waters, but the return journey was like travelling in a different country. It was a land of swamps and bogs and running creeks, and morning fog and slippery tracks.

By the time Giles reached Finke River once more, the water had risen more than halfway to the top of the bank. He crossed with great trouble. Those camped near the bank had moved further away, to higher ground, as a precaution. The next morning, they woke to discover that the river had risen by another two feet overnight. It continued to rise all that day, and by sunset, the river was a hundred yards wide. Those on either bank were cut off from each other. The workers could not continue north, even if they'd known where they were going. Everything was wet. Equipment, clothes, even blankets. Diseases quickly spread; with a campsite packed with people, horses, bullocks, sheep and dogs, effluent was an urgent problem. Flies pestered the horses, driving them 'nearly mad'. And almost everyone suffered from 'bung-eyes'.[4]

The three self-appointed explorers came up with a plan.

Woods would continue his role as forward scout for waterholes and campsites, mapping a route to the ranges. Mills would follow the Hugh River up to the ranges, then work eastwards along the range, while Gilbert McMinn would look for gaps further east. They left on 8 February, each taking a couple of hand-picked companions, including Aboriginal guides.

Mills's group made slow progress up the Hugh. The river twisted back and forth so much, and made the journey so long, that Mills made forays over the plain, looking vainly for waterholes that would allow them to take a more direct route. Just as they reached the ranges, after ten days of slogging around the river's sandy bends, rain began to fall. It kept falling. The ground was so boggy that they could barely move. After being stuck for five days in one place, they ran out of food, so they returned. They'd had trouble reaching the range because there was too little water and had trouble returning because there was too much water.

Meanwhile, Gilbert McMinn had more luck. He tried first to follow the Alice Creek, but this took him into barren wastelands, so he returned, followed the Hugh for a while, then struck away to the ranges. He found a gap through the outer ridges at a place now known as Temple Bar, then crossed a small valley to a gap in the second ridge. Another, wider valley opened before them, bordered on the far side by a high, craggy ridge. The ridge was split by a gorge that perhaps could be traversed on horseback, but was too steep and narrow for drays and wagons. He named that gorge Simpson's Gap, but did not go through it. Instead he camped, then climbed a high hill, where he could see that this valley stretched away far to the east and north-east, where no more ridges were visible. On that hilltop, he wrote in his diary, 'From here there appears to be the possibility of a road . . . The range gets very low and goes to the east as far as the eye can follow it.'

The track he had found zigzagged about, and he had reached the far side of the range, but McMinn believed it was a way through.[5]

He returned south, arriving at the Hugh River campsite on 4 March 1871, the same day as Whitfield Mills.[6] They had wasted more than a month due to floods and the mystery of the MacDonnell Ranges, time that could not be recouped. There was less than nine months until the deadline. The floods had receded, so McMinn and Mills told the crews and bullock teams to start moving north along the Hugh River. Meanwhile, the explorers would go ahead to keep looking for a gap and would report back once they found one.

As John Ross prepared to set out for the north, he realised he no longer had his copies of John McDouall Stuart's maps, which he would need to follow; William Harvey had taken them with him when he was fired. Since Harvey was now camped over at Depot Junction on the other side of the river, Ross sent a messenger to retrieve the maps from him, but the messenger returned empty-handed. Harvey said he had given the maps to Whitfield Mills, camped further along the Hugh River with Alfred Woods and others.[7]

Ross had no time to lose. He knew that Mills had been out exploring and was likely to do so again—with his maps. Ross and his reduced band left the junction on 7 March, their first stop the camp at Alice Creek, which they reached that evening.[8]

Whitfield Mills was not there. Someone at the campsite told them that Mills had left that day on a second expedition north, to investigate the gap that McMinn had found. Ross rode north, struggling through the sandy plain of spinifex and mulga, hoping to find Mills and his maps.

Mills and his two companions reached the MacDonnell Ranges for the second time on 11 March. The water that had bedevilled them last time was now their friend, because they had no need of the endless curves of the Hugh; they could ride to the ranges directly.

About thirty miles east of Stuart's track, and about six miles east of the Temple Bar passage that G.R. McMinn had found, they reached a river. Ross had encountered this river further south-east, and in a shameless act of flattery, had named it the Todd River, after his boss. If Ross had followed it, rather than crossing it, he would have arrived at the place on the bank where Mills now sat on his horse.

Mills could see that the river seemed to enter the range through a gap a short distance north. The Todd is an ephemeral river, but when Mills reached it, there was water. They rode through the gap and found a second gap in the next ridge beyond. Mills named the first gap Heavitree Gap, after the school he had attended in England. When they followed the river through the second gap, they found a hidden grassy valley, dotted with waterholes brimming with fresh, clear water. Mills believed it was a chain of springs. He named the biggest waterhole 'Alice Spring', after Todd's wife. The town that grew nearby became known as 'Alice Springs', an iconic outback town.[9] Of course, the area already had a name: Athurreyurre.[10] Mills believed that the water was permanent, but the Alice Spring is not a true spring, filling only when the Todd River flows. When the river brings water, it bubbles with life, but soon dries out again, and the Alice 'spring' is nothing more than a bed of hot sand, whipped by the dry desert wind.[11]

Mills ventured beyond Alice Spring and discovered a gap in the next, final ridge. They turned south and rode back through Temple

Bar Gap, into the still-wet desert. Within the space of hours, they met John Ross and his party riding north. Mills informed Ross of the gaps in the ranges that he and McMinn had found. Ross demanded that Mills hand over his maps and Mills did so. Ross entered the ranges through Temple Bar Gap and wove through the valleys, probably passing to the north of the Alice Spring.

We can conjecture about Ross's route through the ranges, but we cannot know for sure, because, with no surveyor, he made no maps. Also, on his journey north, somewhere between there and the Roper River, he lost his diary. Ross had come highly recommended as the best available explorer in the colony, but he was prone to losing objects and losing his way. Todd must have rued the passing of John McDouall Stuart.

Mills located his crew on the Hugh River on 19 March. They had crossed the line of latitude that defined their starting point, so he got them to make camp, cut down some nearby trees for poles and commence work on 21 March. They were starting a month late, but at least Mills knew which way to build the line. As it approached the ranges, his crew would take the line through Temple Bar Gap and, from there, to Alice Springs.[12]

26

The Steady, Soaking Rain

Port Darwin to the Roper River, 18 February–5 June 1871

The advance working camp at the Katherine River was running out of supplies. Paqualin had been gone for three weeks, promising to ensure that fresh supplies arrived, but no deliveries had come here, to the end of the track, nor was there any sign of Paqualin himself. William McMinn headed back to Number Two Depot to investigate. On the way, he became stranded on the bank of the flooded Fergusson River. He waited for three days, hoping that it would subside, then simply took the plunge. He swam across, leading his horses by their tethers. One of the horses was swept away downstream and was not seen again. That river alone would explain why no supplies had come.

McMinn arrived at Number Two Depot on 18 February, where he learned that the supply wagon had arrived—the one that was waylaid at Rum Jungle—but it could not go further, given the state of the track. There was palpable animosity in the air. Three days earlier, the work crews here had circulated and signed a petition, demanding pay packets each week, until their return to Adelaide. The contracts stipulated that they would be paid on their return to Adelaide, but they had realised they would never see the on-time bonus and if the project halted, they might see no money at all. Such a demand was impossible to meet, because Paqualin simply did not have bags of cash that could be dispensed as pay packets. The crew grudgingly returned to work.[1]

A week later, the meat ran out, so the crew started killing and eating the bullocks. Doing so saved their lives, but it also meant that they had eaten the heavy transport. And any bullock meat not consumed immediately needed to be preserved with salt. This meant that they soon ran out of salt. The sugar stores were ruined by rainwater, so they were out of sugar, too.[2]

McMinn wrote a formal letter to Paqualin, then walked across camp and handed it to him. He did not want to have yet another argument with the manager: a letter was more official. The letter was a warning, outlining McMinn's concerns. The stores were unprotected from the weather, causing food to be spoiled. The equipment (purchased and owned by the government, as he was quick to point out) had also been left to the elements and had deteriorated. The work teams had run out of sugar and salt, which had been ruined by rainwater. Finally, there were not enough workers to complete the job.

McMinn demanded to know if more workers and supplies were being brought from Adelaide. If his concerns were not answered, he would have no choice but to terminate the contract. Paqualin had no answer, because he did not know. McMinn told him to find out.[3]

Meanwhile, at the Katherine River camp at the end of the track, with both Paqualin and McMinn gone, the workers rebelled. Sheets of rain fell every day, forcing work to stop, but the two team leaders, Tymn and King, wanted work to resume. They wanted the workers to cross the river on makeshift rafts so that they could continue poling south. Once they crossed that river, their connection to Port Darwin, and even to Number Two Depot, would be even more tenuous, and they would be in even more jeopardy. A deputation confronted Tymn and King, informing them that everyone was on strike until fresh provisions arrived.

Tymn negotiated an end to the strike by agreeing to send a small group to Number Two Depot to bring back some provisions, on condition that the others crossed the river and resumed work on the south bank. To everyone's relief, a small delivery of provisions arrived soon afterwards.

But before work could recommence, the equipment needed to be taken across the river. They loaded a wagon, tied a rope to it and, with several men heaving and hoing, tried to pull it across, but the wagon broke away, was swept downstream and was lost. They built a large raft out of pine logs bolted together, under the supervision of a man who was once a shipwright. The raft worked, and after shunting over the remaining gear, the team started construction south of the river on 24 February, in daily pouring rain.[4]

No more bullocks could be spared for food. After poling for ten days in horrendous weather through boggy country, they had only made twelve miles of progress. The workers mutinied. Twenty-nine of them—almost half—quit on the spot and set off on foot, north along the muddy track, towards Number Two Depot and Port Darwin. Their long trek was so miserable that some of them came to wish they had stayed at the camp.[5]

Sick and hungry, the remaining workers tried some more industrial action. Another deputation was formed, and a representative took their grievances to the manager's tent, while the others hovered outside, listening. Their delegate complained that 'there is not enough food to fill our guts'. He noted that they were even out of sugar. Tymn retorted, 'sugar is a luxury, and not a necessity, certainly not to fill your guts'.[6]

Tymn could not solve the problem. After all, he was stuck there, too. He could not simply magic fresh supplies into existence.

Another small load of supplies did come, but morale remained at rock bottom. Malaria, dysentery, bung-eyes, and other nameless maladies beset them.[7]

Quite suddenly, the wet season was over. The rain stopped and the lush grass turned to stubble. Clouds of flies pestered the workers, swarming over the food and making everyone sick.[8]

A spark of good news for McMinn came down the line on 18 March. The *Gulnare* had returned to port that day, bringing the explorer McLachlan from his expedition. They had been gone for months, far longer than McMinn had hoped, because they were waylaid by storms, forcing them to shelter. When the storms finally passed, they went to Normanton in Queensland for resupply before returning.[9] McLachlan reported that the Roper River was navigable by ship for eighty miles. The Roper plan was viable.

McLachlan had explored much of the river by the *Gulnare*'s cutter rather than the ship itself, which waited downstream. They met tragedy one evening while the cutter was anchored by the bank of a tributary. The crew was wakened by screams. The *Gulnare*'s first mate, William Read, had been sleeping on deck with his leg dangling over the water. The crew saw Read's head and shoulders being dragged through the water by a crocodile. Before they could do anything, he was gone. His horrified crewmates rowed furiously for two days back to ship.[10]

McMinn had other business to attend to: Charles Todd had instructed him to meet an explorer named John Ross near the Roper River in April. After delivering his missive to Paqualin, he chose four companions, including the experienced explorer and surveyor Stephen King, to accompany him.

The five of them rode down the track to the Katherine—it was drier now and easier going—and met disgruntled men coming the other way. The party splashed across the river, now subsided, and stayed at the workers' campsite at the very end of the line. After a brief rest there, they left for the Roper River at the end of March.[11]

McMinn and his party reached the Roper River on 4 April 1871. John Ross was supposed to arrive sometime in the second half of the month. Every day at noon, they lit a signal fire to guide Ross to the place.

McMinn was supposed to wait until the end of April, and he would have, if the project had been on track, but it was not. After waiting for a week, he planted a flagpole at the end of a nearby high range, easily seen by anyone approaching, and nailed a wooden sign to it. On the sign, he wrote: *Mr Ross dig half a mile north west. W McMinn.*[12] Half a mile north-west of the sign, they buried hermetically sealed containers with provisions and a letter inside, then made conspicuous markings nearby to indicate exactly where to dig.

Ross and his group of explorers did not perish, but, just like Burke and Wills, they missed the signs left for them, so they missed the buried provisions, after arriving a month late and at the wrong part of the river.

McMinn returned north, arriving at the working camp ten miles south of the Katherine River. It was deserted. He continued to the river and crossed it to the campsite on the other side, where the remnants of the construction team were camped. Most had quit and had returned north. The remaining workers were, once again, on strike.

Paqualin was there, having returned from Number Two Depot.

McMinn opened his pack, got out some paper, a pen and ink, and sat down and wrote another letter. He handed it to Paqualin. The letter stated that, under the powers vested in him by the Government of South Australia, he declared Darwent and Dalwood's contract null and void. Paqualin was henceforth relieved of all duty. McMinn informed all the workers there of the decision and told them to return to Port Darwin, where they would be taken back to Adelaide. For many of them, this was welcome news.[13]

Mc Minn and Paqualin argued. Paqualin pleaded for more time, at least another month. He pointed out that the wet season was over now, the roads were drying and the rivers falling. They would soon all be back at work and making great progress. McMinn wasn't interested. He said he had 'had enough of Darwent and Dalwood's bunkum'.[14]

At least, that's what the records say he said, but McMinn probably used much stronger language than 'bunkum'. Either way, the contract was cancelled.[15]

A worker in Port Darwin wrote: 'After holding out as long as we could, we had to beat a retreat, being fairly starved out 220 miles from Port Darwin. It was rather a strange sight to see the men as they came down in straggling parties, with their half-starved looks and their long, shaggy, dirty beards.'[16]

A supply ship from Adelaide had arrived in late April and another from Timor in May, both too late.[17]

By the start of June, all but a handful of workers had returned to the port. The deadline was seven months away, yet all work on the northern end had stopped. Even so, McMinn was sure he had made the right call, and that under new management—his management—the line would be finished either by the deadline or soon after. He knew his decision would be controversial, so decided to go to Adelaide to explain it, before returning north to complete the project.

He retained a small workforce in Port Darwin of the few he trusted who were willing to stay. They were placed under McMinn's second-in-command, Bob Burton, the former shipwright who had designed the rafts for the Katherine River. He told Burton to go down to the Roper to map some suitable supply tracks, ones that would not turn to slush in the next wet season.[18]

Everyone else, including McMinn and Paqualin, boarded the *Gulnare*. They set sail on 6 June for a slow, sad journey home.[19]

27

A Wilful, Lavish Land

Roper River, May–June 1871

After passing through the MacDonnell Ranges a final time, John Ross and his party crossed a featureless, mulga-strewn plain. Near a place now known as Barrow Creek, they had a hostile encounter with a group of Kaititja men.[1]

The Kaititja men called out to them, beckoning them to come and talk, and one stepped forward, offering a dead possum in goodwill. After a confused exchange, Ross continued, with the men following, indicating with gestures that there was water and a resting place nearby. The party found the place, but were suspicious, so stopped only briefly.

As they departed, the Kaititja followed. They could do so easily because the explorers' horses were ambling at walking pace. Fires sprang up behind the party, then two men sprinted ahead, lighting fires in front of them. Smoke billowed over the party, blown by a fierce wind from the south-east, while the men approached under the smoky cover. It was a coordinated, rehearsed ambush. Another fire was lit near the leading packhorse. As the men came closer, Ross shouted at them and raised his gun as a threat, but the gesture meant nothing to them.

Ross wheeled his horse around and charged towards them, then fired both barrels of his shotgun into the air. The men turned and ran. At least one was hit by the buckshot spray, but Ross doubted it caused serious injury. Giles chuckled later that the buckshot 'would no doubt amuse their medicine-man to extract, and, I hoped, teach them a lesson'.[2]

Quite likely, Ross and Giles were right about the effect of the buckshot; its lethality diminishes beyond a very short range. As for the 'lesson', well, there was perhaps truth in that too, although the lesson is viewed very differently today, because, after all, that's what the weapons were for. The white men carried weapons to defend themselves and, less directly, to teach 'lessons'.

The explorers reached the Roper River on 19 May. The instructions from Charles Todd were to follow a tributary, the Strangways River, leading to the Roper, where they would see signal fires and find William McMinn. Ross thought he had found the Strangways, but it was a different river, the Elsie, which took them to a different part of the Roper, upstream from the meeting place.[3] They crossed the river and kept going north, hoping to run into telegraph construction crews.

Near the Katherine River, they entered some low, rocky hills, where they found poles, but no wire. Their excitement turned to confusion when they realised that nobody was there. Stumps of trees, cut down for use as poles, had sprouts growing from them, revealing that months had elapsed. There were no fresh tracks of horses or wagons or drays anywhere. A piece of tin was nailed to a pole, with pricked holes making the number '202'. It was a distance marker: they were 202 miles from Port Darwin.

They rode along the track in the direction of Port Darwin. After a while, on 6 June, they met two riders coming the other way, who introduced themselves as Northern Territory policemen. They told the explorers that the contract was cancelled and that the workers had returned to Adelaide, leaving that same day.[4]

The hope of completing the line by New Year's Day, only seven months away, was surely out of reach. With that sobering realisation, the explorers continued north to Port Darwin.

28

The Far Horizon

South Australia, June 1871

Across South Australia, the first frenzy of preparation had settled into a steady hum of activity. Imported equipment reached the wharves of Port Adelaide and Port Augusta for cartage inland. Empty bullock drays returned to The Peake, ready for reloading with fresh supplies. Horse-drawn wagons went back and forth between Adelaide and The Peake, threading along the grassy plains at the foothills of the Flinders and at the edges of the salt lakes. Bully beef was manufactured near Port Augusta to feed the far-flung, hungry workers. Straps, blankets, boots, and all other manner of equipment wore out and needed replacing.

It was not Charles Todd's telegraph, nor was it the Premier's. It was everyone's. It was a source of colonial pride and gave a sense of common purpose. People were hungry for news about it, but news was almost entirely absent from the Port Darwin end and sporadic from the centre, relying as it did on camel mail or verbal reports from returned bullock drivers.

But the closest section of the line, Bagot's section from Port Augusta to just beyond The Peake, had roads and villages and farmhouses, so news of progress along it was plentiful—and it was all good. Bagot's crews had struggled in the treeless plains near the salt lakes, but Todd had supplied them with iron 'Oppenheimer' poles, and allowed them to space the poles further apart in those stretches.[1]

A telegraph station had been built at Beltana, fitted out with batteries, relays, and Morse equipment. By the end of June, the line of poles from Port Augusta extended through Beltana and Strangways Springs (the first two stations), to within ten miles of The Peake. The wiring teams were within a week of connecting Beltana to the colony's telegraph network, and construction of the Strangways Springs and Peake telegraph stations was underway.

At Charlotte Waters, Dick Knuckey's team, working at a cracking pace, had erected a stone storehouse and were on track to finish three months ahead of schedule. Knuckey would then take them further north to assist with other sections.[2]

Todd had employed a physician, Dr Frederick Renner, to provide medical services to workers along the line. After leaving Adelaide mid-February, Renner reached Charlotte Waters in April, where he treated his first overland patient for a case of scurvy. At Harley Bacon's depot on the Finke River, he treated an Afghan camel driver who had been bitten by a black snake, which had been kept at the depot as a pet. The man had been sick for a week without any treatment, and was drowsy and weak. Dr Renner applied ammonia orally and through injection, after which the man recovered in two days. It should be noted that the use of ammonia compound for snake bite was discontinued in 1874 after a commission in India concluded that it had no remedial effects. The man may have simply recovered from the bite after another two days' rest, regardless of Dr Renner's treatment.[3]

Further north, along Central Section B, poles had been erected for seventy miles, again on target for completion.

Still further north, near Alice Springs (Central Section C, managed by Whitfield Mills), progress was just as rapid and the few reports that trickled back suggested that relations were good with the Aboriginal people there. It was said that, for the most part, the Aboriginal people kept away from the telegraph camps, but the interactions that did occur were amicable. On one occasion, three Aboriginal men approached some telegraph workers bathing or drinking at a creek, gesturing for them to come closer. When the workers did so, the Aboriginal men gestured for them to put their hands on the ground, which the workers did. The Aboriginal men felt them all over, and seemed either confused or curious about the men's clothing. There followed a friendly interaction in which one of the Aboriginal men fitted a boot to one foot, but discovered that he could not walk properly with it.[4]

The few reports from Port Darwin suggested that there, too, work was proceeding well. The people of Adelaide had every reason to believe that the line—their line—would be finished by the end of the year, as planned.

Queensland's Chief Telegraphist, William Cracknell, fired another salvo in his annual report, urging once more that Queensland join with the British Australian Telegraph Company to extend the undersea cable from Port Darwin, across the Gulf of Carpentaria, to Queensland.[5] Cracknell explained why Todd's overland scheme was doomed:

> The country this line will traverse between Lake Torrens and Newcastle Waters, extending over fourteen degrees latitude, is described as scarcely better than a desert, where little or no timber can be obtained for construction purposes, and during dry seasons, it is for the most part, devoid of surface water, and feed for cattle cannot be obtained.

He concluded, 'All hopes of working a line of this description with anything like regularity must, I fear, be abandoned, at any rate until the country is thoroughly opened up and permanently settled.'

South Australians bristled. Todd needed to respond.

Todd reminded Cracknell that he had previously held out the hand of cooperation, but that hand had been slapped away. At the intercolonial conference of 1870, his colony, South Australia, had offered to partner with Queensland on the cable connection, but Queensland had declined. Now it was Queensland's turn to bristle.[6]

Cracknell was partly right, in that water was scarce through much of the continent's interior. But that problem was rapidly becoming solved. Reliable water sources had been found at Dalhousie Springs,

Charlotte Waters, and Alice Springs, and in some waterless places, wells drew on underground reservoirs. Sure, the dry mulga plain north of Alice Springs was tough going, but even that long stretch was not holding up the work. The arid heart could be traversed. What neither Todd nor Cracknell yet knew was that Todd's real problems lay much further north.

29

The Grey Clouds Gather

Adelaide, July 1871

The first warning of the northern disaster arrived by mail on 3 July, stating that William McMinn had cancelled the contract with Darwent and Dalwood, and intended to supervise the completion of work himself. The letter did not say that the *Gulnare* was on its way, because it had been sent from Port Darwin weeks earlier, via steamship from Ceylon, before the *Gulnare* had left.

Todd asked the contractor Dalwood for his input. Dalwood said that he and Darwent were prepared to continue the work, whatever McMinn had said or done, and they did not accept that the contract was cancelled.[1] Todd sent orders up the line to Woods, manager of Central Team D (north of Alice Springs, in the vicinity of Central Mount Stuart), that his crew should finish their work as quickly as possible, using only ten poles to the mile instead of twenty, then move north to assist. He looked into hiring a steamer from Melbourne to take extra workers and supplies.

Then, on 8 July, the *Gulnare* arrived in port, sending shockwaves through Adelaide.

There had been scant news about the northern expedition after the fleet had left for Port Darwin a year earlier. The sporadic updates that arrived by mail were out of date and contradicted each other. Prior to that day, there had been no sense that it was going so badly that the whole thing would be called off.

As soon as they stepped ashore, McMinn and Paqualin vied for attention, each accusing the other of causing the disaster. On the voyage home, McMinn had written a report on the matter, which he promptly delivered to Charles Todd. He said nothing about strikes, or mass resignations, or a crashed wagon of rum. He made no mention of flooded rivers, flyblown shirts, or the waves of malaria, dysentery, and bung-eye that swept through the camps. Perhaps he wanted to avoid a public mud-slinging match. If so, he miscalculated.

Darwent and Dalwood, their contract in tatters and facing financial disaster, attacked, and they made it personal.

> Mr McMinn carefully abstains from telling the public how much of the delay was due to the Government. He does not give any information as to the difficulties which he threw in the way of the undertaking, or why he should have seized upon stores belonging to the contractors to indemnify the Government for advances which were not made . . .
>
> We cannot be expected to submit quietly to the confiscation of our property and the injury to our character and credit which has been attempted by the ill-considered and oppressive conduct of a public official. The public may not be aware that Mr McMinn himself tendered for the work and was unsuccessful . . .
>
> Mr McMinn (a very young man) was confirmed in his despotic powers, and the public can now see how he has used them.

An account by one of McMinn's aides, portraying McMinn positively but casting the workers in a bad light, was published anonymously in the *Register*. This elicited protests from workers, especially the accusation that they had 'rebelled' and were 'infuriated' at their conditions. It was all a gross exaggeration, they said.[2]

McMinn was too rash, his critics said. Yes, resupply ships had been late, but they had arrived, eventually. And progress was delayed, but that was during the wet season, which was now over. McMinn had sent them packing just as the weather turned and favourable work conditions emerged.

The public was confused. Had McMinn done the right thing or had he acted impulsively? Was it true that he had bid for the contract himself? And if it was true, perhaps he was acting out of jealousy. Was he the despot he was accused of being?

Todd was unwavering in his support for McMinn, certain that he would not have made the call without good reason. Likewise, Darwent and Dalwood supported their manager, Paqualin.

McMinn was naively optimistic that the project could still be completed on time and that work would resume as soon as he returned to the Northern Territory with a fresh workforce. In his report, he said,

> From the experience I have gained of the country traversed, and of the nature of the work, during my supervision of the contract, I am of opinion that it is possible to complete the line within a few weeks of the stipulated period. To effect this, however, extraordinary means will have to be provided, and an energetic party enlisted without delay. It will be well to consider the saving of time possible by procuring the stock required in Queensland.[3]

Technically, McMinn had reason to believe that he would be appointed to run the contract in Darwent and Dalwood's place. The contract had stipulated that if the overseer voided it, then the overseer would take control of the work. But that clause was inserted because the work was conducted in a very remote place; it assumed the overseer would stay put. In returning to Adelaide, McMinn had lost his advantage, giving the government a free hand to choose whomever they liked to take the contract—and they were not inclined to choose him. He was too controversial. He was politically toxic.

The old whaler, John Hart, who had first crossed swords with Todd sixteen years earlier, was still in politics and was the current Premier. Hart's views about the English scientist had evolved. Indeed, he had championed Todd's overland telegraph scheme. It was Hart who proposed the bill to provide Todd with the funds, and it was Hart who had handed Todd total control of the project. But now, given the latest events, he had cold feet.

When the news first broke, Hart hurried to the Governor's residence, only to find that Todd had beaten him there, and the two of them were already holding a crisis meeting. That hardly improved his attitude.

Three days after the *Gulnare* sailed into port, Hart presided over an all-day cabinet crisis meeting. He was in no mood for consultation or consensus; he took control. Todd was inclined to send McMinn back to run the project, but Hart had no interest in doing that. He appointed the colony's 27-year-old railway engineer, Robert Patterson, to the job. There was no committee, no selection panel, and no interview. Hart simply made the decision.

Patterson would be paid £300 above his current salary and would receive a bonus of £1500 if he finished the work on time. Even if he didn't, he would get a £1000 bonus if he completed it by 15 January 1872, £600 if by the end of January, and £300 if by the end of February. But these generous terms were non-negotiable. Patterson had no choice: he was going to the Northern Territory, whether he wanted to or not—and it became clear later that he would much have preferred not.[4]

During his time in the north, McMinn had found a solution to the supply line problem in the Roper River. He urged the government to send the new expedition to the Roper River, not Port Darwin, so that they could quickly restart work.

Todd agreed. In May, believing that the *Gulnare* was on its way to the Roper with supplies, he had written to Hart: '. . . the mouth of the Roper has been surveyed, and found to be navigable for a considerable distance, which has been availed of by sending all the materials for the line, south of that river, round by sea instead of being carted overland.'[5]

Of course, it had now transpired that the *Gulnare* was not 'availing itself' of the river after all, but was anchored in port in Adelaide. Despite having egg on his face, Todd doubled down, urging Hart to send steamers to the Roper River. However, Hart was not interested in Todd's opinion.[6] Hart 'relied on his knowledge of nautical matters', instructing Patterson very precisely that, when he sailed north with a new workforce, he was to take them directly to Port Darwin, not the Roper River.[7]

With the colony at risk of humiliation and financial ruin, the stakes were high. In an unusual move for a premier, Hart took personal control, not just of decision making, but of arrangements and procurement. He moved quickly. The *Gulnare* had arrived in port on a Friday; Hart held crisis cabinet talks the following Monday; he appointed Patterson, secured new funds, and put those funds at Patterson's disposal that same day; then on Tuesday, Hart boarded a ship for Melbourne to acquire ships and supplies at short notice.[8]

Five ships were commissioned to take personnel, equipment, animals, and supplies to the Northern Territory. One of these, the *Aldinga*, was only required to transport the personnel to Melbourne, where they would board the *Omeo*. Todd immediately wrote a message to Woods, in the Central sections, explaining what had happened and instructing Harvey's group—the northernmost crew—to reduce the line to only ten poles per mile in order to speed their progress, so they could hopefully finish early, then help with the Northern Section. The kick-on effect of that was that Harvey's crew would continue for longer than anticipated. Todd despatched extra supplies into the interior.[9]

Robert Patterson was a tall, dour, introverted engineer. He had smarts, but not people smarts. He was a cheerless, melancholy man who, you might say, tended to view the glass as half empty.

He had recently crushed the hopes of lobbyists for an expanded rail network. Political will had been accumulating for a rail extension pushing inland. When Patterson was asked to report on the feasibility, rail advocates hoped that this was just the next step in bringing it to a reality—much like Charles Todd's reports on the possibilities of telegraph. But Patterson saw only downsides. He reported that new rail lines would cost too much to build and bring in too little revenue. With that, the dream of an expanded South Australian rail network was over.

Patterson offered McMinn a place in the new expedition, but McMinn turned it down, sullenly remarking that he 'objected to the position which the government gave him'.[10]

After being sidelined from the big decisions, Todd was brought back into the loop. Patterson was instructed to report to him, rather than to the government directly.

Todd appointed a postmaster for the Northern Territory, John Little, to accompany the new expedition and appointed his orphaned nephew, Griffith Todd, to be Little's assistant.

Patterson's workforce departed in the *Aldinga* on 27 July 1871, with as much fanfare as the previous expedition had received almost a year earlier. Cadet surveyor William Crowder wrote, 'I never shook hands so much in my life and I am sure I promised to write to twenty fellows who I hope will forget about it as I shall.'[11]

In Melbourne, they transferred to the *Omeo*, which took them up the east coast towards Port Darwin.

Part V
Patterson's Journey

30

The Ghost of Expeditions Past

Port Darwin, August–October 1871

From the moment the *Omeo* arrived in Port Darwin, Robert Patterson's expedition echoed the previous, ill-fated expedition.[1] Again, the sleepy settlement was shocked by the unexpected arrival of a ship. Again, the cannon fired a welcome salute.

The Government Resident also arranged a fireworks display for that night, and in turn, Patterson invited the Government Resident and others to a dinner party aboard the *Omeo*. Over the next few days, the other ships arrived: the *Antipodes* (carrying the bullocks), the *Golden Fleece*, the *Laju*, and the *Himalaya*.[2]

Still there was no wharf, so again, the horses and bullocks had to swim ashore. There should have been one. The pylon-driving machine that had been shipped at great expense lay idle with grass sprouting around it. Instead of a wharf, Government Resident Douglas had continued to put all available hands to constructing a spacious stone residence for himself and his family, which was now complete. It had a large verandah, and rose from solid foundations which the Larrakeeyah had helped to build, in return for payments of flour.[3] It was, by far, the most impressive building in the settlement, yet two years later, Douglas's successor described it as 'an ill-devised dilapidated barn' and had parts demolished and rebuilt.[4]

Many of the horses and bullocks died swimming to shore, and many others looked unwell afterwards. They died because there was no wharf. They died so that the government resident could live in that beautiful stone house on the hill.

Again, the residents were caught in a state of indolence. Before leaving, McMinn had instructed his second-in-command, Bob Burton, to continue wiring unwired poles, but in the intervening three months, Burton's team had wired a mere thirty miles.

The inaction was not entirely Burton's fault. The wire needed to be delivered to Southport by ship for cartage inland, but Bloomfield Douglas had objected to the government vessels being used. The ships were under his command, not anyone else's, and he intended to keep them that way. So Burton's team sat idle, while the *Bengal* and *Larrakeeyah* lay anchored nearby, rocking on the waves. Douglas occasionally used the vessels for day trips to nearby beaches and islands, and for sojourns to Timor for supplies and mail.[5] For example, Douglas had organised an exploration of the abandoned settlements at Port Essington and Melville Island in July, travelling to them in the *Larrakeeyah*. They saw no evidence of Aboriginal people living there—perhaps due to a lack of permanent water sources—but they did see buffalo, English cattle, and horse tracks. They found old stone buildings at Port Essington, which appeared to have once been elaborate constructions. The gardens were gone, except for a few pineapple plants. Nothing else remained. The *Larrakeeyah* was returning to harbour when the first ships of Patterson's fleet arrived.[6]

The settlement's main activity was prospecting for gold. McLachlan—the surveyor who had explored the Roper by boat—had sortied about the landscape, supposedly to 'explore' and 'survey', but gold was his true motivation. Likewise, Douglas's expeditions to the islands were driven by the same motive.[7]

Relations with the Larrakeeyah were still good, despite harsh actions by Douglas. In April, a dispute had arisen between an unnamed white man and Binmook, a Larrakeeyah man. Binmook's pet dog became a nuisance so the white settler shot the dog; in return, Binmook speared the white man's horse and the horse had to be put down. Douglas learned about the spearing and decided that the culprit should be held responsible under British law, the crime punishable by flogging. When the police approached the Larrakeeyah settlement, Binmook fled. Douglas ordered that two other Larrakeeyah men be taken prisoner until such time as Binmook handed himself in.[8]

Tensions were high. The Larrakeeyah said they would never give Binmook up and threatened to spear every white person in the settlement if the hostages were not released. But Binmook defused the situation by handing himself in. He submitted to a flogging with a riding whip, then was released.

Surprisingly, after tempers settled down, cordial relations resumed between white settlers and the Larrakeeyah. The continued peaceful coexistence was thanks to Binmook's courage and stoicism. Had he remained in hiding, it could have been a different story.

It is likely that Douglas's hostage-taking strategy was encouraged or suggested by the head of Port Darwin's police, Inspector Foelsche. Douglas actually liked the Larrakeeyah people, naming a boat after them, and even leading them, on one occasion, on a pig hunt. Foelsche was less sentimental and more calculating.[9]

The explorer John Ross was convalescing from scurvy in a hut, having arrived overland only a few days before the *Omeo.* He had intended to return overland to Adelaide, but was too sick, so was waiting for the next available ship. When the *Omeo* departed a week later, Ross was aboard.[10]

Two agents of the telegraph company were also there, preparing for the arrival of the company's cable-laying fleet. One of them, James Squier, was courting the Government Resident's daughter Eleanor. He married her the following year. Eleanor's older sister, Harriet, who had planted the first pole, married a young surveyor named Dan Daly.[11]

Thanks to the previous work, a rudimentary telegraph line was operating between Port Darwin and the Katherine River, two hundred miles away. James Stapleton operated the port end, while a telegraphist named Andrew Howley operated the far end. The small, isolated camp at Number Two Depot was a miserable place, plagued by disease. A nineteen-year-old German, Alphonse Nienabar, had died at Number Two Depot in June after lapsing into a coma, following a series of malaria-induced seizures. He was buried under a palm tree there.[12]

The starting point for work was at the end of the track, on the far bank of the Katherine River. Meanwhile, the remotest crew in Central Australia, William Harvey's crew, was poling northwards, taking the line from Adelaide to a point about 640 miles south of Port Darwin. Patterson's expedition would have to pole and wire the gap from the Katherine River down to the northern end of Harvey's section: a distance of about 440 miles. There were no roads and the terrain was poorly understood. There was a risk that it would be too far for the horses and bullocks to carry their loads. To ease their burden, the animals were sent out with empty wagons and drays, while the *Gulnare* shipped their equipment to Southport for collecting there. That way, the first leg of the journey would be easier on them.[13]

Incredibly, again, the expedition's manager—this time Patterson rather than Paqualin—made rash, risky decisions. Patterson reckoned he could stop somewhat short, because he knew that Harvey had been instructed to continue poling further north once his section was complete. Patterson divided the gap into four sections and assigned four managers. He only had capacity for three wiring teams, so he assigned them to the three remotest poling crews, figuring that the poles of the nearest section, those across the Katherine River, could be quickly wired later. Speed, not quality, was the guiding principle. Finishing the line by the deadline of New Year's Day was surely out of reach, but Patterson was going to do all he could to try.

He encouraged his managers to take shortcuts wherever possible. For example, Todd had specified that the line should have twenty poles to the mile, but allowed that in some locations, like stretches of barren desert, only ten poles to the mile would be acceptable. Patterson told his managers to install only ten poles to the mile everywhere. He even said that they could avoid using poles at all, instead hanging the wire from tree to tree, if trees were available to do it.[14]

It was the prospect of a bonus that drove this madness, the massive, instant-riches bonus of £1500 that Premier John Hart had promised if the line was completed on time. Even if it was completed within two months of the deadline, Patterson would receive a smaller, but still substantial, bonus.[15]

The workers certainly saw it that way. One of the songs they sang had the lyrics:

> Hurry up, Jack!
> If we don't finish this job in seventy-two,
> Patterson's bonus will look pretty blue.[16]

Once again, Charles Todd's agent in Port Darwin was a voice of warning, and again, that voice was ignored. Whereas before it was William McMinn, now John Little played the role. In anticipation of a functioning telegraph line, Todd had appointed John Little as the Port Darwin Chief Telegraphist and Postmaster. Little was no stranger to isolated postings, having run the Robe telegraph office near the Victorian border for several years. He arrived aboard the *Omeo* with Todd's nephew, Griffith Todd, who would be his assistant.

Patterson frequently sought Little's advice. On one occasion, Patterson visited him at midnight, full of worry, wondering if he should abandon the section closest to the Katherine completely—because his workers could return to finish it 'any time'—to prioritise the most remote sections. Little encouraged him to do the opposite: focus on the closest sections, build them properly and leave the remote parts for later. They talked it over for hours, but Patterson made no firm decision, wanting to sleep on it first.

There was a curious disconnect between Patterson's anxiety and his high-risk strategy. When, on two occasions, Patterson told Little that the workers might starve to death, he seemed not to be expressing a desire to prevent it, but was simply worried that his project might run over time.

From the outset, Little was alarmed by Patterson's management and his finish-at-any-costs mindset. He was particularly alarmed by Patterson's plan to leave a gap in the wire south of the Katherine. If the line was laid continuously out from the port, as soon as wires were up, the crews would be in communication with Port Darwin. By intentionally leaving a gap, Patterson's plan doomed them to isolation for months.[17] In his diary, Little wrote: 'I am terribly anxious about the line and feel certain that Patterson's plan will be a failure.' Given the loss of so many animals, he encouraged Patterson to send an urgent message to Adelaide requesting more stock, but Patterson was reluctant.

But Little's pleading did have some effect. Patterson dropped the planned gap in the wire, reduced the number of crews from four to three and reduced the length of line for each crew. He reduced the length of the most distant section and decreed that it be built 'in a substantial manner', meaning no shortcuts. These instructions were sent to the Katherine River, but he had prevaricated for too long. The furthest crew, managed by Burton, had departed down the track, hurrying to reach its starting point before the wet. Patterson tried to organise for the message to be conveyed on horseback, but was told that it could not be done: Burton and his crew had crossed the Katherine River and were already out of contact.

Again, the stock struggled. Many animals that survived the swim to shore died in the following weeks. Reports came up the line of horses and bullocks either dying or having to be abandoned along the track. A month after Bob Burton's arrival at his crew's starting point, up to a third of the bullocks were dead. Not enough bullocks meant not enough drays, and that meant not enough food deliveries down the track.

The construction of the company telegraph hut was delayed by hard ground, and then by a decision to relocate it; the crews were taking too long to reach the Katherine River; the equipment and provisions likewise. Everything was too slow.

31

The Wreck of the *Gulnare*

Port Darwin, October 1871

Patterson knew his expedition was in trouble, but he dithered and prevaricated, asking everyone he could for advice on what to do. He changed his mind and changed it back again.

John Little had concluded from the start that the Roper River plan was the best, and that it had been foolish to bring the ships to Port Darwin, entailing such a long overland journey south to commence work. Patterson eventually came to the same conclusion, possibly after much persuasion and cajoling from Little. The Roper River was the key to success, and maybe even to survival.

Patterson assigned the *Gulnare* to deliver supplies to a place the explorers had named Leichhardt's Bar, about eighty miles up the river and a fairly short distance east of the planned telegraph line. He then sent a telegram to the Katherine River, asking them to despatch a team of bullock drivers to Roper Landing to meet the *Gulnare*, then distribute supplies up and down the line.

Carrying coils of wire, bags of flour and salt, ammunition, and various other supplies, *Gulnare* left Port Darwin on the evening of 5 October, low in the water with its heavy load. There was no moonlight, the tide was strong, and the seas were rough; squalls over the past few days had dragged both the *Gulnare* and *Bengal* westward, and the *Bengal*'s anchor had broken.[1] On the west side of Vernon Island, thirty miles into its journey, the *Gulnare* foundered on a coral reef, where it remained, stuck. The news did not reach Port Darwin for four days. The *Bengal* and *Larrakeeyah* were sent to retrieve the ship's cargo and crew. The *Gulnare* limped back to port, returning nine days after departing. It was deemed to be irreparable and was therefore condemned.

There were whispers that Captain Sweet was drunk on the night of the shipwreck. A marine board enquiry, held the following year in Adelaide, did not blame alcohol, but did blame Captain Sweet, primarily because he was the captain and the captain is always responsible when a ship is wrecked.[2]

It took days to bring the sailors back, transfer the *Gulnare*'s cargo to the *Bengal* and tow the wrecked ship back into port. An urgent message was sent down to the Katherine River, telling the bullock drivers not to go to the Roper Landing yet, but it was too late. They had gone and were out of contact.

More bad news came up the line. The second crew, under the supervision of the explorer G.G. McLachlan, was making very slow progress, and more of the animals had died. The delivery teams under the direction of Bedford Hack were struggling. The crews only had enough food to last them to the end of January.[3]

Little penned a private letter to Todd, to be sent by the next mail ship:

> Upon arrival I found that the line was completed to the Katherine distance 202 miles and working exceedingly well, the sulphate of magnesium batteries being a great success. (Stapleton at Port Darwin, Howley at the Katherine).
>
> The prospects of the line being completed within the time anticipated were I found quite out *of the question owing to the following causes:*
>
> 1. The abandonment of the Roper Scheme;
> 2. Heavy losses of stock on the voyage up and immediately after their arrival here, viz bullocks 28% horses 10%.

He explained to Todd that he had advised Patterson to change strategy, by completing a more modest stretch of line, and by abandoning the goal of connecting it to Adelaide by the deadline.

This was partly an explanation for why the deadline would be missed, and partly a warning about Patterson's poor leadership.[4]

Patterson requested that the *Bengal* take the cargo to the Roper River in place of the *Gulnare*. Bloomfield Douglas reluctantly agreed, but explained that his ship first had business to attend in Java, including a mail run. When the *Bengal* sailed for Java, Little's note to Charles Todd was in the mailbag in the hold.[5]

Near the end of October, the *Curaçao* brought news that the Queensland overland line from Cardwell to Normanton was almost complete, with only a hundred miles to go. Little had privately questioned McLachlan, who had explored extensively around the Roper and the Gulf of Carpentaria about the viability of a Queensland line through that terrain. He concluded, based on that conversation, that it was not viable at all, because so much of the land was susceptible to flooding. In depriving them of the contract, Todd had possibly saved the Queenslanders from disaster: there was never going to be a landline from Port Darwin to Normanton.[6]

However, a cable under the gulf, though it would be expensive, was possible, so news that Queensland's line had nearly reached the coast rang alarm bells. The company agent, Squier, asked for a progress update from Patterson, but was rebuffed. He went over Patterson's head to Bloomfield Douglas, but the Government Resident also refused to tell him anything.

Little lost his temper when he learned of their stonewalling. His diary probably accords with what he said to their faces: 'I see no object in concealing it. It will not mend matters and the cable company will distrust us. Besides, it's known all over the place that we are in a great fix, and the cable officials are taking note of all the tittle-tattle and rumours of the men. It would be much more straightforward to give them an official letter.'

With the *Curacao* about to depart, Little urged Patterson and Douglas to send a call for help to Adelaide. The message could travel as regular mail to Batavia, where it would be transmitted by telegraph to Singapore, then to Ceylon, then be taken by fast mail steamer to Adelaide. Granted, the message would take a few weeks, but it was the fastest method available. Yet neither Patterson nor Douglas was willing to do so, paranoid that the telegraph company would read their private telegram.

Patterson and Douglas concocted an alternative plan: they would send a message, but it would be taken aboard the *Larrakeeyah*—the sailing boat currently in harbour—to Normanton, then be relayed to Adelaide by telegraph from Queensland. Moreover, as postmaster, they assigned John Little himself to carry this important message. When he reached Normantown, Patterson told him not to come back, but to return to Adelaide once he reached Queensland. Patterson and Douglas were trying to rid themselves of this troublesome telegraphist.

Fearing for his life, Little pleaded with them to reconsider. The steamship route was safe and reliable, whereas sending a sailing boat across the Gulf of Carpentaria in the monsoon season, he believed, was lunacy. Patterson was unmoved. He coldly told Little that if he refused to go, then he would be held responsible for any calamities that occurred on the line.

Patterson relented on the *Curaçao* option, agreeing to send a telegram to Todd by the official mail route, but insisted that Little should still go to Normanton as a backup. The possibility of the mail being lost en route to Adelaide was remote, so the only explanation for sending Little to Normanton is that Patterson and Douglas wanted him gone.

In fairness, Little was not popular with workers either. He may have been right, but he was also annoying.

When word got out of the plan to send Little to Normantown, the company agents told Little they supported him in his protests. Colonel Finniss confided to Little that he would report to London that 'no one is in charge here'.[7]

Little was trapped. He wrote in his diary, 'I am fairly between two fires.'[8]

Patterson and Douglas prevailed, despite the company's objections. When the *Bengal* sailed to the Roper River, it would take the *Larrakeeyah* on board. In the Gulf of Carpentaria, the *Larrakeeyah* would be lowered into the water and would sail to Normanton with a small crew, with John Little its only passenger and a letter its only cargo.

32

The Cable Has Landed

Port Darwin, October–November 1871

The large steamship *Edinburgh* arrived in Port Darwin on 25 October 1871, the same day that the *Curaçao* departed for Java. The first British Australia Telegraph Company ship to reach port, it had sailed direct from England, its hull low from the heavy deep-water coils of cable in its huge hold. A year earlier, the *Edinburgh* had been one of several ships involved in the laying of cables from Madras to Penang, Penang to Singapore, and Singapore to Java.[1]

The *Hibernia* appeared three days later, bringing the shallow-water cable. Patterson, Little, and Patterson's manager, Walter Rutt, were taken aboard and given a tour of the ship. Little described how he felt afterwards: 'I was greatly delighted . . . everything is done in a most complete style on these magnificent vessels. The staff of officers for both companies is enormous.'[2]

Another two days later, the *Investigator* appeared, bringing Captain Robert Halpin, the manager of the entire cable-laying project, and a large technical staff of engineers and telegraphists. The *Investigator*, like the *Omeo*, was a steamship clipper: with three masts, it had the option of employing either steam or sail. The *Edinburgh* and *Hibernia* would lay the cable, whereas the *Investigator* would remain in port until the project was complete.[3]

After a handshake with Halpin, Patterson rode away on a horse-drawn wagon the following morning. He had decided to go overland to Roper Landing in order to supervise the delivery of the *Bengal*'s cargo, and also to inspect work sites along the way.

The next day, Little hurried down to Southport to intercept him and retrieve him. He explained that since the *Investigator* would be idle for several weeks, he had sounded Captain Halpin out about the possibility of taking the ship to Adelaide to bring back much-needed supplies and stock; and that the captain was willing to do so.

Patterson reluctantly returned to port, met with Captain Halpin, then reported to Little that there was no deal. Halpin was demanding £8000 for a return trip to Adelaide, far too much money. Little conceded that it was more than he expected, but he pressed for another option: for Halpin to take Little to Normanton in the *Investigator*. As Little saw it, surely that would be far safer than sailing there in the *Larrakeeyah*. But Halpin's price for that was £4000, again an unreasonable price. Little's last-minute attempts to avoid sailing to Normanton had failed.

Patterson returned to Southport to resume his journey inland.

With an entourage of employees and advisors trailing behind, Captain Halpin was taken to the proposed site of the company's telegraph station. It was a short distance away from the main settlement at Fannie Bay, a place chosen by the company's agent, Squier, who had selected it to minimise cable breakage on the shallow, rocky harbour floor. Halpin rejected the site as unsuitable and told them to instead build the station at Fort Point, closer to the colonial settlement. He said that the cable was solidly built and was not in danger of breaking on the sea floor. He then looked about Fort Point for a suitable building to commandeer.[4]

With Bloomfield Douglas's assent, Halpin took possession of a vacant hut. Within days, it was completely fitted out with batteries and telegraph equipment. That hut would soon be the telegraphic link between the Australian continent and the world.

A trench was made from the low-water mark to the hut with shovels and, where they hit rock, dynamite. A man standing too close to the explosion was blinded in one eye by shrapnel.

On the morning of 7 November, a string of boats bobbed on the waves between the *Hibernia* and the shore, bringing the end of the cable. It splashed and thudded onto the beach. Horses were brought in to help with the pulling. The men sang as they pulled, and for a time, there was no sound but the lapping of the water and the singing of the men.[5] They dragged the cable ashore and up the trench until its tip was poking into the hut.

A champagne bottle appeared and a toast was declared to the success of the expedition. Bloomfield Douglas ordered the firing of the Fort Point cannon.[6]

The technicians connected the cable to the apparatus in the hut and sent a test message to the *Hibernia*. It worked! The *Hibernia* chugged slowly out to sea, the cable sliding into the water in her wake.

A company telegraphist gave Little a tour of the hut. Little was in awe. It was fitted with the finest, most advanced equipment possible, and it was all so neat and well organised. His response was, 'The system is beautiful.'

It seemed to take forever for the *Bengal* to be loaded. Little found that the sailors were sitting about, idle, when nobody was watching, so he assigned Griffith Todd to supervise. That sped things up. Little asked Douglas for a horse to assist with loading and unloading, but Douglas told him that no horses could be spared.

The Woolner tribe arrived in early November, waging war on the Larrakeeyah tribe. The fighting necessitated around-the-clock guards on the settlement's perimeter. Douglas organised an expedition to 'drive them away'. For this, he enlisted all the workers engaged at the port, sending them off at dawn. They were back by lunchtime, claiming to have chased the Woolner far away. Given the brevity of the foray, either the Woolner complied with remarkable speed, or the men treated the mission as a paid half-day off work, telling Douglas what he wanted to hear. If they had conducted themselves that day with the vigour of their usual activities, the Woolner had nothing to fear. Douglas, pleased with the report, gave them all a rest day because he was sure they were 'too tired' to work.[7]

The stream of bad news up the telegraph wire—stories of dead bullocks, lost horses, and bogged drays—came to a halt in mid-November, when a severe thunderstorm hit south of Port Darwin, and the line went dead.

The cable and the company's telegraph hut were unscathed by the storm; they remained in communication with their colleagues aboard the *Hibernia* as if nothing had happened. But the Katherine River station was silent. Repairers found and fixed a break and contact was resumed, although with sporadic outages. John Little, coordinating with Griffith Todd, Stapleton, Howley, and the repair team, determined that poor construction was the cause. Every pole had a lightning rod installed, but these lightning rods, which were simply lengths of thick wire, had been put too close to the wires and insulators. Instead of solving the problem, they made it worse. They attracted lightning, which destroyed the line when it hit. All the lightning rods had been installed that way, so they would all now have to be reinstalled.

When the line was working, Howley sent message after message of gloom. McLachlan's teams made only three miles in one day. There were bullock teams stuck fourteen miles across the river. The delivery team that was supposed to meet the shipment at Roper Landing had returned to the Katherine, reporting that an army of one hundred to two hundred Indigenous men had attacked them, killing two horses and forcing them to retreat.

Little confided in his diary, 'This is not work, it is insanity.'[8] He wistfully considered the beautiful *Investigator*, anchored in the harbour, which could be their salvation for £8000.

Then, on 21 November, the company agents proudly reported that the cable had been successfully laid between Port Darwin and Banjoewangie, at the eastern end of Java. Australia was telegraphically connected to the world!

Sadly, the only parts of Australia that the rest of the world could communicate with were Port Darwin and Howley's shack by the Katherine River. A message of congratulations to Captain Halpin arrived from Patterson, who was camped at the Katherine River.

As soon as the undersea cable was working, Squier telegraphed the company's London headquarters, informing them that the overland line would not be operational by the deadline, six weeks away. The cable had been laid; the company had kept its part of the deal. The deadline was only 43 days away, yet Patterson's construction crews were still on their way south, and had not yet started work.

33
Heart of Darkness
The north, November 1871

Patterson did not witness the landing of the cable in Port Darwin. After some tense, fruitless negotiations with Captain Halpin, he hurried back to Southport on the *Larrakeeyah*, rejoined his small travelling party, including his second-in-charge, Walter Rutt, climbed onto the seat of his wagon, and was away. Accompanying them were Edward Rix, a medical officer; Augustus Caesar, a cook; Teddy, a Larrakeeyah tracker and guide; and three others. They were soon joined by Inspector Foelsche, who informed them that a bullock driver named Bowman had died of sunstroke further down the track.[1] Each night, they made camp by the track, sleeping on the ground, arranging mosquito netting around them as best they could.

Patterson was glad to escape the port, writing somewhat cryptically in his journal, 'I often think of the miserable days weeks and months I spent at Port Darwin. The horror of that time can never be expressed.'[2] Patterson was driven by fear of failure. Yet the dead bullocks on the Port Darwin beach; the wreck of the *Gulnare* on a coral reef; the slowness of the crews; the loss of contact with Robert; and Walter Rutt's serious illness all portended disaster for Patterson's expedition.

The first steamy breaths of the wet season came. Through intermittent rain and searing sun, they crossed the Adelaide River, its water low and tame, then arrived at Number Two Depot, where a small telegraph station was in operation. Patterson was hoping for updates from Port Darwin, but a thunderstorm had cut the line. However, the operator was able to make intermittent contact with the Katherine River station, so Patterson received updates from there.

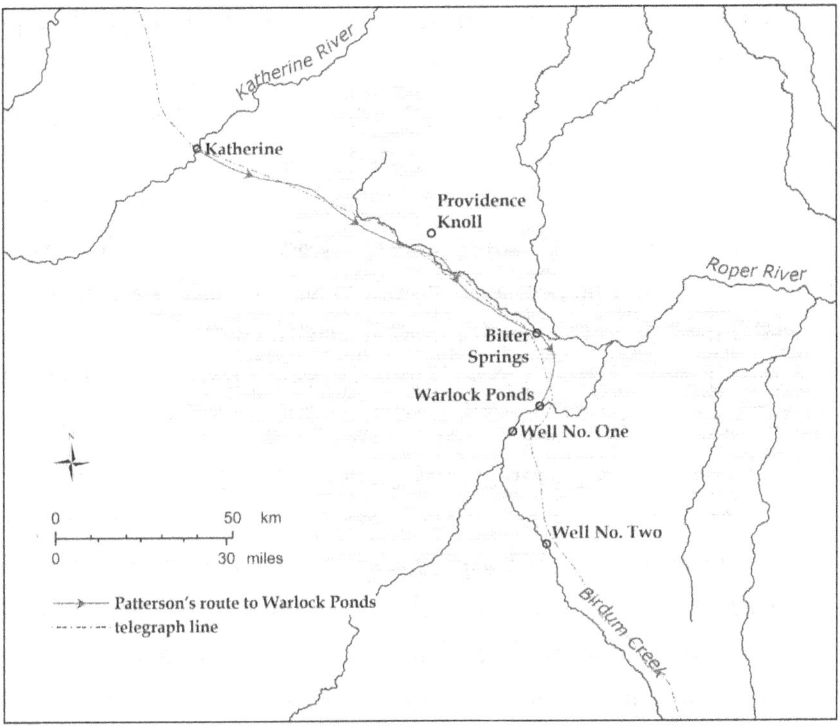

Patterson's journey from the Katherine River to Warlock Ponds in November 1871

He learned that Bob Burton's team had lost six horses on the journey to the Katherine: three dead and three so 'knocked up'—exhausted—that they were abandoned on the track. A wagon had also broken and was left behind.

In came a second report from the Katherine: the team of bullocks and drays bound for the Roper River, which had passed through several days earlier, had returned. They claimed that they had been attacked three times by Aboriginal warriors and forced to turn back.

They may have been telling the truth, but the specifics were surely exaggerated. Much further south, the Aboriginal communities around Attack Creek and Newcastle Waters aggressively defended their territory and would attack intruders. However, the Aboriginal people between Port Darwin and the Roper River were not overtly aggressive. Even the Woolners, the most warlike people in the area, fought only with other Aboriginal tribes, and only sporadically, and despite ongoing fear of them, had never attacked the white settlement. The primary grievance of white men in the area was that Aboriginal people liked to sneak into their camps to steal things.

The delivery team claimed that there were as many as two hundred attackers, whereas other encounters rarely described more than twenty or thirty Aboriginal people at any one time and place. And then, after what must have been a fierce and mighty battle with so many warriors, they fled, their only casualties being two wounded horses. Maybe the white men had been attacked or threatened by a very small group, but felt the need to exaggerate to justify their running away.

At any rate, their running away was a blessing in disguise, because the *Gulnare* was wrecked, and would not have been there when they arrived. If they had persevered, they would have been camped by the river for weeks, and would probably have run out of food.[3]

Patterson arrived at the Katherine River a week later. Here, he learned that the line to Port Darwin had been repaired. The main update was that the departure of the *Bengal* had been delayed and it would now leave on 21 November. Patterson intended to stay at the camp and not proceed until he received positive confirmation that the *Bengal* had sailed.

At the Katherine River camp, Patterson became suddenly and severely sick, with all the symptoms of malaria: muscle aches, fatigue, fever, and chills. Rix, a 'medical officer' but not a physician as such, could only suggest that he ask Dr Millner in Port Darwin for advice. Howley messaged Port Darwin to send Dr Millner to the telegraph office.

Patterson sat in the little telegraph shack by the river, next to Howley while at the Port Darwin depot, Dr Millner sat next to James Stapleton. Millner and Patterson conversed, their words translated through the telegraphists' Morse keys. It might have been the first telehealth appointment in history.

Millner prescribed brandy, but Patterson replied that there was no brandy at the Katherine River camp. Millner prescribed an enema. After asking Rix, Patterson replied that there were no enemas either. Millner listed various other medicines, none of which was available, so in the end, he told Patterson to just get some rest.

Rest did not help. Patterson's symptoms were worse the next morning, so Rix administered chloroform and ether to alleviate the pain. The following day was Sunday. Patterson was so sick that he could not even conduct the Sunday service, which he had hoped to do.[4]

The following Monday, a message arrived that the cable from Port Darwin to Java was now complete. Patterson managed to dictate to Howley a brief message of congratulations for Captain Halpin.

A messenger on horseback arrived from across the river, to report that a team that had passed through a week earlier was stuck in heavy sand, about eighty miles south. After learning of this latest setback, Patterson confided in his diary, 'I am unutterably weary of the whole thing. I see nothing but blackness and suffering ahead and I am afraid the expedition must collapse.'[5]

The wet season sputtered to a start, sporadic thunderstorms interspersed with periods of searing, muggy heat. Some parts of the track were boggy while others were hard and dry, with long stretches without water for the animals. The rivers were still placid, but there could be no comfort from this. A worker who had worked on the previous expedition warned that at this time last year, the Katherine River was no higher than at present, but in the peak of the wet, it was uncrossable.[6]

Walter Rutt's crew was some distance beyond the south bank of the Katherine River, at their starting point for work. Rutt remained with the workers, while Patterson and the other travellers continued south. They took with them an unladen dray and three horses to assist the bogged teams. On the day they left, Rutt was feeling very unwell. His illness progressed over the coming weeks.

The high sandstone plains south of the Katherine were rough going, with scarce creeks and waterholes. They found McLachlan's bullock teams at a place called Billabong Gum Flat. They were now in the catchment of the Roper; indeed, the creek bed they stood in, cradling the billabong from which their horses thirstily drank, was the distant, thin tail of the mighty Roper River itself. Patterson, alarmed by the lack of water on the way, sent a messenger north with instructions for Rutt to build wells between the Katherine River and Billabong Gum Flat.[7]

After delivering the horses and dray, the travellers left the stuck team, continuing south along Roper Creek, camping at the elbow where it turned east. From there the creek meandered towards the coast, swelling from creek to river. The water at this campsite must have tasted dreadful, because it was called Bitter Springs. They left Roper Creek and went south to Warlock Ponds. There was a pretty creek here, not yet named on white men's maps. Patterson wanted to name it 'Elsie Creek' after his wife, but there was already an Elsey River nearby, so instead he named it 'Birdum Creek'. 'Birdum' was his sweetheart name for his beloved Elsie.[8]

Further along Birdum Creek they found Bob Burton's crew, who had received Patterson's instructions to sink wells, and was numbering the wells as they were dug. They were camped at Well Number Two.

Wells, however, were no longer the priority: the *Bengal* was on its way to the Roper, and the delivery teams that were supposed to meet it there had turned back to the Katherine. Patterson sent seven of Burton's bullock teams east, to Roper Landing, to wait for the arrival of the *Bengal*. He told them to hurry.

Near their camp was an old, disused campsite. They were not the first to discover it; the explorer Gregory had found it fifteen years earlier, although he could not explain it. Leichhardt, perhaps. Gregory had found evidence that the campsite was made by Europeans: trees that had been felled with an axe; forked branches stuck in the ground to support tents; and in the ashes, detritus that was European in origin. The ashes and felled trees were still there, but the other signs were gone.[9]

At a camp near Warlock Ponds, a man named Jeremiah Harcus disappeared after going in search of some stray horses, his footprints erased by the rain. For several evenings, rockets were fired into the sky to guide him back to camp, but he never returned.[10]

34

The Voyage of the *Bengal*

Roper River, December 1871

The *Bengal* sailed past Arnhem Land and the lonely, uninhabited Wessel Islands, into the Gulf of Carpentaria. On board were three smaller vessels. Two were cutters: small, fast sailboats for getting to and from shore, or to other ships, or for navigating rivers. One of the cutters was named the *Gulnare*, in memory of the ship wrecked by Captain Sweet some weeks before; the other was the *Dolphin*, perhaps inspired by the numerous dolphins that could be seen in the warm gulf waters. Also on board was the *Larrakeeyah*, a larger, faster sailboat capable of long voyages.

When the skies were clear, everyone slept on deck in the mild tropical air, rather than in the cramped cabin. They did not have much to do, so they spent their time mending equipment, learning knots or other skills, playing cards, betting, and arguing. Thanks to the books provided by the Governor's wife, they also passed time by reading. One book mentioned in a crew member's diary was a comedy, *The World in Light and Shade* by Alfred Whaley Cole.[1]

In calm seas, the *Larrakeeyah* was lowered over the side with a skipper named Meikland, a small crew, and the Port Darwin post-master, John Little. They were bound for Normanton carrying mail, including an important and urgent message from Patterson, requesting more stock and more workers.[2]

As the boats drifted apart, all those aboard the *Bengal* stood on deck and gave the *Larrakeeyah* three cheers for their voyage, and the well wishes were returned in kind. Then the *Larrakeeyah*'s sails were hoist, her bow turned to the south, and she receded to the blue horizon. The *Bengal* sailed west.

That night, a heavy squall forced those aboard the *Bengal* to sleep in their cabins for the first time. At one o'clock the following day, 12 December 1871, there was a total eclipse of the sun, shrouding them in a deep twilight; the dogs on board barked in agitation. When there was a break in the clouds, the captain and some others looked at the eclipse through a piece of smoked glass.[3]

At that moment, at a campsite on Billabong Gum Flat, some two hundred miles to the west, Patterson's group saw the eclipse, too. Patterson wrote in his diary: 'It was a very fine sight. The eclipse was total soon after midday, and it got almost dark, the stars shining out one by one, whilst flames appeared shooting out from the circumference of the eclipsed Sun.'[4]

And at all the far-flung camps of the lonely crews of workers, the sun disappeared behind the moon and, in a strange, disorienting moment, they were thrown into darkness.

The *Bengal* arrived at Maria Island three days later and dropped anchor there. The mouth of the Roper River was nearby, beyond the horizon to the west. The wet season came and there was no more sleeping on deck. The weather was rough and the river's outflow turned the sea a thick, muddy brown.[5]

The following morning, the *Dolphin* was lowered into the water with a skipper, four crew and a load of supplies to deliver to Roper Landing. Captain Sweet assigned a man named Jones as skipper, but Jones was a cantankerous, surly man, and very unpopular with the crew; the others refused to go if he was skipper, so a man named Charles Miller was assigned the role instead.

Miller and his crew returned eight days later, on 24 December, their skins covered in red mosaics of mosquito bites. Miller reported that they had reached Roper Landing but found nobody there. They deposited the supplies on the bank and 'blazed' some trees to mark the spot before returning. He also said that they had encountered a friendly group of seventy Aboriginal people. They had also seen crocodiles.[6]

A creek near the river mouth was so infested with mosquitoes that it was dubbed 'Mosquito Creek'. On Christmas Day, the crew of the *Bengal* saw six Aboriginal men on the shore at Mosquito Creek, gesturing to them. Captain Sweet sent a boat for them, and they came aboard. They were tall, healthy, and good-natured. They carried no weapons, but two of them had visible spear wounds on their bodies. They were all missing their two upper front teeth; on subsequent interactions, it became apparent that this was characteristic of all the men of this tribe. Captain Sweet provided them with a meal of meat and biscuits. The crew traded with the men, taking fish hooks, turtle shell, and twine.[7] The sailors dressed the Aboriginal men in some spare clothes, which they seemed to enjoy. Then some of the sailors played music and others danced. The Aboriginal men caught on quickly, copying the dancing. Then, after eating and dancing and trading, they were taken back to the shore.[8]

The Aboriginal men returned three days later, accompanied by another man, and were fed and entertained as before. One crew member, William Crowder, wrote in his diary that he tried to learn their language, and took notes of what he learned. Unfortunately, while Crowder's diary still exists, his linguistic records do not.[9]

As the boat transported them back to shore, one of the men stole a rowlock, and they all ran off. Because of the theft, Captain Sweet decided that they would not be allowed on board again.[10]

Captain Sweet sent the two cutters on expeditions up and down the wide river mouth, plumbing and charting the water depth, and dropping buoys to mark navigable channels, in preparation for taking the *Bengal* upriver. In doing so, he realised that McLachlan's maps of the gulf and the river were rife with errors.[11]

The river itself filled them with awe. Crowder wrote in his diary:

> It is a splendid river and it seems a great absurdity for the South Australian government to pass it by and go to a dirty dry hole like Port Darwin, which is not a patch on it, and I firmly believe that if ever another township is formed in the Northern Territory The Roper will be the place for it.[12]

35

The Pitiless Blue Sky

The Peake to Alice Springs, November–December 1871

Six telegraphists gathered at The Peake Station in late November. As the line was nearing completion, it was time to place staff. Each of them had been handpicked by Charles Todd for their knowledge and experience of the science and practice of telegraphy. Four were assigned to run telegraph stations along the line: Charlotte Waters, Alice Springs, Barrow Creek, and Tennant Creek.

The telegraphists were supposed to be supplied with batteries for their stations, but the batteries were delayed. They left anyway, hoping the wagons would catch up. By the time they reached Charlotte Waters, the first station where one of their number would stay, the battery wagon had not caught up, so a decision had to be made. Their supervisor, Ben Clarke, knew that Todd, and indeed the entire colony, had one priority above all others: the telegraph line must be operational by New Year's Day. Clarke told the telegraphists assigned to the three furthest stations that they must press ahead on their own, and that he would follow with the wagons and the batteries. Those three were Johannes Mueller, headed for Barrow Creek; Richard Watson, for Tennant Creek; and Carl Kraegen, for Alice Springs. Clarke did some quick calculations. He figured that if they left immediately and travelled for thirty miles each day, then all three of them would reach their respective stations on time. Clarke had been given instructions on how to find water along the route, which seemed fairly straightforward, so he wrote out a copy for them, and also a copy of the general instructions for following the route. Then he sent them forth.[1]

The telegraphists went with no maps, only those handwritten directions. It was summer, which by definition meant that it was searingly, scorchingly hot. For most of the first day, they failed to find any of the waterholes mentioned in Clarke's instructions. In the late afternoon they reached the Goyder River, where they found water. They drank deeply, then made overnight camp.[2]

Late the following day they reached the Hugh River, but it was dry, so they pressed on, looking for a waterhole that was supposed to be at Alice Creek (this was not the well-known Alice Springs, but a small tributary of the Hugh). This was recorded as a reliable source of water on the maps of the explorer John Ross, but as Alfred Woods had found to his irritation, there was often little or no water there at all. At any rate, they did not make it to the Alice Creek by sunset. They made camp and slept thirsty, consoling each other that Alice Creek was close by, and they would find it in the morning.

Keen for a drink, the men packed up and continued at dawn. They were so excited about the prospect of reaching the Alice Creek waterhole that they sang songs as the rode along. But by mid-morning, they realised that they had somehow missed Alice Creek, so they turned back to find it. They followed track after track, doubling back after every false lead to follow the next. The horses were as also thirsty, distressed and tired. One lay down in the dirt and could not be coaxed to its feet. They left it behind, planning to return to it with full waterbags after they found water.

Near a small, dry creek bed, they saw a piece of tin nailed to a tree, with a message hammered into it with nail holes. The sign said that there was water at the junction of this nameless creek and the Hugh River, about a mile away. They hurried down the creek to the junction, but this part of the Hugh River, at least, had only a bed of dry pebbles and hot sand.

They knew—in fact, Todd had advised as much—that sometimes water can be found in the dry creeks and rivers by digging. So two of them dug the sand with their hands and tomahawks and knifes. But still no water.

They cut back through the scrub and reached the telegraph line, where they could go no further. They were spent. Kraegen had not assisted with the digging; perhaps they needed one person to mind the horses while the others dug. For that reason, he had more energy than the other two. The three of them agreed that Kraegen should continue alone to find water, fill the waterbags, then return. He promised he would be back soon, then rode away.

He did not return by nightfall.

There was moonlight, and the other two felt somewhat better after a rest, so they continued in the cool of the night, looking for Kraegen. Morning came, and with it, another day of brutal heat. The remaining two men reached a marked waterhole named Rocky Creek, but they found no water there, and no Kraegen either, so they continued until sunset, finding nothing.

The next morning, they knew they were close to death. They shot one of their horses and drank as much of its blood as they could. They filled their quart pots with blood, but when they tried to drink it later, it had congealed hard in the pots. They now had only one horse.

One of them later wrote of his experience:

> We thought we should never get over the plain; but we did. We sat and suffered; the poor horse crawled, and doubtless also suffered. He seemed to go at the rate of about half a mile an hour—he could not have gone a mile an hour—but whether one or the other it seemed an eternity before we got to the timber. On we crawled, until on rising a bank we saw the bed of the Hugh once more. The horse pricked up his ears, mended his pace, reached the steep rocky bank, and all of a sudden (thank the Lord!) we saw water. A small pool 18 inches by 30, and only a foot deep, but water.[3]

They stayed by that small puddle all the following day and night, 'swigging water like a couple of dilapidated fishes'. From there, they travelled to the Finke River, where they met Ben Clarke and the wagons.

Karl Kraegen had arrived in Adelaide in 1853 from Germany, aged twenty-one. He went to try his luck on the Victorian goldfields, then moved to Sydney, where he gained a reputation as an engineer and innovator. He and his friend Gustavus Kopsch, who had emigrated with him from Dresden, performed Australia's first display of electric lighting in Sydney in 1863. He then became the Chief Telegraphist at Albury, where he constructed a time ball, partly funded from his own pocket. His wife died in 1871, only a few months before his journey to Alice Springs, leaving him the sole parent of three small children, whom he left in the care of his wife's family in Goulburn, New South Wales.[4]

His body was found at the base of a telegraph pole by a line repairer. He was lying face down, his hand on his hat, as if shielding his face from the sun. His body was wrapped in a blanket, a grave was dug, and after a short ceremony, Kraegen was buried. An inscription, punctured in a plate of tin, was nailed to a plank which served as a headstone. It read:

> In memory of C.W.J Kraegen, aged 40, who perished here for want of water, about 12/12/71. Buried 20/12/71.[5]

His three orphaned children remained in the care of their grandparents in Goulburn.

36
Hart Tumbles
Adelaide, November–December 1871

Premier John Hart had a problem, and its name was James Boucaut.

A lawyer by profession, Boucaut had previously played at politics, entering parliament ten years earlier and in 1867, at the age of 34, briefly becoming Premier. He was the youngest person in the colony's short history to do so, holding office for a year before losing his seat in the next election. Now, after winning a by-election in October, he was back and he was causing plenty of trouble.

Soon after stepping into the chambers, Boucaut sank a bill that provided religious instruction for prison inmates. There should be a separation between church and state, he declared, and the proposed bill violated that separation. After clocking up that quick victory, he went after Hart himself, tabling a no-confidence motion.

Boucaut found wide support, particularly on the issue of government spending. The colony's budget was in the red, largely because of the collapse of the Northern Territory expedition and the subsequent cost blowout for the overland telegraph line. And when it came to overland telegraph, Boucaut had other lines of attack. He had questions—or rather, accusations—regarding the appointment of Robert Patterson, who, he believed, was given the overland telegraph job because he was a mate of Hart's. Boucaut reminded everyone of a speech that Patterson gave at a recent railway station opening, in which he gushingly praised Hart, and a report by Patterson that gave Hart the political ammunition to kill the proposed rail line extension. Boucaut admitted that, sure, Patterson was qualified, but then again, so were plenty of other people. So why him?

And then there was the matter of the bonus. Boucaut wanted to know, 'How was it, when there were so many men able and willing to take charge of the Northern Telegraph party on more moderate terms, that Mr Patterson should have been offered a bonus of £1500, especially considering the state of the public finances?'

Boucaut answered his own rhetorical question with another, even more inflammatory one: 'I am led to ask whether this appointment was not a reward for past services.'[1]

This was an outright accusation of corruption—of both Hart *and* Patterson.

Hart's Treasurer laughed in derision. Boucaut retorted, 'I do admire the Treasurer. He is like an old rat. The harder you pinch him, the better he fights.'

Then Boucaut told Hart and his ministers, to their faces, that their time was up:

> . . . the position of the ministry is that of an old, withered, and decayed tree. Their days are numbered, and only a little time is left to them on that side. The sound of the woodman's axe is in their ears, and it requires no blow from my hand to bring them down.

Boucaut claimed that the rotten tree needed 'no blow' from him, but he delivered the blow anyway. His no-confidence motion passed, and the Hart ministry tumbled. But there was a sense that Boucaut had gone too far with the corruption allegations. Hart was finished, but Boucaut did not have the numbers to form a ministry to replace him. There was a power vacuum.

To fill the void, one of Hart's ministers, Arthur Blyth, cobbled together a reshuffled ministry out of the wreckage of the old. Almost as soon as Blyth was sworn in as Premier, Boucaut pushed another vote of no confidence. Blyth was crippled.[2]

In this midst of this chaos, on 28 November, Patterson's telegram landed like a bomb.[3]

> The Telegraph expedition is breaking down through excessive loss of stock by deaths at port Darwin, through disasters attending the passage of the dry country between the Katherine and the King, and through knocking up of stock generally. The schooner *Gulnare* which should have arrived at the Roper with rations for the relief of the various parties by the end of October struck and stranded on a reef of West of North Vernon Island . . . About 120 bullocks out of the 500 shipped are dead. In the remainder many are useless and 75% badly knocked up. Average rate of travelling for the first 160 miles 7 miles a day. Subsequent rate not 4 miles per day.

For everyone in Adelaide, it was déjà vu.

Blyth acted swiftly. Horses and food were purchased at short notice, at whatever price they were available. Three vessels were commissioned. Two of the ships, the *Omeo* and the *Tararua*, were cargo steamships. Todd purchased a third ship, the steam-powered tug boat *Young Australian*, to assist the larger vessels.

It would have been foolish to leave Patterson in charge of the expedition on his own, given Boucaut's accusations. Blyth's chief secretary told Todd, 'You will have to go yourself and do it.'[4]

In his letter, Patterson had asked that the ships go directly to the Roper River. Since John Hart was no longer in power, there was no objection, and that's where they were sent.

There was another vote of no confidence, parliament was dissolved and a snap election held in December. Blyth's government scraped in with the barest of majorities, but Boucaut immediately began chipping away at their numbers. Blyth could hear the woodsman's axe.[5]

37

Tidings on Birdum Creek

Roper River catchment, December 1871

While Patterson was on Birdum Creek near Well Number Two, three travellers arrived from the south, two white men and a black man. They had come from William Harvey's crew, Section E, carrying a letter addressed to William McMinn, government overseer of works.

Patterson explained that McMinn had left the Northern Territory several months ago and was now in Adelaide. Harvey's team did not know this, or about anything else that had occurred, because they had been out of contact with the world for many months, having left Adelaide more than a year earlier and receiving news only as fast as a camel could carry it.[1]

The travellers' leader, Burt, reported something of great interest to Patterson. On their journey, they had met some drovers, who were bringing several thousand sheep overland from South Australia, hoping to sell them here in the north. Burt reckoned the drovers and their flock would reach nearby Warlock Springs in about three weeks. This was unexpected, wonderful news. If thousands of sheep were on their way, maybe the workers would not starve to death after all.

Yet Patterson's mood was barely lifted by this change of fortune, because he focused, gloomily, on a terrible story that Burt told. Apparently, the drovers had been led by two brothers, Ralph and John Milner, but John Milner was dead. Along the way, somewhere near Attack Creek, John Milner had been murdered by a black man.

Burt said that he and his two companions had also been attacked, in their case by 150 men near Newcastle Waters. They were 'compelled to fire', then to flee for their lives.

Patterson wrote in his private diary:

> I much fear we shall have to shoot a score or so of them before we can establish a funk of the white man in the native mind. The cold blooded murder of Millner by the blacks at the termination of my section will not induce us to treat them with unwarrantable leniency should they attack any of my parties. Packard's ill-advised retreat from the Roper will only have emboldened the natives and lead them to deeds of greater daring.[2]

Aboriginal warriors did not kill any construction workers, so Patterson found no reason to 'shoot a score or so of them'. Yet tension was increasing between white and black, particularly on remote tracks far from settlements and the main camps. As for the killing of John Milner, that had nothing to do with race relations, but instead was a variation on a tale as old as time.

38
The Drovers
September 1870–December 1871

Ralph Milner had first gotten the notion to cross the continent after hearing about Stuart's success. Around that time, Milner drove a flock of sheep across inland South Australia, found countryside amenable to farming, and became a squatter.[1]

When he heard about the overland telegraph project, he decided to give it a go. He could sell those sheep in the north and make a tidy profit. He wife had recently died and he had no desire to stay on the farm. He persuaded his brother, John, to join him, with seven other stockmen. They also hired an Aboriginal couple, Charlie and Fanny, as guides. They took livestock consisting of about 4300 sheep, 160 horses, 150 goats, 17 working bullocks, and 25 dogs. They also had two spring carts, two bullock drays, and one large horse wagon. Because of the carts and the wagon, it would be the first crossing of the Australian continent of a wheeled vehicle.[2]

They left in September 1870, about the same time as the construction crews were leaving Adelaide, although they encountered no crews until they reached the north. The travelling was easy at first, because they simply followed the tracks of the telegraph construction teams or explorers all the way to Central Mount Stuart. After the tracks ran out, they navigated using a copy of John McDouall Stuart's journal.[3]

There were long stretches without water, where the grass was scarce and scorched by sun and wind. They crossed stony plains and tablelands and sandhills. They camped at lagoons and gum-lined creeks, and little muddy waterholes. In February, on a hard, arid road, they were hit by a thunderstorm and the wagon got bogged. The bullocks broke two yokes from straining to pull the wagon out of the mud, but they eventually got it free. The days were so hot that they would sometimes travel at night. Their progress was slow and methodical. When they found an appropriate place to camp, they would leave the sheep to graze while they scouted north, looking for the next watering hole, then return and herd the sheep on.[4]

South of the MacDonnell Ranges, they encountered Whitfield Mills and his companions; the first people they had met associated with the telegraph. This was a stroke of luck, allowing them to pass into the range and to camp at the Alice Spring. They stayed in the ranges for several weeks, because Milner had sent two men back to the Finke River to collect some revolvers and cartridges he had arranged to be delivered there. While they waited, the ewes lambed, increasing the flock to more than 6000 sheep. While there, they were pestered by a plague of rats.[5]

Beyond the ranges, they came to enormous boulders known as the Devil's Marbles. A grassy weed they had not seen before was abundant there. The sheep grazed on it, but it was poisonous, and half of them died.[6]

Fanny was feisty, and more skilled than Charlie at many things. She could ride, drive, and fetch horses as well as any of the men. She argued frequently with Charlie, on one occasion chasing him with a burning stick. Because she was beautiful, she attracted the attention of Aboriginal people they encountered, but, according to one account, 'she only laughed at them as she did Charlie'.

Near Attack Creek, a tall, powerful-looking Aboriginal man took a shine to Fanny and started to hang about their camp. But Fanny distrusted the stranger, telling the others, 'Wild fellow no good!'

The others motioned to him to clear out, but John Milner admired him and allowed him to stay. He said the man was 'a fine specimen of a native'.[7] Ralph was away at the time, scouting forward, looking for the next suitable campsite.

One afternoon, John Milner was resting in the shade of a tree with Fanny nearby. The tall stranger appeared, carrying weapons, and began encouraging Fanny to leave with him. She refused. He persisted, so she hit him in the head with a stick. That made him angry.

It's not clear exactly what happened next. Maybe John Milner got involved, maybe he tried to protect Fanny, or maybe he was just a channel for the tall stranger's rage. Arthur Ashwin, one of the drovers, claimed that John was lying on the ground with his back to the tall stranger. But one way or another, the tall stranger hit John Milner in the head with his club.

Milner's dog, Dick, attacked the stranger. Ashwin heard the commotion and came running with his revolver drawn. The man raised a boomerang at Ashwin. Ashwin fired. The tall man ran away.

Fanny jumped on a horse and galloped to the camp to summon the others, while Ashwin stayed with the dying Milner. The party later found a trail of blood left by the escaping stranger, but found no body, and never saw him again.

They buried John Milner at the base of a nearby tree. For a grave marker, they hammered his name, age, and date of death into a bit of tin, then nailed the tin to the trunk.[8]

Charlie, distraught, painted himself and issued challenges into the wilderness to come and fight, to give him a chance to get revenge. Seeing this display, Fanny told Charlie he was a 'big fool'.

39

The *Bengal* or Bust

Roper River, December 1871–January 1872

Before heading to Roper Landing, Robert Patterson returned north to check on progress along the line.

On a bright note, the wire had been strung across the Katherine River, and was complete for another fifty miles south of there. James Stapleton had established a mobile telegraph station at the end of the line with a pocket relay. Unfortunately, the line between the Katherine River station and Port Darwin was down again, but Stapleton was able to communicate with the Katherine.[1]

Disease was rife in Walter Rutt's camp, and Rutt himself was emaciated and weak. In Patterson's eyes, 'he is shockingly reduced—he looks as if he were wasting away, and he is certainly the most haggard looking man of the whole expedition.' Rutt was irritable and impatient with everyone, snapping at subordinates over trifles.[2]

The delivery teams led by Bedford Hack had barely made it across the Katherine. A bogged dray was chained to 30 bullocks in an attempt to pull it out, but the chains broke and the dray was left on the far side of the river. The track between the Katherine and the port was too boggy to traverse. They were cut off; their hopes of survival now riding on two things: the arrival of the *Bengal* and Ralph Milner's sheep.

Wracked by malaria and staring at defeat, Patterson was physically and mentally low, writing in his diary: 'I am continually depressed with the weight of low thoughts, failures, neglects and wandering forgetfulness, and my feelings and desires one often dead . . . Day by day I become more dissatisfied with myself, and I pray for the sanctification of Thy Will for without that is right I can do nothing.'[3]

Yet a few days later, he wrote, 'I am continually being surprised at myself and the good spirits I keep in.'[4]

It was raining almost constantly.

Patterson made for Roper Landing: first south to Warlock Ponds, then east along the south bank of the Roper. As the light faded on Christmas Eve, he found the campsite of Ralph Milner and his shepherds by a swamp near the river. In nearby grassland they had 3000 sheep.

Also at their campsite was Dick Knuckey, who had been the supervisor for Central Section A. His section was complete, so he had gone north with several of his crew to assist with other sections. His workers joined Harvey's crew, but Knuckey did not stay with them. He kept going north, rode across the gap to the northern section, and here he was, willing to do whatever was needed.

Dick Knuckey was a godsend. He was a talented rider, explorer, worker, telegraphist, and leader, and he would be of invaluable assistance in the months that followed.

On Christmas Day, Milner and Patterson left the campsite together, riding east to survey the track to Roper Landing. Patterson wanted to find a route for his wagon; Milner wanted to search for a bullock dray he had abandoned in that direction. They were sopping wet within minutes of leaving, the water up to their knees on horseback as they crossed flooded creeks. They found two abandoned bullock drays belonging to overland delivery teams, and Milner's dray, none of which could be salvaged. They concluded that Patterson's wagon would not make it to the landing. They arrived back at the campsite in driving rain.

Patterson's hopes of dining on mutton for Christmas lunch were dashed. He described the meal in his diary: 'it consisted of some half warm sweet tea, very weak and a bit of cold sodden black damper made from damaged flour brought all the way overland from South Australia'.

Milner apologised, explaining that they had killed a sheep to eat, but the rain had ruined the meat.

Patterson purchased one thousand sheep from Milner and arranged for him to deliver them to the various crews along the line, a third going to Rutt, a third to McLachlan and a third to Burton. Patterson also purchased 60 of Milner's horses.[5]

They parted company; Milner to go west, Patterson east. Milner's flock had to go a mere 30 miles, but even that short distance was impossible. Fierce rains came; the creeks rose higher; the flats turned to lakes. Milner and his shepherds retreated with their sheep to higher ground, stranded like everyone else. The sheep were not delivered to the starving construction crews for several more weeks.[6]

Patterson left most of his group behind with the wagon, continuing on horseback with Inspector Foelsche, a farrier named Bayfield, and Augustus Caesar, the cook.

They met a bullock team camped on high ground. The team had tried to go to Roper Landing, but the plain beyond this high ground was flooded and could not be crossed with bullocks and drays, so they were waiting for the water to subside.

Patterson and his companions pressed on, sploshing across the plain. They saw an Aboriginal man trailing them. At camp that evening, men returned from retrieving a stray horse reported that they had seen many armed Aboriginal men hiding nearby. Patterson, Foelsche, and Bayfield took turns to keep watch during the night, fearing an attack, but no attack came. The only threat that night was the relentless, pitiless rain.[7]

They reached Roper Landing on 30 December. Nobody was there. No bullocks, no workers, no stores, no *Bengal*. There was a message for them, probably hammered into a piece of tin, saying that the campsite here was at risk of being flooded, so everyone had moved downstream to the junction of the Roper and Hodgson rivers. They went through 'frightfully rough country', with reeds higher than their heads, reaching the campsite—the new 'Roper Landing'—in the late afternoon.[8]

The forty men at the camp were in a sorry state. They were almost out of food. They had enough flour to last two more days. When that was gone, the only remaining food was jerked beef, which at this camp was called 'stringybark'. The irony: these men were supposed to save the others from starvation, but they themselves were at risk of starving to death.[9]

They had not seen the *Bengal*, although they had found a note, stating that a boat from the *Bengal* had arrived three days before them and would soon return. But they had been waiting for almost two weeks, and the boat had not returned.[10]

The next day was Sunday, so Patterson held a very wet church service, attended by about half the men, on the bank of the swollen river.

Monday was New Year's Day, the deadline for completing the line. It was raining hard, and the river rose higher. That day, they consumed the last of the flour, save for a few handfuls. What had happened to the *Bengal* was anybody's guess. Maybe the ship was on its way up the river and would arrive at any moment; maybe it had returned to Port Darwin; maybe it had sunk; maybe pirates had taken it. Anything was possible.

Patterson decided that he needed to go down the river to look for the *Bengal*. He ordered the men to dismantle a wagon and convert it into a raft. They wrapped the chassis in tarpaulin to make it waterproof and lashed empty ten-gallon barrels underneath for buoyancy. A small mast was installed and a tent fly rigged up as a sail. Oars were fashioned out of fallen branches. The finished raft was carried to the water's edge.[11]

Patterson announced he was going to take the raft in search of the *Bengal* with a select, trusty crew. He then named the men he had chosen to accompany him. Those men flat-out refused. He asked others, who also refused. If the *Bengal* was there at all, it was likely to be at the mouth, eighty miles downriver. Starving to death looked like a better option than setting out on that raft.

Four men volunteered.[12]

Standing by the raft in the mud and the rain, Patterson gave a speech. He christened the raft *Elsie*, after his wife, then produced a bottle of sherry and invited everyone to 'drink to the success of the *Elsie*'. Then they loaded the raft with supplies, pushed it into the water, climbed in and were swept down the river.[13]

They made fast progress in the strong current. Once Roper Landing (as the new campsite was thereafter called) was out of sight, Patterson revealed to the others that he had brought the last of the flour.[14]

When the light faded, they used the oars to steer to the riverbank and lashed the raft to a tree. They tried to light a fire, but their matches were damp and would not spark. They loaded Patterson's gun with gunpowder and a rag, then fired it, igniting the rag. It burned long enough for them to light their pipes, and as they smoked, they were happy for a moment, but the pipes were soon out and they lapsed into gloomy silence. A howling wind picked up. They tried to sleep on the raft, but it started to fill with water. They put their oilcloths and blankets on the ground, but as soon as Patterson lay down, he sank several inches into the slush. They lay shivering on the boggy ground, bitten by mosquitoes, with the wind howling and the rain falling on them all night.[15]

By daybreak, the river had risen and they had to wade out through waist-deep water to get to the *Elsie*. They climbed aboard, untied the raft from its mooring, and pushed off again into the current. They had three days' supply of meat and five days of flour, after which they would be done for.[16]

The rain eased and they looked for a place to land, in order to try again to light a fire and cook some food, but Aboriginal people on the bank saw them and shouted at them, following their raft for several miles. Patterson and his crew were afraid they would be attacked if they landed, so they kept going until they were well past the threat, then pulled over to the bank, tied the raft, and tried again to light a fire. They eventually succeeded, but went through almost all their matches in doing so.[17]

One of the others, an old bushman, knew a recipe for brewing fake coffee. He roasted some flour in the tin of the 'meat billy', boiled some water and added it to the flour, then sweetened the concoction with a little sugar. They roasted some ham in the ashes, along with the remains of the previous night's tinned meat. Patterson was unwell. He had a headache and his skin was hot. He could barely eat any of the food but drank plenty of the fake coffee brew.[18]

The next morning, they got some fire going in the meat tin and took it with them so they would have fire that night, then they set out again in the *Elsie*. The downstream river was in flood, stretching for miles to either side.[19]

Some while later, they passed Elsie's Bluff ('named after my darling', Patterson commented in his diary). There, they saw the masts of the *Bengal* in the distance, at the mouth of the river about five miles away.[20]

Patterson and his crew on the little raft rowed towards the masts of the *Bengal*. Or rather, the four crew members rowed, while Patterson, as captain of the *Elsie*, peered anxiously ahead. A boat approached them from the direction of the *Bengal*. When the two vessels were alongside, Patterson and the boat's coxswain introduced each other. The coxswain, Miller, said that he was taking his boat upriver to Roper Landing, to see if anyone had arrived there yet. But it was just a reconnaissance, nothing more. They were not transporting provisions.

Patterson ordered Miller to return to the *Bengal* immediately and to tow the *Elsie* behind him. This gave Patterson's crew needed relief from rowing; their hands were blistered from using the rough bush oars.[21]

They climbed aboard the *Bengal* at sunset and were greeted by Captain Sweet. Patterson demanded that Sweet explain himself. Why had the *Bengal* not gone to Roper Landing? Sweet replied that the current was too strong. They were still pushing upstream, but had made only two miles of progress in the past five days. Patterson noted sarcastically, 'A rate of progress rivalling even that of the bullock teams.'[22] He ordered two boats loaded with supplies, to leave for Roper Landing the next day at first light.

The three crew of the little *Elsie* slept under cover for the first time in weeks. Patterson praised God for saving him, writing in his diary: 'Before going to sleep I did not forget to thank my Heavenly Father for His love and care for me—I do trust that my life may show forth His praise.'[23]

In the days that followed, supplies were shunted up to the landing in the *Bengal*'s cutters, although the boats were small, so only a fraction of the cargo was moved.[24]

Over the next ten days, while Sweet's crew loaded boats and rowed them to Roper Landing and back, Patterson spent all day, every day, writing letters to his wife, Elsie. There was no way to send them, so they accumulated in his bag.[25]

Eight Aboriginal men visited the *Bengal*, swimming from the shore with logs, which the sailors believed were for fending off crocodiles. They visited every day, increasing in numbers. On occasion, they tried to bring two women aboard with them, but that was strictly against the rules and the women were turned back to shore. Eventually the Aboriginal visitors became so numerous and disruptive that Sweet banned all further visits.[26]

On a windy, squally evening on 14 January, a light could be seen further down in the river's reaches. Patterson fired his carbine and a distant blue light flared in response. It was the *Larrakeeyah*. A boat was despatched to the vessel and returned with the Port Darwin telegraphist, John Little.

The *Larrakeeyah* had sped across the gulf, getting to Normanton in only two days. From there, Little had travelled 120 miles inland to the end of the Queensland line, where he made contact with Adelaide, before returning to the boat. On the return journey, they were caught in a cyclone and were forced to take shelter in the lee of an island for two weeks. From his correspondence with Adelaide, Little had quite a lot of news.

He told them that Lady Edith Fergusson, who had so kindly donated all the books they were enjoying, had died. They all agreed that it was very sad.

In politics, the Hart government had fallen, replaced by the Blyth government, which was already looking unsteady. They all agreed that it was no surprise; anyone could see that was coming.

Todd and the new Premier Blyth had sent three ships to the Roper River with horses, food, and more workers. The ships were the *Omeo* (again); another barque named the *Tararua*; and a tug steamer, the *Young Australian*. This was excellent news.

But Little's most explosive update was that Charles Todd himself was coming to the Roper River aboard the *Omeo*. Patterson was thunderstruck.

When he viewed Little's correspondence with Todd, Patterson was miffed by Todd's tone and attitude. For example, he learned that Todd had described Patterson's message, delivered via the *Caraçao*, as 'unnecessarily alarming'. Clearly, he did not grasp the seriousness of the situation!

Patterson also gleaned that Todd was unjustly blaming him for the stock losses, believing that Patterson must have 'overdriven' the animals, and that he must not have rested them enough in Port Darwin. But most of the losses had occurred before any work had started, caused by the animals having to swim to shore.

Patterson was bewildered. Why was Todd coming at all? Was he, Patterson, going to be fired? Had the government lost confidence in him? As revealed in his daily diaries, Todd's impending arrival played over and over in Patterson's mind.

The *Larrakeeyah* returned to Maria Island to await the arrival of Todd's fleet. Patterson visited Roper Landing in one of the cutters, then, with John Little and a small crew of sailors from the *Bengal*, sailed down to Maria Island to join it.

Part VI
Todd's Journey

40
The Estafette
Adelaide, January 1872

The *Omeo* was at Port Adelaide, being loaded up for the third time for an expedition to the Northern Territory. Fifteen wagons, two wagonettes (smaller, two-wheeled wagons), horses, tents, tentpoles, crates, cases, wheels, swags, bags of potatoes, bales of hay, barrels of flour, even a lathe.[1]

Two more workers on the line had died in the latter part of the year. Far north of the Territory border, and north of the MacDonnell Ranges, a group of workers climbed Central Mount Stuart for no reason other than curiosity. The camp's cook, Charles Palmer, turned back, feeling unwell. He felt unwell for several days afterwards, then collapsed at the campsite and died.[2] The other death was a bullock teamster named George Middleton, who had returned to the town of Blinman to collect supplies. While there, he complained of feeling sick, lay in bed at the inn for two days, then was found dead. The local doctor certified the cause of death as tuberculosis.[3]

Despite deaths, disease, thirsty explorers, floods, and stony desert tracks, construction proceeded apace, and both the Southern and Central sections were on course for completion, either by the deadline of January first, or soon after. Only in the north had everything gone awry.

Every day from now that the line was incomplete, the colony had to pay the British Australian Telegraph Company £70. For each month, that amounted to around £2000 or more. That was on top of the extra costs for salaries, food, and equipment. The missed deadline increased, rather than removed, the urgency—the line had to be finished as quickly as possible.

Todd came up with a scheme to stop the financial bleeding, even as work continued.

William Harvey's crew, bolstered by Dick Knuckey's crew, was poling and wiring north across the long, final gap. Meanwhile, Patterson's crews, presumably, were extending the line from Port Darwin southwards.

At some point, the gap could be bridged temporarily by a horse courier service, otherwise known as an estafette. Once that was in place, people in Adelaide would be able send and receive telegraphs with people in New Delhi, London, Paris, New York, and all places of the world linked by cable.

The estafette would work like this: a person delivers a message to the Adelaide office, where a telegraphist sends it down the line in Morse code. The message passes through relay stations such as Charlotte Waters and Alice Springs, until it reaches a mobile, temporary station at the end of the line. There, it is written in pencil on a slip of paper, carried on horseback to a mobile station at the other end, tapped out again in Morse code, then travels around the world to its destination. The horse couriers would leave from each end of the line every Tuesday. For the general public, the experience would be the same as any other telegraph service, although the messages would take longer to reach their destination.

The estafette would solve three problems. First, the line could start generating income right away; second, it would reduce public anger about the late completion; and third, it would stop the bleeding of cost from the daily late fines. Todd could claim too that the telegraph line was operational, even if part of the line was horses and mailbags instead of wires and batteries. The colony could then declare that its part of the deal had been met and thereafter discontinue its punishing late fines.

Todd contracted a man named Ray Boucaut—the politician James Boucaut's brother—to run the estafette. Months earlier, Todd had appointed telegraphists for all the inland stations, and he knew those telegraphists were on their way to commence work. According to the latest reports, the last stretch of unwired line between Adelaide and Alice Springs would be completed by New Year's Day. At least, then, the southern and central parts of the line would be complete.

The first message from Alice Springs had been arranged to be sent on New Year's Day. It was not sent then, but arrived on 3 January, the day before Todd's departure on the *Omeo*.[4] The message simply said that the Alice Springs telegraph station was operational, and that the entire Central Section was complete. This showed what could have been: if it wasn't for the collapse of the northern expedition—twice—then the line could have been finished only three days over time.[5]

Then a second message came through, reporting that Carl Kraegen, the Alice Springs telegraphist, was dead, having never reached Alice Springs. These messages were sent by another person who had temporarily taken his place.

41

The Black Prince

Adelaide to the Roper River, January 1872

The *Omeo* was the pride of the South Australian fleet. Brought to the colony in 1859, it was built in England to carry passengers and substantial cargo.

The *Omeo* was a striking, beautifully made vessel, around a hundred yards in length. It was a barque—a standard three-mast sailing ship—with a steam engine fitted. It was a hybrid: it could travel either by steam power or wind power, although the 80-horsepower steam engine was not strong, given the *Omeo*'s 800-ton bulk, and struggled in strong currents.[1]

The stairs down to the stateroom were lit during the day by a stained-glass window above; and in the stateroom itself there were velvet cushions, white enamel panelling, mouldings made of gold, and dining tables and chairs made from polished cedar. A hallway led to a ladies' room and eleven comfortable staterooms for those who liked to travel in style.

Naturally, Charles Todd was assigned one of the staterooms, as were the senior managers and their wives, and some paying guests travelling to Port Darwin.

There were also more than 80 cheap beds where most of the workforce would sleep on the journey, but aboard the *Omeo*, even these were quite comfortable.[2]

Down in the hold were the horses, with the extra provisions to feed the stranded workforce.

The ships' captains were instructed to sail to the mouth of the Roper River, unload the livestock there, then proceed to Port Darwin to unload the equipment and provisions. That was the official brief.

However, in an informal meeting with Blyth, Todd raised the possibility of taking the *Omeo* and other ships up the river itself, to Roper Landing, as advised by Patterson and others. Blyth told him to use his judgement, but there would be no official support for him if he did.[3]

They stopped in Newcastle Port to load coal and animal fodder. The voyage would be long, so much coal was brought aboard and the hold was filled, with more to come. Extra piles of coal and fodder were heaped on the *Omeo*'s beautiful deck.[4]

A strange passenger boarded the *Omeo* at Newcastle. He was an adventurer, explorer, and horse thief named Andrew Hume. He was, he said, a cousin of the famous explorer Hamilton Hume, the man from whom the Sydney–Melbourne highway gets its name. That claim was probably a lie.[5]

Four years earlier, the police near the New South Wales town of Baradine were searching a forest after reports of a bushranger gang in the vicinity, where they found only one man: Andrew Hume, riding a stolen horse and in possession of a revolver. Under questioning, he told them that he had acquired the revolver from notorious bushranger Captain Thunderbolt, and that other bushrangers knew him by the alias 'The Black Prince'. Giving no satisfactory account of how he had acquired the horse, he was sentenced to ten years' imprisonment for robbery under arms. After serving four years, he wrote a remarkable letter to the gaoler, alleging that he had evidence of the fate of the Leichhardt expedition.[6]

Hume claimed that, in 1862, after working on a Queensland station for a while, he travelled west across the continent, 'crossing all the rivers running north'.

> Passing them I came to small dry plains, and with difficulty succeeded in reaching the falls, where, as I got plenty of water,

> I stayed with the blacks until I happened to find a man who had been amongst them some time. While with him I was shown the under named marks, the first of which was on one tree; the second on another about 100 miles distant:
>
> L C
NOV 1847
DIG
+
>
> L C
AUG 1848
ROCK
+
>
> These are facsimiles as well as my memory can trace them now. Underneath the first tree was a bottle containing letters. In the rock, or rather the hollow of the rock, close to the second tree, were papers rolled up in a saddle-bag, some of which were written documents, and some appeared to be maps or plans. I placed the letters which are found under the first tree with the others under the second tree. After doing this, I promised the white man who was with me that I would either bring them to Sydney myself or let the Government authorities know where they were. I must not omit to mention that I found a quadrant, telescope and thermometer with the articles concealed in the rock under the tree.[7]

The white man, whose name he never asked, refused to return east with him, because he was too old to make such a long journey.

Hume's story held up surprisingly well under prolonged questioning. He was evidently knowledgeable about the places he described, and only a couple of minor discrepancies appeared in his story, discrepancies he could easily explain. He declared that if he was taken to the north coast, he would be able to find the marked trees and retrieve the hidden items.

These were sensational claims. The flames of public excitement were fanned by the curator of the Geelong Botanical Gardens, a former travelling companion of Leichhardt, who gave Hume's claims credence. The curator recalled a doctor with the Leichhardt expedition named Lewis Classon, hence the initials LC on the trees.[8]

But another of Leichhardt's former travelling companion dismissed Hume's claims as patently false. Havendon Hely reminded people that this was not the first time a criminal had tried to get a reduced prison sentence by claiming knowledge of Leichhardt's fate. John Garbutt, confined on Cockatoo Island, had persuaded the chaplain there that Leichhardt was alive, held captive by a band of runaway convicts who had established a secret colony inland from the Darling Downs. But unlike Hume, Garbutt was unable to sustain his lies under questioning.[9]

The authorities gave Hume a chance to deliver on his promise. His sentence was remitted, and he was sent to retrieve the strange white man and the saddlebag under the rock.

Hume came aboard the *Omeo* with two horses: one for himself and one to bring Classon. Todd was handed instructions that he must provide Hume with any resources he required, including blankets, provisions, and firearms.[10]

42

Todd's Fleet

Bowen to the Roper River, January 1872

Bowen, on the eastern Queensland coast, was the last port of call before the Roper River. After the *Omeo* anchored in the evening, Charles Todd went ashore in a row boat, accompanied by the second mate and two others. It was midnight and the little harbour town was asleep, but a light shone from the telegraph station window. Todd's knock was answered by the telegraphist on duty, who had been expecting him. He handed Todd two telegrams from William Cunningham, Todd's second-in-charge in Adelaide, about official matters. Todd had hoped there would also be something from Alice, but there was not.[1]

The telegraphist tapped out Todd's responses. Todd baulked at sending a personal message to Alice on a public line, so instead, he sent one to Lizzie, his oldest child.

The telegraphist offered him a drink, gratefully accepted. After an hour or two of conversation, Todd walked Bowen's quiet streets, seeking the others. They had found a fruit shop, woken the owner and pestered him to open his store 'early', which he had done, and now they were carrying sacks of fruit down to their boat at the jetty. It was first light by the time they pushed off and dawn when they reached the ship.

Somehow, while in Bowen, Todd had purchased a doll for his baby daughter, Nina.

The *Omeo* stopped at several islands along the way. On one, near the Great Barrier Reef, they found a ruined hut, some empty beer bottles, and writing carved into a stone. The inscription had the cryptic words: 'Sacred to the memory of the A.E.E.'[2]

A foray was made onto Booby Island in the Gulf of Carpentaria, established as a maritime post office. The idea was that ships passing Booby Island would leave letters for passengers and crew of other ships, or surplus food, or collect mail and food. In a cave on the island was a zinc box marked with the letters 'A.P.' and in this box the mail was supposedly stored.

It was a strange system, but not unique. Galapagos Island served as a mail drop-off and collection point for two centuries, originally with a box painted with the words 'Hathaway's Postoffice', and later with a barrel. In *Moby Dick*, Hermann Melville described the practice of whaling ships carrying mail for one another, which they would pass on directly if they met.

Booby Island was no Galapagos. The chosen cave was exposed to the weather; the zinc box had been left open by a previous visitor and was half full of water; the letters inside were ruined. Some stores that had been left behind by other ships were decaying among the guano and bird corpses.[3]

They crossed the gulf, and when they anchored on the evening of 26 January, Todd could see Maria Island on the horizon to the south-west. As they steamed towards it the next morning, a boat under canvas came into view, anchored in the island's lee. It was the *Larrakeeyah*, and its skipper, Captain Sweet, was soon on deck, giving a verbal report to Todd.

At the same time, a white flag was seen on Maria Island. Sweet explained that Patterson and Little had come down the river in a cutter (the *Dolphin*) and were camped on the island. Patterson and Little were on the deck of the *Omeo* the next morning, sunburned and covered in mosquito bites.

Todd was at an impasse. The plan, devised in Adelaide, was for the *Omeo* to discharge her animals and cargo here, at the mouth of the river, or onto Maria Island, then proceed to Port Darwin. The animals and cargo would then be taken up the river by other ships, including the *Tararua* (also on its way from Adelaide) or the *Bengal* (which had come down from Port Darwin under Patterson's instructions), with the help of the *Young Australian*. But none of those other ships was here: the *Bengal*, apparently, was stranded halfway up the river, and the others, for some reason, had not arrived.

The horses were the most urgent problem. Several horses had died on the voyage and Todd did not want to lose any more. The coastline near the river mouth was swampy, completely unsuitable for landing them. They could be landed at Maria Island, but Patterson, who had been camped on the island for a week, strongly urged Todd not to. That left Todd with the option he had privately discussed with the Premier before leaving: taking the *Omeo* up the river. He asked Captain Sweet for his opinion.

Over the past week, while waiting for the *Omeo*, Sweet had been taking soundings of the river mouth and dropping buoys; he believed that it could be done. Patterson, knowing firsthand the dire situation on the line, was adamant that the *Omeo* needed to go upriver with the supplies. Todd was persuaded.

But the *Omeo*'s captain, George Calder, objected. His employer had never agreed to such a thing, and furthermore, the ship's insurance would be voided. Todd assured him that if the *Omeo* was wrecked, the government would pay.

Calder protested that if, by a miracle, he took the ship up the river and back down again, it would need to be surveyed for seaworthiness as soon as possible; he could not possibly then continue to Port Darwin, as agreed. Todd reluctantly agreed to annul the contract once the ship arrived at Roper Landing. Getting the goods up the river was paramount. The ship's private passengers could continue their voyage to Port Darwin aboard another ship.

Calder asked for that in writing, so Todd wrote a letter, providing full indemnity to the *Omeo* in case of accident on the Roper River, and relieving Calder of his contract thereafter. He had no formal authority to do any such thing, and if it had all gone wrong, he could not have been sure the government would back him, so the letter was possibly worthless. The Premier had secretly told Todd he should do it if necessary, but that it was Todd's risk to take. Regardless, the letter persuaded Captain Calder.[4]

First, the *Larrakeeyah* approached the river, the crew making depth soundings, then Captain Sweet raised a flag signalling all clear and Calder nervously guided the *Omeo* forward. It seemed as if they were entering a long lake instead of a river; a fast-moving lake that was trying to expel them. The *Omeo* strained against the current.

They made slow progress. Eight miles one day, twenty the next and four the day after that. The third day was the slowest due to shallow, muddy banks and a neap tide. The landscape was stunning, with lush grasslands, paperbarks, distant ridges, and spectacular skies from which storms struck, then dispersed, then struck again. On moonlit nights they saw crocodiles floating down the current like logs.[5]

Todd was enthralled by the Roper. In a letter to Alice, he wrote:

> The banks are thickly lined with trees of various descriptions—Gum, paper bark, acacias, and a very fine ficus, being the most conspicuous. The country is splendidly grassed, and quite green of course, this being the wet season, it is however subject in many places to heavy floods from the overflowing of the river.
>
> How it is that so little should be known of what is really one of the finest rivers in Australia I cannot understand, and I should have thought it would have been selected without hesitation as the site for the Northern Territory Settlement. It must become a place of importance . . .[6]

And some days later:

> I am still on board the *Omeo*, but in a river never yet, or before, traversed by a steamer. I have, therefore, the honour of

> opening to the commerce of the world a new and very fine river, destined, I should think, to become of considerable importance as this portion of northern Australia is occupied by enterprising settlers.

He was intrigued by glimpses of Aboriginal people on the shore. A man sitting cross-legged, immobile on a stump, watched the steamer go past. One small group followed them all day, hurrying along the bank as the steamer laboured upstream, then when the *Omeo* dropped anchor for the night, setting up camp nearby, so as to follow them again in the morning.[7]

Twenty miles from the river mouth, they found a suitable place on the bank to land the horses, in dire need of a break from the hold. The horses had to swim to shore while the men stood waist-deep, herding them. There was a flurry of panic when a crocodile glided into view, but the crocodile took fright at the strangers and swam away.

Todd assigned a man to stay with the horses for a few days, as long it would take to return and collect them. The *Omeo* steamed away up the river and immediately ran aground on a sandbank, where it was stuck for several hours.

At about this time, Patterson and Todd had their first chance to talk privately.

Patterson wanted an excuse to resign. If Todd were to usurp his authority, he would resign; if Todd landed the horses at Maria Island, he would resign; if Todd refused to take the *Omeo* up the Roper River, he would resign. Brooding and waiting for Todd's arrival, he had rehearsed the scenarios in his head (as revealed in his diary and letters to his wife). He was so convinced that either he would quit or Todd would get rid of him, that he had carted a box of all his documents with him to Maria Island and hidden the box there, until the game had played out. It seems that he hoped to spite Todd by taking the documents back to Adelaide, rather than hand them over to his enemy. Hence, he did not want the box on board, lest Todd seize it after his resignation.

This proved to be a miscalculation. Todd was disarming, promising that Patterson was still in charge as 'chief officer', with Todd having final responsibility.[8]

This wordplay did not mollify Patterson. As Todd stood on the deck admiring the view, Patterson sat hunched in the cabin, writing a letter to Todd. In it, he reminded Todd that he had been appointed directly by the government as 'Commander of the Expedition', and that he was answerable only to the government, and that there was no mention of the 'Superintendent of Telegraphs' in any of the documents. He admitted that he had consulted Todd on various matters before leaving Adelaide, but that was only because of 'long established friendship and respect for yourself'. He demanded to know: 'Am I to be regarded as Commander of the Expedition as heretofore or have the Government lost confidence in me and despatched you to undertake the active supervision of the work?'

Patterson gave the letter to John Little for delivery to Todd.

Todd had no choice but to respond likewise, but he made Patterson wait three days for a reply. In his letter, Todd reminded Patterson that he *was* mentioned in Patterson's agreement with the government and that Patterson had been instructed, from the start, to report to Todd, to seek his advice, and to keep him apprised. Patterson's guff about keeping him informed out of friendship and respect—as if it was a favour—was nonsense.

Todd also reminded Patterson of his alarming message in November, claiming that the expedition was 'breaking down' and that without intervention, 'the expedition must inevitably collapse'. Surely, he could have seen what effect that might have politically?

Then followed a quick bit of pandering from Todd: 'I am indeed so impressed by the care and forethought used by you as far as I have been able to judge, that I should personally view your return to Adelaide with unfeigned regret.'

Patterson was unconvinced. He went back down into the cabin, penned another letter and delivered it the next day. He derided Todd's response as 'evasive and foreign to the points raised by me'. Then Patterson spelled out his question plainly: 'Am I to be regarded as Commander of the Expedition with the same powers as before, or is it intended to reduce me to a lower position than that with which I set out from Adelaide?'

Apparently, the title mattered, so Todd relented on that, replying, 'I recognise you as Commander of the Northern Territory Telegraph Expedition, subject however to my control as head of the department.'

Patterson was prepared to resign in high dudgeon. He had fantasised about righteously storming back to Adelaide, but Todd would not give him a reason to do so.[9]

They steamed on towards Roper Landing, while Patterson silently lamented his hidden box, far behind them on Maria Island. He had sought to sabotage Todd, but had sabotaged himself.

Charles Todd and Alice Todd (nee Bell) in 1855, the year they were married and moved from Cambridge, England, to Adelaide. STATE LIBRARY OF SOUTH AUSTRALIA (SLSA)

King William Street, Adelaide, in 1865; a small but growing city. SLSA

Queens Wharf, Port Adelaide, 1872. Several shipments of personnel, supplies, livestock, and equipment left from here to Port Darwin for the construction of the line. SLSA

Adelaide Observatory. After its construction in 1860, the Todds lived here until Charles's death in 1910. The observatory was later demolished to make way for an extension to a school. SLSA

The observatory telescope, installed in 1873. SLSA

The Todd's three oldest children, Lizzie, Charlie, and Hedley. SLSA

Charles Todd in 1871. SLSA

Horses and wagon travelling north with supplies for construction workers on the overland telegraph. SLSA

Bullock teams could carry heavier loads than horses, transporting heavy equipment such as poles and wire along the line. SLSA

An overland telegraph camp in the MacDonnell Ranges. (LIBRARY AND ARCHIVES NT) PETER SPILLETT COLLECTION

Workers at the jetty at Roper Landing, 1872, photographed by Captain Sweet. SLSA

A ceremony was held after the planting of the first pole in Port Darwin in 1870. Photograph taken by Captain Sweet. SLSA

Landing the cable at Port Darwin in November 1872, photographed by Captain Sweet. SLSA

Port Darwin telegraph station, 1875. SLSA

The settlement at Port Darwin in 1870. The building at the top of the hill is the Governor's residence. SLSA

Four senior managers at the Roper River in 1872, photographed by Captain Sweet. From left: A.J. Mitchell, Robert Patterson, Charles Todd, John Little. SLSA

Three ships at Roper Landing on the Roper River in early 1872, photographed by Captain Sweet. The ships are the *Tararua*, the *Bengal*, and the *Omeo*. SLSA

The Alice Spring on the Todd River, near the telegraph station at the town now known as Alice Springs. DAVID DUFTY

The Hugh River on the plain south of the MacDonnell Ranges. The Todd, Hugh, and Finke rivers are ephemeral desert waterways, running only after rare periods of heavy rainfall. DAVID DUFTY

The MacDonnell Ranges. INGO OELAND/ALAMY

The Alice Springs Telegraph Station is now a reserve and a telegraph museum. DAVID DUFTY

A partition ran through the Eucla Telegraph Station on the border of Western Australia and South Australia due to colonial politics. Each colony provided its own staff and equipment for its side of the partition. These pictures show the Eucla station from the South Australian side (top, SLSA) and the Western Australian side (bottom, STATE LIBRARY OF WESTERN AUSTRALIA).

Charles Todd in 1900. SLSA

Richard Knuckey, who led the construction team around Charlotte Waters, and who accompanied Charles Todd on his journey south across the continent. SLSA

William Whitfield Mills found a pass through the MacDonnell Ranges at a place now known as Alice Springs. SLSA

Robert Patterson, in charge of construction of the northern section of the line, after the first attempt at that section ended in failure. SLSA

Captain John Hart, retired whaler and controversial politician, crossed swords with Charles Todd over his grand plans for telegraphy in the colony. SLSA

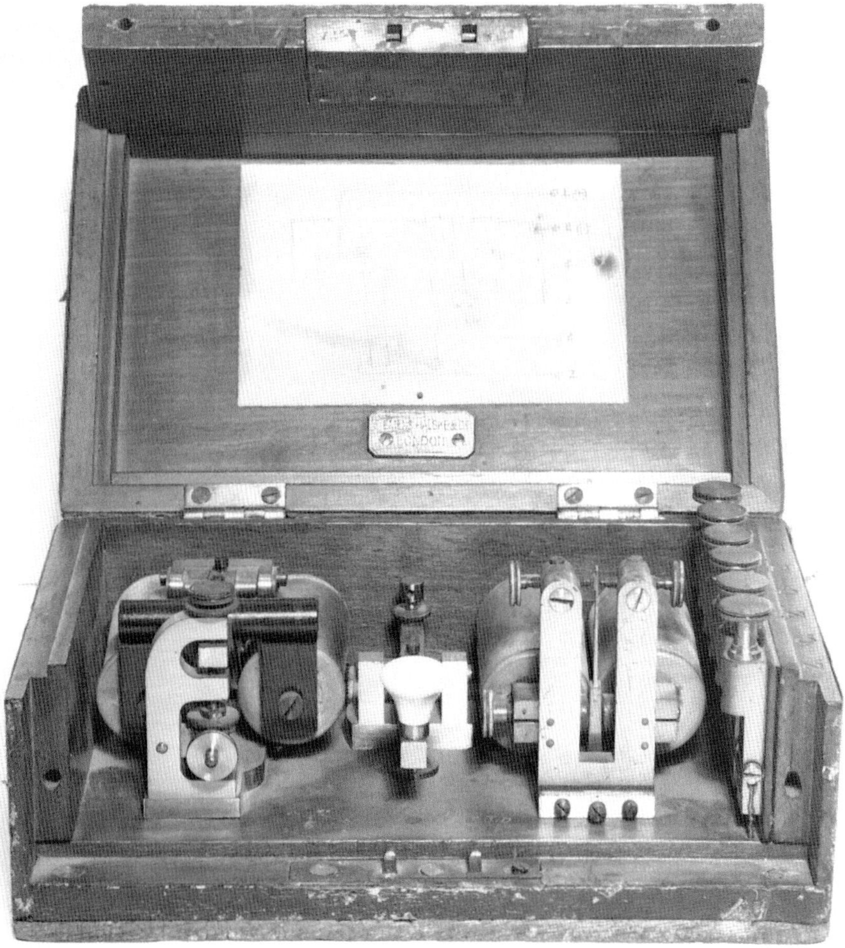

This portable telegraph transmitter, known as a 'pocket relay', was the device that Charles Todd used near Central Mount Stuart on the day the line was completed. SLSA

Telegraph equipment used in a telegraph station. SLSA

Charles Todd (centre) with staff at the post and telegraph office in Adelaide. SLSA

Alice Todd in 1890. SLSA

Charles Todd with five grandchildren 1900. SLSA

43

The Mighty Roper

Roper River, February 1872

The *Omeo*'s engines pushed the ship against the rushing current, as the river's level rose and fell, as distant storms emptied into the catchment. The water level would rise, lifting the ship as much as thirty feet in a matter of hours, then quickly dropped again. The ship grounded on a sandbank, but floated free on a surge.

Todd was entranced by the scenery. The banks were lined with several species of trees, sometimes covered with vines. Beyond the banks were lush plains, green hills, and, beyond them, distant glimpses of higher ranges. The clouds would burst, then break, the sun glinting on low-lying mists. Then the storms would return in sheets, blinding their view past the banks.

Near an island in the river named Hawks Nest Island, the ship grounded again. While they were stuck, a boat came from upriver carrying the *Bengal*'s first mate, who said that the *Bengal* was stuck a short distance away.

There was a high bank nearby on the shore and the skies were clear. Four women from the *Omeo* were taken ashore with some clothes to dry. While they were busily hanging their washing, five Aboriginal men approached, completely naked, calling out to them in a friendly manner. The women shrieked in horror, running to the river's edge and calling for help. A boat was sent to fetch them, while men still aboard the ship readied guns 'in case they meant mischief', but by the time they reached the shore, it was clear that the Aboriginal men meant no harm. They were simply curious.[1]

The men were invited onto the boat, dressed in sacks (not for their own sake but that of the agitated women) and taught how to shake

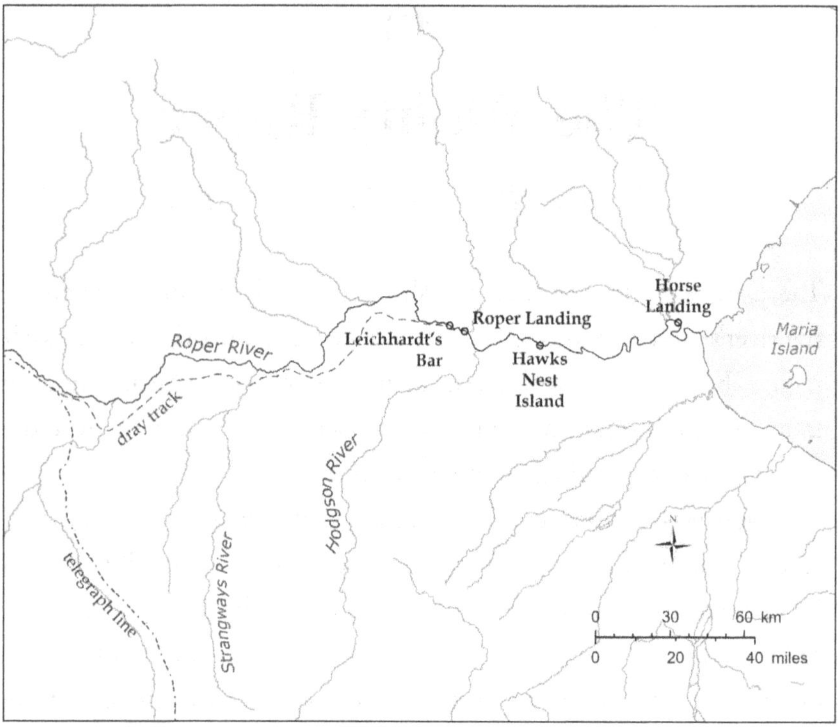

The Roper River

hands with the ladies. The men visited again the next day, staying for several hours.

The *Larrakeeyah* appeared. This was surprising, since Todd had instructed Sweet to wait with the *Larrakeeyah* around Maria Island until the other ships arrived. Sweet explained that he had waited for two days but they did not come, so he had returned up the river. Todd sent him back down again.[2]

A third boat approached! This was the cutter that Patterson had taken down to Maria Island. After losing sight of the other boats and ships, its crew had returned a different way through the lower reaches. They told an alarming tale of an encounter with a Malay prau, which they believed was a pirate ship. The prau seemed to stalk them for a time, then sailed directly at them. The cutter's skipper fired his revolver into the air as a warning shot, but the ship bore down on them, so he fired directly at it. He missed, or believed he missed, but circled away.[3]

Todd conceded that the ship might have been a pirate ship and might have been hostile, but even so, he disapproved of the decision to fire a weapon at it.

Three days later, the *Larrakeeyah* returned, escorting the *Young Australian*.

Built nineteen years earlier in the London's Blackwall shipyards, the *Young Australian* was neither young nor Australian. It was a smallish ship made of sturdy wood and steel, housing a gigantic steam engine. Everything about it, from the side-paddle wheels to the jutting arms, hooks, and chains, was functional. Tough and stocky, it would have been better named the *Blackwall Brawler*.

Chains were fastened, and the tug pulled the *Omeo* off the sandbank. Once the *Omeo* was free, the *Young Australian* was fastened to the *Bengal*, which, being a sailing ship, could not fight the currents without help. The three ships then headed upstream towards the landing. But soon after getting underway, Captain Calder steered the *Omeo* onto another sandbank.

Impatient to get to the landing, Todd hopped onto the *Bengal*, promising that the tug would return for the *Omeo*, just as soon as the *Bengal* was safely delivered. Patterson clambered aboard with him. They arrived at Roper Landing later that afternoon.[4]

The landing was on the southern bank, surrounded by water on most sides, in a junction between two rivers, the Roper and the Hodgson. Debris clung to nearby trees from when the water level was higher. Even now, the Roper was a full 130 yards wide, flowing strongly. Under the direction of the camp's manager, Stephen King, the men had made a jetty by cutting several nearby trees at the same height, with the tree stumps acting as the jetty's pylons. No pushing the stock into the water here: the horses clopped across the jetty with ease.

King had also overseen the construction of a wooden storehouse. Todd was impressed, describing the muddy camp as 'a respectable township in embryo'.[5]

There was higher ground to the south, along the Hodgson, where the bullocks were being kept. There was a bluff there, called Matilda Bluff. Patterson had given the privilege of naming it to John Little, who had named it after his wife; Patterson had already named some nearby cliffs 'Elsie Cliffs' after his own wife. Little climbed the bluff and described the spectacular view:

> The two rivers could be seen like silver threads in an undulating green and lightly timbered park. Further back ranges and table-lands were visible, having a pimple-like appearance on account of the haze. Bold, rugged, red, ironstone bluffs were nearer at hand, and through a gorge between Elsie Cliffs and Matilda Bluff the Hodgson could be seen winding down from the tableland.[6]

While all hands busily unloaded the ship, Todd hopped back on the tug, which returned to the *Omeo* and towed it up the next day.

The *Omeo*'s passengers stepped ashore to the muddy campsite, hauling suitcases. Their disappointment at not being taken to Port Darwin was not lifted when they learned they would be sleeping in tents.

Morale was low all around; the landing workers had been living in mud and tents for six weeks, subsisting on jerked beef, with rain dumping from the sky every day. The passengers, crew, and workers on the ships were travel-weary and stir-crazy.

On the evening of the *Omeo*'s arrival, Todd announced a celebration. Rum was served to all the workers. Todd made a speech, reiterating the importance of the project and explaining why he had come to the Roper. Under Patterson's gaze, he said he was not taking over, but merely supporting Patterson. Someone called for three cheers for Todd and then three cheers for Patterson. Knowing how obsessed

Patterson was with his wife, Elsie—and even though she was far away in Adelaide—Todd then called for 'another cheer for Mrs Patterson!' This blatant ruse actually worked: Patterson was quite pleased by the gesture.[7]

While the workers celebrated outside, Todd hosted a dinner party aboard the *Omeo* for a select group: the ships' captains, the managers and the passengers. Here, not rum but bottles of champagne were opened. Todd was careful to place Patterson at the head of the table, referring to him as the chair of proceedings. It was a terrific evening. Todd happily confided in a letter to Alice, 'It passed off first rate—cemented friendships, and brought about a good feeling amongst the different elements of the Expedition which I trust will be productive of good results.'

They all drank much champagne. Late in the evening, Todd jokingly called someone to order for making an overly long (but no doubt heartfelt) speech. Patterson was not too drunk to overlook what he perceived as Todd's indiscretion towards him. After all, wasn't he the chairman? It was therefore his place, and not Todd's, to call people to order. He recorded in his diary that Todd 'insisted on usurping my functions as chairman . . .'[8]

The candles were extinguished and the revellers went on deck to enjoy the night air. Patterson stumbled to bed.

The remaining business for Charles Todd to attend to was this: send the *Omeo* back to Adelaide; get the *Omeo*'s passengers to Port Darwin aboard the *Bengal*; bring the horses from Horse Landing; and await the third and final ship from Adelaide, the *Tararua*, which was bringing more supplies and more horses.

The *Omeo* left on Tuesday, 13 February, piloted by the *Young Australian*. A handful of men whose 'services are no longer required' were sent aboard. Also on board was a very sick man named Thompson

Naisbit, who Todd believed would never recover. He arranged entry for Naisbit into the Adelaide hospital on his return.[9]

The *Omeo*'s passengers glumly watched the *Omeo* disappear down the river. Captain Calder, who had promised to take them to Port Darwin, had cheerily abandoned them in his hard bargaining with Todd. Their misery was lightened somewhat by the *Bengal*, after the captain opened the ship's bar for all the hapless residents of Roper Landing, selling alcohol to them at exorbitant prices.[10]

The ships sped down the current, reaching the mouth in two days. The *Omeo* had a mailbag on board for delivery to Adelaide. Todd had been writing a long letter to Alice during his travels, adding to it whenever he had spare time. He wrote a few concluding paragraphs before folding it and sealing it in an envelope.

> The weather is very trying—very hot—and damp a regular vapor bath, with thunderstorms of great intensity, furious gusts or gales of wind, and torrents of rain—then fierce sunshine. The storms are grandly awful—the sunsets magnificent but dripping at every pore with our clothes completely saturated, it is difficult to enjoy life especially when worried and harassed on all sides—long letters to write—angry disputes to settle—and jealousies to calm—such is life with me now—but by the blessing of God I hope to succeed . . .
>
> And now dearest Alice good bye—wishing you and all my dear ones every blessing—I am,
>
> your affectionate Husband
> Charles Todd

They anchored near Maria Island, going ashore for firewood to feed the voracious appetite of the steam engines. Perhaps Patterson hoped to retrieve his document box, but he had hidden it on the south of the island, not the western end where firewood was being collected.

On their way up the river, Todd was worried that rising waters put the horses at risk, so they stopped at Horse Landing to board twenty of the horses. The man Todd had put in charge, George Deane, told a harrowing story of an encounter with the local Aboriginal people, with whom they had been getting along quite well until recently.

He claimed that while the others were out, the Aboriginal men took the opportunity to sneak up on him. They had stolen an axe and had used it to fashion a heavy club, which one of them brandished as they approached. Todd recorded in a letter:

> . . . he fortunately saw them and fired his revolver, which brought back the rest of the party from the bank, on the appearance of whom the rascals made off and were not seen afterwards.[11]

In running away, the Aboriginal men dropped the large club, which Deane kept. Todd did not learn for sure whether the Aboriginal men meant harm, or, if they did, why.[12]

The tug was not designed to transport livestock, so the horses were cramped in the afterdeck, their heads above the cabin skylight. Todd was confident that the *Young Australian*, with its powerful engine, could easily fight its way up the current in the space of few hours. In this, he miscalculated.

The current was stronger than ever and the steamer ran out of wood. The *Young Australia* had to anchor overnight while the crew foraged for wood on the river bank. While they were at anchor, a wild thunderstorm hit. The horses panicked, stomping about with their hooves and causing the boat to rock side to side—almost capsizing it—which drove them into a greater frenzy. One horse leapt up and smashed through the skylight, its forelegs becoming stuck in the shattered remnants. Men rushed to free the horse, mindful of not being crushed or trampled to death while doing so.

Between the lashing rain and the frenzied horses, nobody slept.[13]

The next morning, Aboriginal men called out to them from the river banks, raising one arm and then the other, while shouting loudly. They seem to want the ship to stop, but given the horse situation, Todd could not allow that.

The *Young Australian* arrived back at Roper Landing in constant, heavy, driving rain. The river had risen sixteen feet, causing worries that the entire camp would be flooded out. The jetty, almost underwater, heaved in the current, while men swam about reinforcing it with wire.[14] Malaria was rife. The day before their return, a worker named Daniel Kavanaugh had died from 'fever'. As Kavanaugh's illness had progressed, another worker wrote in his diary, 'I went to see him, and I never saw a man so fallen away in his life.' They made a coffin, buried him and held a funeral service.[15]

Todd caught malaria, keeping his symptoms in check with a daily dose of quinine, accompanied by a glass of sherry to disguise the quinine's bitter taste. When he had attacks of vomiting and trembling, he would medicate with brandy and water.[16]

A week later, Todd and Patterson were back at Maria Island, aboard the *Young Australian*, while the *Larrakeeyah* patrolled north each day, looking for the next and final ship, the *Tararua*. Away from the river, they were free of mosquitoes, but the ship was infested with ants that had come aboard with the firewood.

44

The Arrival of the *Tararua*

Roper Landing, March 1872

They waited for more than a week for the *Tararua*, in a frustrating, idle torpor. They killed ants, swatted mosquitoes, fished (with success), and debated all kinds of topics. In the hot, steamy days on the deck of the steamship in the Gulf of Carpentaria, they sought mental escape: conversation and lively debates; reading books; and writing long letters to loved ones. Todd's inner life on the Roper is revealed in his long letters to Alice. He told her what he was reading: *Culture and Anarchy*, a philosophical work by Mathew Arnold.[1]

He wrote that once the Roper business was finished, he would go to Port Darwin—which he did not relish, because he would be the guest of Government Resident Bloomfield Douglas, who was a bit too aristocratic for Todd's tastes.

He confided to Alice:

> I shall have to study etiquette, as Douglas wears spotless white and is a great swell. He has written to say he quite expects me to put up at his house, or the 'Residence' as it is called which I suppose I must do—tho to tell truth I would rather be at the Telegraph Office & be more my own master. I am sorry to find he is very much disliked, owing partly to his intense selfishness (so at least it is said tho he is certainly most hospitable) and partly to his assumed tyrannical tone toward his subs.[2]

From Port Darwin, he daydreamed about travelling to Timor, explaining to Alice, 'Timor is a Dutch settlement that is said to be well worth seeing. In that case I may buy two Timor ponies for the boys. They can be got for about two pounds.'[3]

He fretted that the *Tararua* would never arrive, imagining all kinds of possibilities:

> The steamer (*Tararua*) may have never sailed from Pt Adelaide, or she may have come to grief in the intricate passage of the inner route (inside the barrier reef) and Torres Strait—or she may, which is hardly possible, have arrived off the river while I was going up after the departure of the *Omeo*, and finding no one waiting have gone on to Pt Darwin.

In fact, this third scenario is what had happened. The *Tararua* had arrived at the river mouth, found no ships waiting, so the captain had concluded that 'Roper had been abandoned', a thin excuse for high-tailing around the coast to Port Darwin. But on this issue, Bloomfield Douglas actually showed leadership, refusing to allow the captain to land the supplies and horses. The decision was tough on the horses, but once landed, there was no way to get them aboard again, there still being no jetty. If the horses were bound for the Roper, the Government Resident declared, then that's where they should land.

An exception was made for Todd's nephew, Griffith, who was allocated seven horses for inspecting the line. After those seven were landed, the *Tararua* steamed away in disgrace.

Late in the evening of 3 March, there was a cry of 'Steamer's light!' aboard the *Young Australian*. They heard a gunshot, then saw rockets in the sky and a bright blue light, as the *Tararua* signalled its position. There was delirious excitement on deck. Patterson actually grabbed Todd around the waist and danced with him.[4]

Their joy was partly because they were sick of waiting and partly because the *Tararua* brought a mailbag of letters from home. Among them, a letter to Charles from Alice. Sadly, although some of their letters have survived, that one did not. But some of it can be inferred in Todd's reply, which he wrote over the next few weeks. Alice knew that after discharging its cargo, the *Tararua* would be returning to Adelaide, so she asked him to come home aboard it.

But to his wife's dismay, when the *Tararua* arrived in Port Adelaide some weeks later, Todd was not aboard, having elected to stay at the Roper River. The captain brought a letter from him, which said, in part: 'I wish I could return in the *Tararua* as you anticipate, but there no chance of that. I cannot do so without jeopardising everything. I have indeed a most difficult task to accomplish. The officers & men are all more or less disheartened.'[5]

Patterson had two opportunities to retrieve his document box from Maria Island. The first was when he, Todd, and some others went to the island by boat, to explore and kill time while they waited for the *Tararua*. Unfortunately, the surf was rough, and, as they were leaving the island, a squall swamped their boat, damaging it. They had to walk five miles around the island—until they were out of the wind—before another boat from the steamer could retrieve them.

The second chance arose because the *Tararua* was out of fuel, so a group went ashore to collect firewood. Again, Patterson joined them, but as he reached the shore, he had an intense bout of malaria and lay on the beach until it was time to go.

In his diary, he wrote about how much he wanted that box, but after these visits to the island, never mentioned it again. In all likelihood, he never got it back. Perhaps he fretted that Todd would think poorly of him for losing all the official documentation—after all, he fretted about a great many things—but he need not have worried about that. Todd already thought he was incompetent. Todd wrote to Alice:

> He is not fitted for this sort of work, and is too easily disheartened. He spends too much time in reading, instead of moving amongst his men, and is always writing to his wife and others—but at the same time I thought it better to avoid if possible the extreme measure of suspending him and after some correspondence managed to settle matters amicably and hope soon to have things on a more satisfactory footing. He is gentlemanly and now he knows that my intentions towards him are not hostile he will work with me—I hope, zealously.[6]

45

Sending Supplies

Roper Landing, March 1872

To the surprise of many, Andrew Hume could converse with the Aboriginal people who lived near Roper Landing. One traveller, on his return, said that many at Roper Landing believed Hume's story. 'He speaks the language of the natives fluently, was recognised by them, and was evidently made very much of.'[1]

Todd was sceptical of Hume's story, but he liked him, so he offered him a job on the line until such time as he was ready to make a start on his quest.

The storehouse was full of supplies for delivery inland. Packhorses and bullocks grazed on high pastures nearby, but the track to the west—if it could be called that—was wet, boggy, and flooded. They just had to wait. And while they waited, faraway clerks, sitting at desks in Adelaide and London, tallied the rising cost: £70 per day, every day.

The wet subsided in March. Todd sent a supply team westward on 16 March, led by the surveyor Stephen King and explorer Alfred Giles, with twelve other men, and 60 laden packhorses. Hume went with them.[2] With utter ingratitude, Hume complained to others how poorly Charles Todd was treating him, as he was meant to provision him for his expedition, but had not done so.[3]

The day they left, the rain started again, causing Todd to worry that they would soon be stranded.[4]

A week later, Todd sent out a second team, placing Patterson in charge of the team—or rather, politely suggesting to Patterson that perhaps he might want to take charge.

Rid of Patterson's company at last, he complained again to Alice:

> I am glad to be free of Patterson and can get on twice as well without him. He never works unless for some personal benefit and is dreadfully selfish. He has robbed me of my gun, taken all the saddle straps, wanted all my coffee and I don't know what besides. Notwithstanding all this I think I have acted wisely and for the best interests of the Government in retaining him here.[5]

Todd's reasoning was that, if he had fired Patterson, it would have gone badly back in Adelaide. Patterson and others would have accused him of wanting to rob Patterson of the glory.

Just as Todd feared, the delivery team became stranded near Leichhardt's Bar, where they camped on high ground for a week before continuing.[6]

The packhorses could not traverse the deep, boggy patches laden with their heavy loads, so the teamsters would unloaded the packhorses, carry the load through the bog themselves, lead the horses across, then load them up again. Even with this system, they lost two horses that had become hopelessly stuck in deep mud. An extensive patch of mud could not be crossed, so they made camp again, to wait for it to dry out.[7]

While they were camped there, Dick Knuckey arrived on horseback. Knuckey explained that he was trying to reach Roper Landing, to try to procure supplies for stranded inland crews that were almost out of food. They had been subsisting on 'short rations', which was three pounds of flour and six pounds of tinned meat, per person, per week, for six weeks and were slowly starving. There was no sign of the long-awaited deliveries from Port Darwin.[8]

Giles was able to show Knuckey the hoped-for supplies, which could not be delivered until the mud had dried out. Knuckey camped with them for one night, then continued to Roper Landing.

There, in the upper reaches of the Roper Valley, Todd's plan of maintaining peace with the Aboriginal people broke down. Aboriginal men shadowed Giles's men, stole their tools, and acted in a hostile manner. Believing the Aboriginal men intended to kill them, Giles's men 'set the dogs' on them on one occasion, and on another, when spears were raised, fired at them.[9]

Dick Knuckey arrived at Roper Landing with four other riders and several packhorses just as Todd was sitting down to dinner. Todd was quickly impressed by Knuckey, describing him to Alice as 'one of the most energetic officers we have'.[10]

46
Providence Knoll
Roper Creek and Daly River, January–April 1872

Some of the construction teams were stranded together, at high ground near the upper western reaches of the Roper, at a place they called Union Camp, simply because it was the happenstance union of several groups. Included was Bedford Hack, his bullocks, and bullock drivers: the very people who were supposed to deliver food down the line. There were about eighty men in the bedraggled, makeshift camp. When the delivery team from Roper Landing arrived, the men there were so weak that some could barely stand. There had been one death, a man named Thomas Hawkins, in late March.[1]

Ralph Milner's sheep arrived at around the same time. The sheep were in a poor state, small and weak, their heavy fleeces full of dirt and grass seeds. They needed to be shorn. Milner produced some shears, and the Union Camp cook gave lessons in using them.

Three hundred sheep were despatched north, where another crew, led by Walter Rutt, was stranded. It took the shepherds and sheep a month to get there.

Those stuck at Union Camp had a rough time, but Rutt's camp had it the worst.

Rutt's team had been poling south of the Katherine when the nearby creek, a tributary of the Roper, burst its banks on 3 January. They had moved their horses and cattle to a nearby hill, then carried their food, blankets, and equipment there over three days, as the waters rose up to their waists. Rutt named the place 'Providence Knoll'. As the waters rose, it became an island, trapping them in the monsoonal sea. They were stuck on Providence Knoll for three months.[2]

When they set up camp there, Rutt had already been sick for weeks, with fever and dizzy spells, and was barely able to walk unassisted. That did not prevent him from ruling his tiny island empire with an iron fist. Before they had stopped work, Rutt had suspected a sick employee of malingering, so he reduced the employee's pay, 'until I found his work up to the mark'.[3]

As the supply of bully beef dwindled, the pile of empty tins was put to use, fashioned into metal decks of playing cards. Euchre was the card game of choice.[4]

Rutt put them on reduced rations. Their daily diet consisted of flour, biscuits, and tinned meat. He decided they should kill and eat some of the bullocks. When each animal was killed, the meat was preserved with salt, but they ran out of salt after bullock number four. A worker named Glazebrook refused to prepare some bullock tripe for consumption, so Rutt fired him. But there was nowhere for Glazebrook to go: he was stuck there with the rest of them, with nothing to do. Eventually the others pleaded with Rutt to rehire Glazebrook, which he did, on condition that Glazebrook apologise for his insubordination.

Rutt was a devoutly religious man. He did not drink alcohol and he believed that dancing was sinful. When he occasionally caught men singing and dancing, he became upset and angry.

A delivery of sheep arrived across receding floodwaters in early March. Rutt's men could now dine on mutton, but they were not saved yet. The water was still too high to move their horses and remaining books, or to resume work. There was no point in moving south, to Union Camp, only to be stuck with the others, and going north meant defeat.

They were all sick and scrawny. At the end of March, a man named Ned Privett, whose health had been dire, died, despite last-minute attempts to revive him with wine. He was a grey-haired sailor who had entertained them over many evenings with stories of his adventures.

They buried him under a tree and auctioned his possessions to raise money for his wife and children.[5]

After Privett's burial, a group of Aboriginal people approached with friendly overtures, which were gratefully received by the grieving men. Rutt disapproved and instructed the telegraphist Stapleton to frighten them away by firing his revolver over their heads.[6]

A week after Privett's death, Patterson arrived by horseback, informing them that provisions were on their way. He announced that the men were now back on full rations, but were also back to work, with a pay rise. There was more good news: the delivery drays coming up the track were not just bringing more flour, tea, and salt, but also treats such as preserved potatoes and jam.[7]

Even the resumption of work was welcome to them, because the tedium was driving them mad.

There was another stranded crew, far to the south, that was even more isolated than the one on Providence Knoll. Bob Burton's advance party had left the Katherine in late September, passing through the high plains south of there, past Roper Creek and Warlock Ponds, on its way to the Daly River.

Burton, worried about long dry stretches of travel, made his men dig wells as they went. It was tough, gruelling work, the wells being very deep, and it slowed them down. Then, three days after they commenced poling, heavy rain hit, swamping the campsite. This was the same deluge that had forced Rutt's crew, further north, to take refuge on Providence Knoll.

There was no longer any purpose digging wells, so they travelled southwards, reaching Daly Waters, their designated starting point, on 30 December. They were out of contact with the others, and, due to a navigation error, were not where they thought. Nobody knew where they were.

They commenced poling, with frequent stoppages due to heavy weather. They followed Birdum Creek—or what they thought was Birdum Creek—only to discover that they were on a different creek. Several miles of poles had been planted in the wrong place.

The creeks were overflowing, the track they had come along was flooded and their expected food deliveries did not arrive. Small groups went back up the track to get supplies, but the waters rose higher and those groups did not return. Thirty-six men remained, stuck, unable to work or move. They consoled themselves that, if things got dire, they could eat the bullocks. The camp's mood was desperate when, one morning, they woke to discover that the bullocks had escaped during the night, back up the track. Attempts to find them and bring them back failed. A week later, Burton himself rode out on his horse and returned the next day with the bullocks.

The group was on one-third rations. Even with killed bullocks and caught fish, their diet was meagre, and they lost up to a quarter of their initial body weight.[8] One of the men wrote in his diary: 'It is wearisome work waiting here, nothing to do, nothing to read and never hear anything of the rest of the world. It is more than 3 months since we heard from any other place under the sun. I think I have nearly had enough of this sort of work.'[9] On another day, he simply wrote, 'All quiet today. We merely vegetate.'[10]

The explorer Alfred Giles found them on 28 March. He was greeted by gaunt, thin men in dirty, worn clothes. Giles noted how clean and tidy the campsite was. Keeping it clean was a way to stay sane. He also noticed hundreds of small fish drying on lines between the tents. His arrival was the most exciting thing that had happened in weeks, but Giles had yet more exciting news: others were on their way, bringing a flock of sheep. The thin men took off their hats and cheered.[11]

The rain had stopped then, and the ground dried quickly. A delivery of supplies carried by packhorses arrived within days of the sheep, bringing flour, sugar, and tea. Just as exciting as the food was the arrival of mail from Roper Landing, including newspapers. Burton's men at Birdum Creek had been cut off from the outside world for five months and were hungry for news. The newspapers were somewhat disappointing, some being more than a year old, the earliest being from March 1871—before they had embarked.[12]

47

The Mystery of the Missing Boat

Roper River to Port Darwin, April–May 1872

The *Bengal* left Roper Landing on 3 April with the *Omeo*'s abandoned passengers, who were finally bound for Port Darwin. The ship was escorted down the river by the *Young Australian*, which Todd was aboard, so that he could farewell the *Bengal* once it was safely out to sea.

The river was no longer a cauldron. The ship glided so smoothly on the water that it seemed as if they were motionless, while the trees on the riverbank slid past on either side.[1] Out in the gulf, somewhere near the river mouth and Maria Island, they held a party aboard the *Bengal*, joined by Todd and the *Young Australian*'s captain and crew. There were speeches, warm wishes, hearty toasts, and farewells. Then Todd was back aboard the tug, while the *Bengal* headed north and vanished across the blue horizon. Todd would soon make the journey to Port Darwin himself aboard the *Young Australian*. But he would not leave until he had seen all the delivery teams leave Roper Landing, carrying their vital supplies inland for the stranded workers.

The tug turned and chugged back into the river mouth, toward the landing. Captain Lowrie warned Todd that the *Young Australian* did not have enough fuel to reach Port Darwin.

At a convenient rise, Todd sent four men ashore to camp and chop wood to feed the tug's voracious appetite, both men and firewood to be retrieved when the ship returned in several days' time. Besides axes, saws, and rations, they were equipped with a boat, four revolvers, and two rifles.[2]

Two days later, at Roper Landing, he realised he needed two of those woodcutters to join a delivery team about to leave for the line, so he sent the *Young Australian* down to get them. On the way down, the captain anchored the tug by the riverbank overnight. As they were eating breakfast, all four woodcutters appeared on the bank. They had walked seventy miles upriver from their camp, attempting to walk all the way to Roper Landing.[3]

When they arrived at Roper Landing, Todd asked them to explain themselves. He wrote:

> They reported that they had been surrounded by the blacks who had cut their boat adrift during the night, & then while they went to look for it the blacks robbed their camp leaving them no alternative but to attempt to reach the main camp on foot, following the river a distance of 70 miles. They were very fortunate in seeing the boat sent down for them . . . They were followed by the blacks and had to swim several wide creeks which swarm with crocodiles or alligators.[4]

Todd was furious, and considered capturing and holding a black man as hostage until the others returned the boat. But that turned out to be moot, because the woodcutters were lying.[5]

After despatching the delivery team, Todd left Roper Landing on 21 April aboard the *Young Australian*, bound for Port Darwin. As they neared the woodcutters' abandoned campsite, four black men hailed them, indicating their wish to come aboard. Todd let them on and they rode with them, until the ship anchored for the night near the campsite. Here was Todd's opportunity to 'secure a blackfellow', if he had really wanted to, but he did not take it. Instead, he talked to them.

In the four months since the arrival of the workers at the landing, and the *Bengal* at the river mouth around the same time, communication between white and black along the Roper had improved rapidly. Todd told the Aboriginal men about the boat being cut adrift, and about the four men walking up the river. He described their response: 'They expressed the greatest concern, assuring me that they slept up the river [a] long way from the scene of action—though they had evidently seen the four white men and told us that they had gone up the river—the rope they said had probably been bitten by a "gunambow" or alligator.'[6]

In the morning, Todd inspected the woodcutters' campsite, accompanied by the black men and others from the ship. They found the cut painter rope by the water. The cut was clean. At the campsite itself there were footprints, indicating that Aboriginal people had visited the camp, but the flour and meat were untouched, as were the axes and swags.

As Todd inspected the evidence, the four Aboriginal men told him that the footprints were from another tribe from the coast and suggested that the white men shoot them. After they departed, members of the coastal group visited. First, two black men cautiously approached, and indicated that others would soon arrive. Todd described the visit:

> Accordingly in an hour or two, nine men came to us, the foremost three, who were fine strapping fellows, carrying a beautiful bunch of white feathers from the white crane which frequents the river. They approached with great confidence, and on my invitation came on board & remained till the evening. The chief—or *bungowah* as he called himself—was a fine well made man—intelligent & friendly but somewhat impudent and when thwarted exhibited violent temper—they all indignantly denied having cut the boat adrift and before I showed them the cut painter they said the rope must have been bitten by an alligator.[7]

Neither group was behaving as if they had stolen the boat or had any hostile intentions towards the woodcutting camp. Both groups were friendly and had willingly and trustingly come aboard the ship; both had discussed the issue with Todd and tried to help. At the campsite itself, nothing had been stolen, even though Aboriginal people had clearly inspected it after the woodcutters fled. And the painter rope appeared to have been cut with an axe.

Todd concluded that one of the woodcutters had cut the rope. The boat must have been tied insecurely and it had drifted off during the night. To divert blame, the woodcutter had cut the rope himself, to make it seem as if the boat had been stolen, then alerted the others, creating fear and panic, and causing them to abandon the camp.

Near the campsite was a small woodpile, which they loaded onto the *Young Australian*. It was not nearly enough to get them to Port Darwin.

Because of the lack of fuel, they had to keep stopping along the coastline, so parties could go ashore to cut more firewood. As a result, they met several coastal Aboriginal communities, which they would not have met if the steamer had started with a hold full of fuel.

The Aboriginal people asked for tobacco—which they called 'torn-bucho'—and alcohol. When Todd gave them rice instead, they knew what it was. These coastal people were familiar with trading vessels. For centuries, Malay traders had been coming in search of trepang and turtles, and trading with them. And indeed, the campfires of Trepang fishers were visible on the northern coast.[8]

The *Bengal* was steaming out to Java as the *Young Australian* approached Port Darwin on 8 May 1872. Both ships stopped so that the mailbag aboard the *Young Australian* could be transferred to the *Bengal*, which would deliver it to Java, from where it would go to Ceylon, and then to Adelaide. Todd scrawled a quick note to Alice and popped it into an envelope before the mailbag was taken to the *Bengal*. After landing in Port Darwin, he wrote a longer, more considered letter that was sent on another ship four days later.[9] Todd wrote to Alice that he was 'agreeably disappointed' in the place.[10] It was certainly beautiful, with a magnificent harbour, and the country was green and lush from the recently ended wet season. There were abundant crops, including sugar bananas, sweet potatoes, melons, and a variety of tropical fruits.[11]

Todd's nephew, Griffith, was mightily glad to see him. Todd had swung him a job as assistant telegraphist to John Little. Due to unforeseen events, what should have been a minor position to learn the ropes had become a major undertaking. Griffith had been running the telegraph station in Little's absence, and had recently travelled to the Katherine River and back to fix breaks in the line. The company sent a field instrument and one of their staff to accompany Griffith, a generous act, given that the repairing party were on short rations while away.[12]

Here, for the first time, Todd was in telegraphic communication with England. Morse code pulsed down the line at speeds approaching the speed of light, but there were more than a dozen stops along the way, the first being Banjoewangie, on the eastern tip of Java; the second being at the other end of the Java landline, where it was transmitted on the Java-to-Singapore underwater cable. At each of stations, Todd's messages were re-transmitted by telegraphists, so that every message took almost twenty-four hours to travel from Darwin to London, and every reply took the same in return. Compared to a mailbag aboard a steamship, it was miraculous. There are no records of him using the opportunity to contact his family, although he may have. Instead, there was a flurry of business with Francis Dutton, the colony's London agent, with general updates and orders for more iron poles.

The downside of the visit was Bloomfield Douglas's insistence that Todd stay at his residence. The view from the house was lovely, as it was built atop the cliff by the ocean. And there was love in the air: Douglas's daughter Nelly had been married a month earlier to

Mr Squier of the British Australian Telegraph Company and planned to soon move into the telegraph office.[13]

The problem was Douglas himself. His leadership of the fledgling colony was erratic. He was depressed and drinking heavily, his binges notorious. He was suspicious of everyone, and harboured a fear of Inspector Foelsche; he was sure Foelsche was planning to arrest him, despite the trooper's assurances that he was not.[14]

Shortly before Todd's arrival, a trade ship had diverted to Port Darwin because a mutiny was brewing among some of the crew. Douglas sentenced the two leading culprits to a week in detention, then hired them both as troopers. Pirates as police officers: what could possibly go wrong?

But worst of all, Douglas had the gold bug. He was corruptly using his position, and all the resources at his disposal, to prospect for gold and to corner the ownership of goldmines, should mining ever take off. He could not see the beauty around him, blinded by lust for what he imagined lay under it.

Far to the south, William Harvey's crew had completed the line to Attack Creek, finishing a complete line of poles between there and Adelaide. Wiring teams had installed most of the wire, with only a few unwired sections remaining, including one near Alice Springs and another near The Peake. Meanwhile, with fresh horses and provisions from the Roper, the northern crews were pressing southwards. At the current pace, the line would reach Daly Waters within five weeks.

The costs were piling up: £70 per day, every day. Before leaving Roper Landing, Todd took steps to accelerate the start of the estafette.

Stephen King had been criss-crossing the land with a small team, scouting ahead for the best route for the line, and noting waterholes and potential tracks for bullocks and wheeled vehicles. King was carrying written instructions from Todd that, once he reached Daly Waters, he was to start the estafette. With most of the exploration done and the route mapped, King was now helping with the deliveries from Roper Landing and was on his way south, with rations for the most remote crew, Robert Burton's, near Daly Waters. For a long time, nobody even knew exactly where Burton's men were camped. King had failed to find them on a previous excursion, but they had now been located.

Todd also wrote a message to Burton, to be delivered by a courier on horseback, notifying him that King was on his way.

Todd's letter to Burton said, in part:

> After delivering his loading, Mr King is to organise a horse express service for conveying telegrams between the ends of the wire establishing communication with Port Darwin and Adelaide, and it is of the utmost importance that this service should be established as quickly as possible. I wish you to render him every assistance in your power by detaching all the men and horses you can spare.[15]

From the Port Darwin telegraph office, Todd notified both Dutton and the Chief Secretary of South Australia that the estafette would start early.[16]

A parcel arrived for him from Alice, with an accompanying letter describing its contents, but some things she mentioned, such as recent issues of magazines he enjoyed, were missing. Even the Postmaster-General, then, was not immune from postal theft.[17] His family photographs were his evening comfort; each night he would plan his trip home, although the plan was always the same: he was going to ride from Port Darwin to Port Augusta, inspecting the entire line.[18]

But when he tried to acquire a good horse for his overland trek, Todd's plan came undone. No horses were available. Bloomfield Douglas explained that every single horse was needed at the port and not one could be spared. To ride home, Charles Todd would have to return to Roper Landing, so on 22 May, he stepped aboard the *Young Australian.*

48

Black and White

Roper River and inland, May–June 1872

There was paranoia in the campsites, as the news of John Milner's death travelled by word of mouth up and down the tracks. He was, they said, 'murdered by blacks'. That three-word summary was wrong: Milner was killed not by a group but by one man acting alone. That man happened to be an Aboriginal man, but the circumstances were more about jealousy and love than skin colour. But these subtleties were lost; Milner's death was seen as a salutary lesson about the danger of trusting Aboriginal men.

On Patterson's return journey to Roper Landing, while camped near a creek, several Aboriginal men walked into the camp, wanting to talk. They were unarmed, but several other men were seen hiding nearby in the creek, leading Patterson to believe they were up to trouble. Patterson wrote, 'They yabbered away for a quarter of an hour in the most unintelligible manner and the only thing we could make out was an earnest desire on their part to furnish us with quantities of the fairest and most beautiful of their tribe.'[1]

Patterson did not trust them, so he fired a rifle into the air, frightening them away. He arrived at Roper Landing three days later.

On the north bank, across the river from the landing, was an Aboriginal camp. One night in late May, several Aboriginal men swam quietly across the river. The dogs barked. White men scrambled about, firing revolvers into the night, hitting nobody. When morning came, clothes were missing.

Patterson sent a boat across to recover the clothes, putting a Northern Territory trooper named Davis in charge. As they approached, the Aboriginal men appeared, laughing and taunting them, but as soon as the boat's bow sliced into the muddy embankment, one gave signal and the others scattered into the scrub. That one man remained on the river bank. He threw down his spear and strode towards Davis, grinning.

Davis decided to arrest him, but was unable to communicate what this meant. He tried to lead the man to the boat, but the man would not comply. Davis wrestled him to the ground, then with the help of the others, tied his hands behind his back, put him in the boat and took him back to the landing.

During his time in Port Darwin, Patterson had been a guest of Bloomfield Douglas, where he no doubt heard about the taking of Aboriginal hostages and how successful this was in gaining custody of the true culprit, in return for their release. Patterson took a leaf out of Douglas's playbook, by holding this man—who was apparently a leader—hostage until the clothes were returned.

Other members of the tribe appeared on the far bank, calling out to the hostage in distress. Two brave young men swam across the river in a vain attempt to rescue him. One of them, who turned out to be the leader's son, was also captured.

Patterson ordered that the captives be chained to a tree. He tried to communicate the plan to them, that they would be released in exchange for the clothes, but they did not understand.

The young man called out to the women on the far bank. Some of them jumped in and swam over. Patterson concluded that the man was offering the women in exchange for his freedom. He may have completely misunderstood, but that conclusion forced him to admit defeat. It was hopeless. His 'hostage' strategy was an embarrassing failure.

Patterson released both men, who were then served a hearty dinner and given packages of biscuits to take back for their families.

Later that year, after returning to Port Darwin, Trooper Davis disobeyed the Government Resident's ban on swimming in the Port Darwin harbour. He swam out to what he believed was a log, but it was a crocodile. Hearing his screams, others nearby hurried to rescue him, but they were too late. He was dead, his neck broken by the crocodile's jaws.[2]

The very same day that Davis arrested the Aboriginal leader, another story of conflict emerged much further south.

A small group of explorers, led by the surveyor Stephen King, were camped at Frew's Ironstone Ponds, on their way south. Three men—two white men and a black guide—arrived at their camp, quite agitated. They were 'hawkers', or travelling merchants. One them, Chawner, had a badly injured hand. A week earlier, Chawner had slung his shotgun in a tree while camping. When he retrieved it, a branch caught the trigger, the gun discharged and buckshot hit his left hand. They had buried their merchandise for safekeeping, then hurried north, looking for a doctor.

On the way, they stopped at Newcastle Waters, where they hoped to give their horses a drink. A large group of Aboriginal men forbade them from using the waterhole, but also tried to prevent them leaving. It appeared they had been taken prisoner, for reasons mysterious to them. The three quickly mounted their horses and fled, leaving most of their equipment behind.

To King, Chawner seemed to be as distressed by the incident at Newcastle Waters as by his injury. Chawner swore that after his hand was healed, he would return to 'give the blacks fits'. The views of his black guide on the matter were unrecorded.[3]

The merchants continued north, seeking a doctor for Chawner's bandaged, bloody hand. The explorers went south, worrying about hostile Aboriginal groups, Chawner's tale fresh in their minds. They kept a fire burning all the next night, and took turns keeping watch, just in case. But there was nobody at Newcastle Waters, even though the mud was covered in human footprints.

King's party continued south, camped again, and entered the low, scrubby Ashburton Ranges, looking for a route suitable for bullock drays. They followed one promising route, but it entered a wide, uncrossable quagmire, so they doubled back and tried a different way. In a forest of thick lancewood, they were ambushed by several Aboriginal men armed with spears and boomerangs. One of the explorers, William Crowder, fired and believed he hit a man. The man dropped the spear he was about to throw and disappeared into the lancewood.

One Aboriginal man came within 30 feet of King, the explorers' leader, but another explorer fired before he came any closer. The Aboriginal men fled and could be heard calling out. Perhaps they were summoning help.

The explorers believed they had hit 'two or three'. They doubled back and crossed the range another way. They did not see those Aboriginal men, or any others, on the rest of their journey.

49

To the End of the Line

Roper Landing to Renner Springs, June–July 1872

Roper Landing had changed in two months. The rain had stopped, the river was low, the creeks had subsided to a trickle, swamps and bogs had transformed into lush valleys. Delivery teams were ready for the cargo that had been unloaded from the *Tararua*.

Patterson, back from supervising inland deliveries, was displeased with Todd. As he said in his diary, 'My affairs with Todd are not yet settled.' He was most aggrieved by Todd's instructions to Burton and King to start the estafette, partly because they countermanded his own instructions, and partly because he had not been consulted. If he had been consulted, he would have said not to do it, that the gap was too wide and the country too dangerous. He had therefore cancelled Todd's orders. In his written explanation, he said that obeying Todd's orders 'could not be carried out without involving certain failure to success of expedition'.[1]

To keep everything on the record, he handed Todd several official letters outlining various grievances, and a copy of his correspondence with Burton. In these letters, Patterson's indignation was in full flight.

> In forwarding this correspondence I cannot refrain from expressing my extreme surprise at the step you have thought fit to take. On your arrival at the Roper I only consented to remain in the Northern Territory in connection with this work on the express stipulation that I should retain the same position and powers with which I set out from Adelaide. . . .

> If I am to be subject to the interference now so unhappily commenced and my offers are to take instructions from you at a distance when I am personally on the work—a copy of the instructions, in this case, not even having been supplied to me—it will only remain for me to forward my resignation of the command of the expedition as commanding only in name and not by virtue of the responsibility the position should entail and the powers and control supposed to be involved therein, and I must be content to wait until my return to Adelaide for the seeking of redress as may be possible for me.

Todd was itching to start the estafette, but the last thing he wanted was drama. As usual, he was diplomatic and placating, conceding as much as possible, and probably more than he should have, to calm Patterson down.

He acknowledged that, if it was true, as Patterson claimed, that the express would have involved 'certain failure'—then *of course* he had done the right thing, at least until the two of them could consult about it.[2]

In fact, Patterson's cancelling of the estafette's start was quite hypocritical, because two weeks earlier, while at Daly Waters, he had sent several messages, including one to his wife, across the gap via a despatch rider.[3]

Todd left Roper Landing on horseback on 13 June, accompanied by Patterson and a journalist named Richard Wells, who had accompanied Todd to the Roper River and to Port Darwin and back.[4]

On the first night out, a messenger arrived at midnight to tell Todd that a merchant ship, the *Lucy*, had arrived with mail. He left the others and hurried back to the landing, only to find that the *Lucy* was down the river at Hawks Nest Island, so he went down by boat, purchased some of the *Lucy*'s cargo from its captain, and read the mail. The most important item was a letter from Alice. From the landing, he rode as quickly as possible, returning to the campsite by nightfall.[5]

They reached the line and rode south along it. Todd was disappointed that the poles were all spaced so far apart: only ten to the mile rather than twenty. Patterson reminded him that he had allowed that to be done wherever it was deemed necessary.

Away from the Roper, water was scarce. Creeks and billabongs that had teemed with life only weeks earlier were dry or reduced to small, muddy puddles. They reached Daly Waters, the end of the line from Port Darwin, in the late afternoon of 22 June. Here, a telegraph station had been set up and was operational. Messages could be sent to Port Darwin or, for that matter, around the world. Todd learned that the *Omeo* was chartered to collect the workers in October.[6]

Here, also, was Ray Boucaut, whom Todd had contracted to run the estafette, starting from the south. The estafette was ready to go: Boucaut had met a man named John Lewis, who had brought 25 horses inland hoping to sell them, so he had hired Lewis, his horses, and a few other men as courier riders. They were down at Tennant Creek, on the other side of the gap, waiting for the word to start. Boucaut himself had delivered a bag of mail from Adelaide, which included telegrams for Todd and Patterson.

Todd told him to commence the estafette.

For the next day and a half, Todd made full use of access to the telegraph line, messaging Port Darwin and London. Business telegrams arrived from London to addressees in Adelaide. These were bundled into Ray Boucaut's bags for delivery across the gap. The telegraph line was operational.

On the afternoon of Monday, 24 June, the same day that the estafette started, the line went dead. The Port Darwin office reported that the signals from Java had completely stopped. The underwater cable had broken.

The late fees had been accumulating at £70 per day since New Year's Day, now totalling £12,180. The tally stopped there. With a broken cable and with Todd's estafette running, the company could make no more financial demands.

Ray Boucaut delayed his departure by a day, just in case the signal restarted, but it did not. He departed with the mailbags at 2 am on Wednesday.

Todd, Patterson, and Wells were joined by Walter Rutt, healthier but still gaunt. Rutt was going to rejoin his crew, which was helping build the final stretch of line south of Daly Waters. The next Sunday, at Rutt's camp at Auld's Ponds, Todd 'read service' but it was attended only by Patterson, Wells, and Rutt. They continued south, through dense mulga and hedgewood.

'It will be very difficult clearing,' Patterson observed.[7]

Two days later, just after dawn, they met an estafette rider coming north. He had camped nearby with some bullock drivers who had plied him with brandy, and he was still drunk. He had fallen off his horse twice since he started that morning and, in Patterson's words, 'presented a very dilapidated appearance'. It was Dick Knuckey!

They arrived at a poling camp near Newcastle Waters and Todd told the men to set off firework rockets and light the blue distress lights to entertain the local Aboriginal people. It was believed that this region had the highest population density of Aboriginal people, so Todd intended to establish good relations.

The further south they went, the drier and flatter and hotter the land became, a featureless plain of red dirt dotted with mulga. The floods and mosquitoes of Roper Landing were almost a dream. As they neared Renner Springs, it was as if there had not been rain for a thousand years. Renner Springs was the current depot for Bob

Burton's lonely crew, which had been trapped and isolated for five months further north.

The meeting with Burton was unpleasant. Todd said that the poles his crew had planted were too far apart and would have to be infilled. Burton objected that he had only been following Patterson's instructions, but Todd was adamant: whatever the reason, the problem needed to be remedied. Then, once finished, they had to walk to Roper Landing, where the *Omeo* would take them home.

Todd gave a speech to the assembled men at camp, praising their bravery as they suffered the manifold trials of the wet season. Two of his travelling companions laughed during the speech. After the others had gone, Todd asked them what they had found so funny. They informed him that his audience had not been Burton's crew, but were the delivery teams from Roper Landing, most of whom had arrived with Todd aboard the *Omeo*. Burton's crew, the ones who had been trapped for so long, were camped further down the river.

Patterson was overjoyed. That night, he wrote with glee in his diary: 'Burton's real wet season party were miles away, we have passed them without seeing them. Todd has never seen them at any time, and now he never will.'

Patterson also penned a letter to be delivered to Burton's camp, apologising to the workers there for the extra work they would have to do, explaining that it was because Mr Todd had changed his mind.

It is therefore not a surprise that Todd was not much liked in Burton's camp. The mood was sour when they learned about the extra poling and they did not believe that a ship would pick them up from the Roper River; this was believed to be a ruse to keep them on the line during the next wet season.[8]

When Todd announced his intention to continue south to Adelaide, someone warned him about the long stretches without water. Indicating his travelling companion Richard Wells, he replied, 'That can't affect me, as I am carrying Wells with me!'[9]

Todd and Patterson were getting on each other's nerves. Patterson recorded, 'Mr Todd is getting awfully wearisome and I am looking forward with unaffected delight to seeing the last of him.'[10]

Patterson was not alone in his resentment of Todd. One worker wrote, 'Mr Todd's orders . . . are spoiling the whole affair, and I bet the government will wish they had never sent him to the country.'[11]

Another took pleasure, some days later, in news of Todd's discomfort: 'Express came down today from the Tomkinson. They bring very good news. Mr Todd is at Tennant Creek and short of tea.'[12]

50

Across the Gap

Renner's Springs to Tennant Creek, July 1872

Todd, Patterson, and Wells had a new travelling companion: Dick Knuckey, whose brief career as an estafette rider was at an end. He asked to join Todd on his overland trek to Adelaide.

Patterson was a miserable bore, carping about how poor quality the line was, how it would not last, that white ants would destroy it, that the wire would never survive the wet season: that the whole undertaking was a failure.[1]

The poles were unwired beyond Renner Springs. Most were small and crooked, their path zigzagging back and forth across the hard ground. Todd commented, 'ninety per cent of the poles are miserable things, but I believe sound. Line crosses broken rangy country, many angles to keep a fair road through the gaps'.[2]

Then there were no poles at all. This was the gap, shrinking daily.

They came to the beginning of the southern section of wire near Attack Creek on 18 July, where a temporary telegraph station was operating. While Todd busied himself corresponding with Adelaide, Patterson went to bed early complaining of a headache and nausea. He wanted to return north, but they did not have enough rations for such a journey.

The line to Adelaide dropped out, apparently due to a fault near The Peake. The party rested at Attack Creek awhile, waiting for restoration of the line. It was good country. Water was abundant and wild animals thrived. They realised why the local Aboriginal people would want to keep it to themselves. Wells later wrote, '. . . it is not improbable . . . that they feel aggrieved at being disturbed in the occupation of their favourite places of resort.'[3]

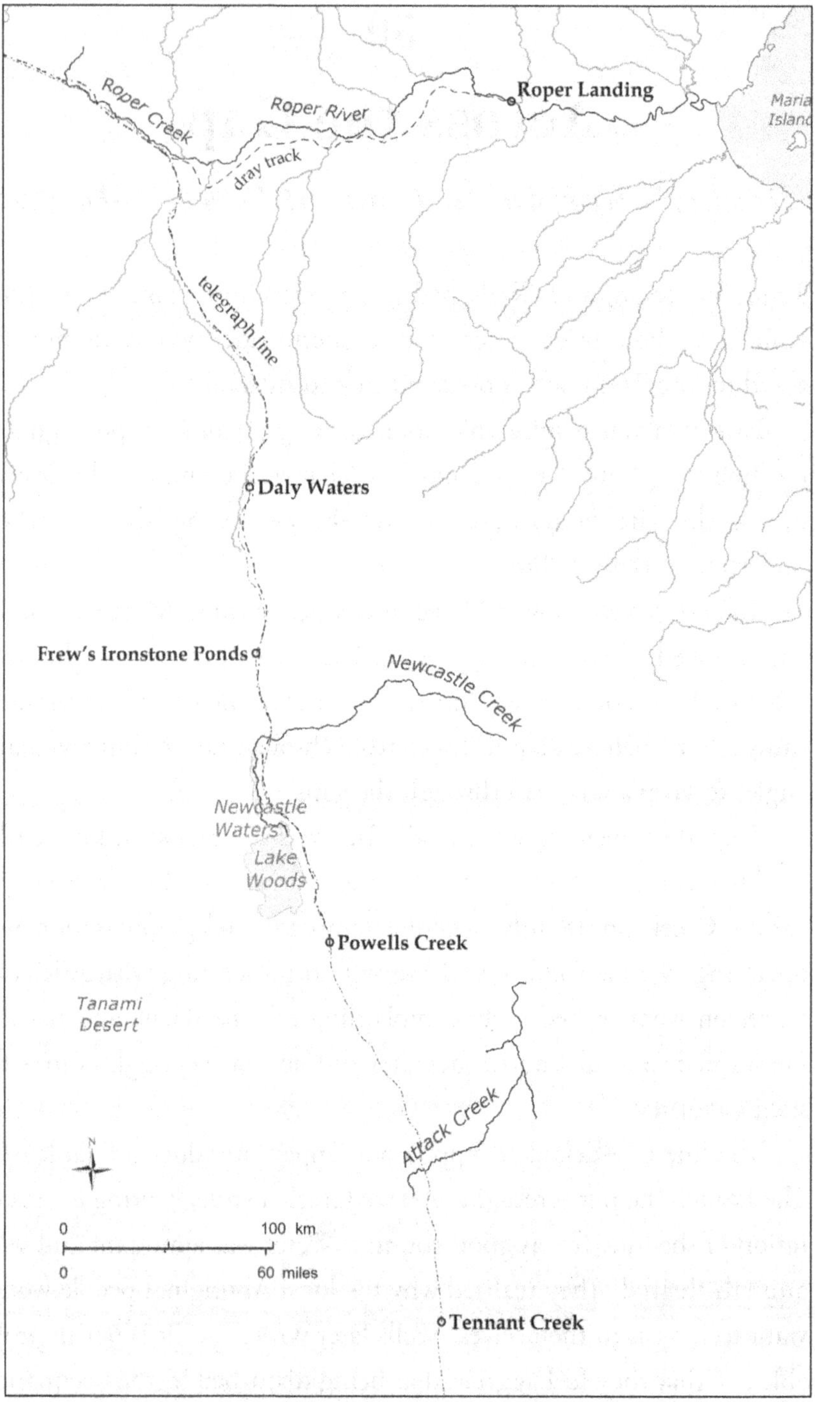

The Route taken by Todd and Patterson from Roper Landing to Tennant Creek

Patterson's health was deteriorating. At Tennant Creek, he loaded up with spare rations and returned north across the gap on 30 July, taking Augustus Caesar the cook and another with him. Concerned that he was planning to head directly back to Roper Landing, Todd reminded him of the need to finish the line and insisted that if he was leaving, he must arrange for someone to supervise in his place.

When Patterson rested that afternoon by the Phillips River, he hung a hammock between two trees, carving the name 'Elsie' into one of them. He then proudly made a sketch of the tree, commenting in his diary, 'The only instance I know of in the Northern Territory where the name feminine is to be seen carved on a tree.'[4]

Near the South Tomkinson River, Patterson passed bullock teams and poling teams engaged in finishing the final sections of the line. His health was getting worse.

While making camp at North Tomkinson River, he was struck by fever and a burning headache. Although it was still daylight, he crawled under some blankets and 'grovelled' there (as he put it) until morning.

Todd, Knuckey, and Wells continued south to Barrow Creek, where the small staff assembled to meet them, and someone made a speech of gratitude and praise for Todd. The line to Adelaide was working intermittently, allowing Todd to catch up with business back home. Thanks to the estafette, he was also able to liaise with Little and others in Port Darwin.

Bloomfield Douglas messaged Todd that he had heard rumours that the Roper Landing storekeeper, Fred Davis, was selling grog on the sly. Douglas was planning to visit Roper Landing aboard the next available ship to investigate the matter.

Todd knew Davis well and trusted him. Furthermore, what Douglas didn't realise was that the system of selling the grog was better than giving it away, because it gave the storekeeper more control—it meant that drunkenness could be kept in check. Todd sent a private message to Davis across the estafette, warning him that Douglas was coming and that if he was selling spirits, he should stop. He then replied to Douglas—also via the estafette—that he had warned Davis to stop. He also notified Patterson. On this issue, at least, Todd and Patterson were in agreement.

They were also partly in agreement on Todd's plan to order iron poles to supplement the wooden poles. Patterson believed these Oppenheimer poles were the only hope of saving the line from collapse. Todd didn't agree, but many of the original wooden poles were substandard would need to be replaced eventually. With all the working crews on the line, now was the most cost-effective time to do it. Todd had written to Oppenheimer earlier in the year about getting more poles, and at Barrow Creek he received Oppenheimer's confirmation.

Problems and tasks of all kinds vied for his attention. Water sources around the Daly River were dry. Estafette riders quit, demanding payment. The line south of Port Darwin was working at night time, but not in the daytime; Little was investigating. Cunningham wanted to know when the join would occur. Camels, horses, packages, letters, stores to be dispensed with, ships to charter and send, purchases made, purchases requested. He was busy, busy, busy.

In an estafette mail run, a message from a line manager arrived for Todd, with an urgent question:

> C. Todd, Esq.:
> Who do you recognise as second in command in this expedition
> I ask this as Mr Patterson has been and is still ill with fever.
> Please say.
> A.J. Mitchell.[5]

The obvious answer to the question 'who is second-in-command?' would have been Walter Rutt, but Rutt was in poor health too. It was a good question: who was actually running things up there? But the end was in sight; the project was nearly over; it just needed to stay on track for a little longer, then Patterson's health would no longer be an issue.

That same mailbag contained several messages from Patterson, probably having banked up, waiting for the estafette service. Patterson was, apparently, on his way to Rutt's camp, further north. Excerpts from them include:

> I am fearful of not being able to make camp before paroxism comes on in which I am helpless for eighteen hours and nagging ague. Have you anything more for me before I start.
>
> I am much enfeebled and reduced by fever, which is getting more weakening upon me. The intermittent paroxysm is due at 2 this afternoon and I must be in camp before then. Have you any questions to ask me before I start. If I do not get better soon I shall be quite helpless I want to make sure of getting on to Rutt at least hope to be there on Tuesday or before.
>
> I finished Dr Renner's medicine a week ago and I could not wait for him since which time I have been gradually getting worse. If I can get to Rutts camp all right I can be carried down to Roper if I do not get better.[6]

Aside from his failing health, Patterson also sent an update on the wiring: 'The last joint will be made Thursday, possibly on Wednesday but I can't promise it.'[7]

Five days to go! Todd notified John Little, urging him that he must get those problems on the Port Darwin to Katherine line fixed by next Thursday. He notified Cunningham and the next day, he notified the Premier, Ayers. He wanted to know, should there be a formal opening ceremony? If so, he would like to do that from Alice Springs, which he would be able to reach by Sunday.

Ayers replied, 'The government do not think it necessary to have any formal opening.'

There were two reasons not to. First, Governor Fergusson had gone to Melbourne for two weeks; and second, the cable to Java was still out, so it might seem anticlimactic. The word from the company was that the cable would be repaired any day, so it made sense to wait for that.

A senior bureaucrat, Josiah Boothby, made contact, saying, 'I am delighted to hear of immense progress made. Do you now regret going?'

Todd replied, 'Many thanks . . . I will arrange if possible for Adelaide and Port Darwin electrically to shake hands at noon on Thursday but I can tell you better tomorrow.'

The next day, he, Knuckey, and Wells resumed their journey. They acquired a buggy in Barrow Creek, allowing them to travel in relative comfort, giving their bodies a break from the saddle.

51
The Join
Central Australia, August 1872

At midday on 22 August 1872, on a plain south of Frew's Ironstone Ponds, two wiring teams linked the wires from the north and south. An hour later, a message arrived in Adelaide from the Port Darwin office, confirming that the line was complete. The message also stated that the cable from Port Darwin was still out of action.[1]

Right away, Cunningham hoisted the Red Ensign, the British naval flag, atop the post office tower. Word spread like fire. Consulates flew their own flags. Reporters arrived, scribbled notes, then hurried to their presses. A public holiday was declared. Offices closed.

The Chief Secretary arrived at the telegraph and post office, where he was informed that the line to Port Darwin was dead.

Patterson had cut the wire.[2]

Patterson was camped at Frew's Ironstone Ponds that morning, still sick. He knew the line would be joined that day south of there. He wanted to make the final join himself, but was too sick to ride there. Instead, he dragged himself out of bed and rode a short way east, to a length of the line already complete, accompanied by Howley the telegraphist and a handful of others.

At midday, tapped into the line with a pocket relay, Howley announced that the join had been made. Patterson dictated a message for Howley to send to Adelaide, informing them that the line would be completed at 3 pm. He then ordered some wiring technicians to cut the wire. Their tension released, the cables whipped and coiled into the air, then landed in the dirt. Hooks were fastened to each loose end. Then they all sat under the shade of a bush, waiting for the appointed time.[3]

It was almost three o'clock when Howley, still tapped in, received a message from Adelaide, from the Chief Secretary himself! The message was an order to connect the wire without delay.

Three o'clock came. Patterson picked up one end of the wire and dragged it towards the other, but the wires were heavy and still under some tension. He could not lift them to pull them together. The others helped. Half pulled on one wire, half on the other, with Patterson between them, grasping each hook as it came within reach. He pushed the wires into contact. An electric current ran through his body! He cried out in pain, dropping the wires. The others laughed.[4]

They tried a second time, with Patterson insulating his hands with a handkerchief. This worked. The wires were joined and the line was complete . . . again.

As a substitute for a 21-gun salute, the crew fired 21 shots from their revolvers into the air. Patterson broke a bottle of brandy on a pole, although some suspected the bottle contained cold tea.

Howley, listening in, heard a message from Port Darwin to Adelaide. It was from Dr J.S. Millner, the 'acting' Government Resident for the Northern Territory. No telegraph message explained his assuming this role, but Millner was acting in the role because Bloomfield Douglas gone to Roper Landing. 'In the absence of the Government Resident, I have the honour to congratulate Her Majesty's Government on the completion and opening of the Overland Telegraph Line. May it prove the harbinger of prosperity to the whole colony. God save the Queen.'[5]

Millner's message lacked the flair of the first American transmission—'What hath God wrought?'—but it ticked all the boxes. The Chief Secretary sent a similarly bland but happy reply.

In Port Darwin, a party commenced in the crowded little telegraph office, where they raised glasses in a toast. Squier, the company representative, said he regretted the breaking of the cable but promised them that he was 'in hourly expectation of the current being restored'. Captain Halpin had returned in the *Investigator*, which was equipped with deep-sea grapples.[6]

Next came a message of thanks from the Chief Secretary to all who contributed. 'In the name of the Government of South Australia, I beg to thank you all for the untiring exertions and energy displayed in prosecuting the important work this day satisfactorily concluded.'

Howley intercepted the message for the small gathering near Frew's Ironstone Ponds. It is clear from his diary that Patterson believed that the Chief Secretary's message was to him personally, but no publicly recorded telegram from that day mentions Patterson by name. He did not know Morse code, so he was reliant on the telegraphist, Howley, to take all the messages for him. Maybe Howley was afraid that Patterson would be insufferable if he was denied his moment in the limelight, and told him what he wanted to hear.

With the deed done, Patterson rode back to camp and climbed into bed, suffering fever.

It is unclear exactly when Patterson had the wire cut. Before going to sleep, he wrote in his diary, 'Howley arrived about nine this morning with the information that the wiring parties would meet about noon thus leaving only the place where the wire is cut abreast of Frew's Ponds, and where I arranged to make the last joint.'[7]

Confusingly, he wrote 'the wire is cut' (present tense) even though he had personally rejoined it that afternoon. He was tired and sick, so his vagueness is understandable. But the timing matters.

Historians have taken that diary entry to mean that Patterson cut the line a day earlier. Therefore, by re-joining it, he was the one who connected Australia to the world. But was he?

A line worker named William Crowder wrote in *his* diary the next day:

> The wire was joined yesterday at 12 o'clock on plain by ours and Rutt's wiring parties and communication through. But as Mr Patterson who was at Rutt's camp wanted to be at the joining of this great line he had it cut down there and another joint made but ours and Rutt's wirers were the real joiners.[8]

In Adelaide, the *Evening Journal* reported:

> At 1 o' clock today the Government received a message direct from Port Darwin, intimating that the last length of wire had been stretched, and that uninterrupted communication across the Continent had been established.[9]

The official messages were sent after three, but the editor and the line worker claimed the line was working soon after midday, maybe with some test messages bouncing back and forth.

It was not until 1908, thirty-six years later, that Patterson's claim to fame emerged, when a journalist interviewed the delivery rider Bedford Hack, who saw him make the join. But it was too late for him to bask in the glory, because he had died two years earlier.[10]

Patterson's little ceremony at Frew's Ironstone Ponds went unreported. Nobody knew about it.

That same morning, Todd made a late start from a campsite south of Barrow Creek, following a small river south. There were patches of frost and the day was cool. Grassy expanses gave way to spinifex, with its glassy, cutting spikes. Emus roamed. The poles were made of sturdy timber which would last some time. Here, as in many other places, Todd found that white ants had attempted to climb the line but their tracks were abandoned.[11]

He arrived at Tea Tree Well, near the eastern foot of Central Mount Stuart, around 4 pm. Todd tapped into the line and learned that it was finished, and that messages were flying back and forth between Adelaide and Port Darwin.

As soon as it was known that Todd was on the line, the Chief Secretary contacted him:

> We opened the line at 1 p.m. this day as it was completed, and the public, from my previous notifications, fully expected it today. I took that opportunity of sending a message in the name of the Government of this country, thanking the officers and men of the construction party for the praiseworthy efforts and untiring diligence they have displayed in bringing to a successful conclusion this great work under your able superintendence. Accept my congratulations that your troubles are now over.[12]

A flood of messages came, congratulating him and wishing him well, from the Mayor of Adelaide, the Secretary of the Chamber of Commerce, Adelaide's various foreign consuls; Cunningham, his trusty second-in-command; Dr Millner; and others. He replied to as many as possible.

He stayed awake, hunched over the pocket relay, until midnight, until the cold night air had given him a headache and he was too tired for any more messages. He wrote in his diary, 'This is indeed a happy day for me.'[13]

Then he slept.

52

The Long Ride Home

August–October 1872

Todd, Wells, and Knuckey arrived in their buggy at Alice Springs on 1 September.[1] There was a telegraph and post office, built of stone, by the Todd River, next to the 'Alice Spring'. The river was flowing, had been since Mills had found the place a year and a half earlier, but Todd doubted it was permanent. The telegraph staff were pleased with the place. There was water, grassy fields, and, they said, abundant ducks.

The stone walls had gun loops for shooting rifles from inside, as a defence against possible attacks by Aboriginal people, but those loops were never used. The nearby Aboriginal communities were peaceful and mostly stayed clear of the telegraph station.

The cable to Java was still broken. The *Investigator* had determined that the break was somewhere near Sandalwood Island.[2] But the steamer's grappling gear hit snags and was lost, forcing it to go to Java for repairs and to refuel with coal.[3] Replacement grappling gear was sent to Java from England.[4]

Todd arranged for Alice to attend the Adelaide post office, so that he could talk to her; Charles sat with a Morse key under his finger, tapping messages to Alice, but Alice did not know Morse code. Down in Adelaide, she sat beside a telegraphist who translated the incoming dots and dashes. There was no privacy. They could not say all the things they wanted to say.[5]

He left Alice Springs on 6 September, following the line at the bottom of the ridge, 'like a large wall', along a grassy flat and through Temple Bar Gap. From there, it was a long ride across the mulga plains, across the Hugh River then Finke River, both of which had running streams, to Charlotte Waters, a two-week journey.[6]

Todd's route from Tennant Creek to Adelaide, following the telegraph line

Two groups of travellers passed them going the other way, hoping to find gold up north. When they made camp in the evenings, some Aboriginal men helped them gather firewood in exchange for food.[7]

Dick Knuckey had built Charlotte Waters station before riding north. For him, arriving there was like coming home. There, for the first time, Todd and his party saw white people and black people living together, the local tribe having taken up residence in the surrounds of the telegraph station. Wells later published an article about his travels, in which he said, 'if the blacks continue to be encouraged and employed by the white people at Charlotte Waters, it will not be a bad plan for the government to send up a supply of blankets to that place. It is often very cold and the natives have scarcely a rag to cover them.'

An exploring expedition had passed through only days before, led by Ernest Giles (not related to the three Giles brothers employed in the construction of the line).

There was a large bundle of mail waiting for Charles, including six letters from Alice, which she had sent over several weeks. Four of the letters had been sent before his conversation with her from Alice Springs.[8]

In one, she wrote, 'I have not heard from you for more than a month. 5 weeks tomorrow and it seems such a long time . . .'

In another: 'I have the map of the Overland Telegraph from the Office nicely mounted hanging up between the Hall door & the Dining room door that I may constantly watch where you are my own dear one.'

And: 'Sometimes when I think of your return I feel so happy and elated I dare not think too much of it.'

And in another: 'Oh how I have longed for you lately . . .'

And: 'Good night dear one. I wish you could have as comfortable a bed as we all have.'

And: 'Won't I spoil you when you come home.'

Besides her longing, her letters overflowed with news, gossip, and stories about the children. At campsites after long day of riding, he read them over and over.

They conversed by telegraph again while he was at Charlotte Waters, but again, it was awkward with so many ears listening.[9]

Two weeks later, he arrived at The Peake. There were two more letters from Alice waiting there, the second one written as he was leaving Alice Springs.[10] 'I am afraid I shall get rather excited as the day for your return approaches.'

Alice told him that the youngest child, Gwenny, was now vaccinated against smallpox. This was a relief to her, as there had been an outbreak in Melbourne. She wrote, 'If small pox comes here it would be dreadful indeed as there is so much destitution.'[11]

For most of the journey, there had been no point in him writing to her, because he would reach her before any letter. But there was a mail service from Mount Margaret, so on their arrival there, he posted her a letter:

> . . . although it was very pleasant to be able to have a telegraphic chat with you, I could not by telegraph say all I could wish, nor express myself so affectionately as my heart prompted me. I was a long time without letters from you . . .
>
> Your letters, so loving as they are, make me long for home and I shall not loiter on the road—there will be much to say on both sides, and as I shall see you so soon it is not necessary for me to give you a recital of my adventures . . .
>
> I don't feel so strong as I could wish—but I look very healthy and well, and believe a little relaxation this next summer will do me good. I should so like to take you and dear Lizzie to Melbourne and Tasmania and hope the Government or Parliament will be sufficiently generous to justify our taking this

> trip together. I would like to go to England, but must not think of that just yet.
>
> . . . and now dearest Alice I must say good bye—with fondest love to all, especially to my own dear wife.[12]

In Beltana, he learned that the Port Darwin-to-Java cable had been repaired on 20 October. The evening after transmissions resumed, the Adelaide sky was lit by fireworks. No details about the cause of the break were made public but now that it was fixed, nobody cared.

At last, Australia was telegraphically linked to the world.[13]

53

Goodbye to the Roper

Roper River to Brisbane, September–October 1872

An emigration took place in central and north of the Northern Territory, as workers drifted, mostly on foot, to Roper Landing. There, the *Young Australian* ferried them down to Maria Island, where they camped and waited for the *Omeo.*

Bloomfield Douglas was at Roper Landing, having arrived aboard the *Larrakeeyah.* Patterson, whose health had improved on his journey from Frew's Ponds, found Douglas in a sorry state. He wrote in his diary, 'I saw poor old Douglas lying down on a locker half intoxicated and looking like a wreck of his former self—he shook hands and kissed me on the cheek and entreated me to take care of him . . . I was profoundly touched to see him in so sad a plight.'[1]

Douglas did not have his spectacles and so could not read his letters, so Patterson read them out to him. One of them brought the news that his youngest son, who had been ill, was now healthy and running about. Douglas burst into tears and sobbed for so long that Patterson had to stop reading. He wrote later, 'Poor Douglas! I am afraid he is irretrievably gone.'[2]

Douglas slept all the next day at Roper Landing in Patterson's hammock, and ate only soup, which Patterson fed him with a spoon.[3]

The workers made rough camp on Maria Island, where they had time to kill waiting for the ship, so they explored the island and raced each other naked on the beach. The fun ended when Patterson arrived.

He reprimanded them for relaxing instead of cutting firewood for the *Omeo*, and docked them all a week's pay. He told the assembled men—fully clothed for the occasion—that if they did not resume work by Monday (this being Saturday), they would all be fired. Then he climbed into the boat and was taken back to the *Young Australian*, moored nearby, where he slept in relative comfort.[4]

Bloomfield Douglas came down from Roper Landing in the *Larrakeeyah*, which anchored near the island. If anything, he had deteriorated further. Patterson wrote 'He is looking very much broken and was in a state of muddledom all the evening. He has not left the *Larrakeeyah* today & is suffering I imagine from delirium tremens'.[5]

The *Omeo* anchored at Maria Island. The first business was to load the firewood the men had cut and to transport cargo for Roper Landing to the *Young Australian*, anchored nearby. With those tasks complete, the *Omeo* sailed east at dawn on 11 October. Already aboard were passengers from Port Darwin, who had heard about a new gold rush, but were quickly disappointed and were returning home.

It was just as well that the Government Resident did not return Patterson's visit, because there was a huge amount of alcohol stored aboard the *Omeo*, being sold at the midship bar. Patterson, partial to a drop or two himself, complained, 'The drunken men made the night hideous last night with their blasphemy and horrid oaths—I did not get to bed till midnight and I was up at five this morning.'[6]

Rutt, who abhorred alcohol, was appalled, ashamed of his workers. But he was mistaken, because few 'overlanders' were partaking; most of them were trying to sleep too. The trouble was mainly caused by some passengers from Port Darwin. Sidney Herbert wrote, 'I had no rest during the night, because of disturbances due to alcoholic effects of those who thought they were having a good time.' A cyclone temporarily dampened the revelry, but the till was ringing again when the clouds cleared.[7]

As the *Omeo* glided up the Brisbane River, the men washed and cleaned and put on their finest clothes for a day and night's leave. They strolled through gardens by the river's edge, hired horse-drawn cabs, splurged at fruit shops and visited pubs. Many were back on deck by sunset, but others—stir-crazy after a year in the wilderness and three weeks at sea—partied on. Several got so drunk they were put in the police lock-up overnight.[8]

Patterson called in on Cracknell, privately denigrating the overland telegraph line to him and predicting that it would fall apart in the next wet season. Patterson's relentless pessimism was his curse. He could not bring himself to praise Todd or Todd's project, instead portraying it as a failure.

In a surprising act of goodwill (considering the rivalry) the City of Brisbane hosted a dinner for 'all officers and men', but Patterson had withheld that information from all but the most important, senior officers. The *Omeo* left in the morning, the hammocks and bunks below nursing a great many sore heads. Patterson travelled separately, paying his own way back to Adelaide on commercial passenger ships.[9]

A week after Patterson's departure, Brisbane's *Telegraph* paper published a blistering attack on the overland telegraph:

> From information obtained from Mr Patterson, we learned that the makeshift line at present in use is so badly 'built' that there is no possibility of relying upon it for any length of period. For a very considerable portion of the distance, the track life through a country which is excessively liable to floods in the rainy seasons . . . and the posts on which the wires are hung are anything but substantial. In many cases, they are hollow, and the white ants will have a splendid opportunity for making their way to the top, and eating away the wooden insulators which have been used for a considerable distance along the route. Although the fact is not officially admitted, it is well known in Adelaide that the line, as erected, is only temporary . . . An estimate has,

> we believe, been made of the probable cost of constructing a substantial line . . . at £600,000.[10]

The Queenslanders' solution was, of course, to run a new submarine cable to Normanton, connecting to Queensland's telegraph network.

Part VII
Connection

54
Homecoming Hero
Adelaide, October 1872

Tired and sore, Todd and Knuckey left their horses in Burra, where they caught a train to Adelaide.

The timing of Todd's arrival was supposed to be a secret, but word had leaked out. When the train stopped at Riverton, they stepped onto the platform to find a crowd waiting for them. The station was adorned with festive flags and the crowd applauded as Todd emerged from the carriage. Someone delivered a prepared speech to him on behalf of the town, lavishing praise on Todd, who managed a few appreciative words in response, then returned to his carriage.[1]

A larger crowd was waiting for them at Adelaide station, cheering as they emerged. Hands were outstretched for shaking, including those of the Premier Henry Ayers, Cunningham, and several old friends. Ayers said some very kind words, then announced there would be a public holiday to celebrate the completion of the line. Alice was not there. Overcome with excitement and nerves, she could not face the crowds, so she waited for Todd at the observatory.

When the news of Todd's arrival reached the harbour, ships hoisted flags and bunting. He was taken by carriage to the new post office, which he had been planning for years. When he'd boarded the *Omeo* in January, it had still been under construction. The gathered staff applauded as he entered. The new telegraph room, which he had never seen, was bedecked with flowers.[2]

He met privately with Cunningham, then, at last, went home to Alice and the children.

Two nights later, Todd hosted a function at the post office for all postal and telegraph staff. His main motivation was to publicly thank

Cunningham, and to highlight his role in running the Post Office and Telegraph departments while Todd was away. The staff had even chipped in to buy Cunningham two silver plates. Champagne was served, followed by speeches.[3]

The night after that, Todd hosted a dinner for all the managers and senior staff on the line. More speeches.

As Ayers had promised, a public holiday was declared for 15 November, with a banquet for all officers and men held at Town Hall that evening. There were simultaneous banquets held in Melbourne and Sydney, and one in London on the same day. There were many speeches. Across the street from the Town Hall, a fireworks display was launched from the Post Office balcony.[4]

Two weeks after the banquet, a reunion dinner was held at Town Hall for all the workers on the line. Todd and Cunningham had installed telegraph machines in Town Hall, so that congratulatory messages could be received and read out during the dinner. Speeches, speeches, and yet more speeches.

On that occasion, the Governor announced to the diners that Todd had been conferred an auspicious title by Queen Victoria herself. He was now Companion of the Order of St Michael and St George (usually abbreviated to CMG), a prestigious British award for foreign service and diplomacy. Some said that it was not enough—that Todd should be given a knighthood.

No bonus had ever been promised to him, because he had needed no encouragement. He was, after all, the political driving force behind the telegraph project. Yet there were public calls to pay him one. Ayers decided to pay a bonus, not just to Todd, but to anyone who contributed, depending on their seniority: £1000 for Todd; £500 for Patterson; half that again for senior managers; and so on down the line, with much smaller amounts going to everyone else, some labourers receiving only £15 to £20.[5]

55

Patterson's Curse

Adelaide, December 1872–August 1874

The Brisbane article that denigrated the line, quoting Patterson as its source, theoretically could have arrived in Adelaide by telegraph the day it came out, but it didn't. Telegrams were costly, so editors exchanged only the most important stories. Instead, the article arrived the old-fashioned way: by ship, in a bundle of newspapers.

Rumours were circulating that the line was dodgy. Charles Todd hosed down claims that it was badly built, that it would be washed away in the wet season, that white ants were destroying the poles. In a report to the Premier, he wrote, 'How, and by whom, such reports originated, I am at a loss to conceive.'

A few days later, a letter arrived from a member of the public, F. Basedow of Tanunda, with a copy of the Brisbane *Telegraph* article enclosed. The letter said, 'A perusal of the *Telegraph* . . . a copy of which I hereby forward, will give you a clue as to the origin of those rumours.'[1]

So Patterson was the source. Todd was not surprised. He had no option but to notify Premier Ayers.

Ayers summoned Todd to give a response. That was easy, because the article was riddled with factual errors. For example, Todd pointed out that the claimed costs were much higher than reality. Ayers made no comment either way, but announced he would hold a formal enquiry into the allegations in the *Telegraph* article.[2]

Todd issued a challenge to Ayers: 'Personally, I court every enquiry; and should any doubt be entertained on any point in connection with the work, or its control, for which I can be held individually responsible, I am quite willing to place my resignation in the hands of the government.'[3]

Critics claimed vindication. They pointed out that the line had failed earlier that year near Charlotte Waters. Todd replied that that the Charlotte Waters break was caused by lightning strikes on the iron poles, shattering the insulators. This problem would not recur because he had commenced the reinstallation of lightning conductors on the poles.[4]

A delegation of senior managers, including Dick Knuckey, Bob Burton, Whitfield Mills, and others, visited Todd to demand that he refute the slanderous allegations going around. Todd said he had already done so, in a report to government. Reporters were in attendance, so Todd threw it back on the managers. He asked them to refute the allegations on the spot, which they did.[5]

Knuckey, Todd's friend who had ridden with him down the line, said:

> I have seen perhaps more of the line than anyone else in the room. I have ridden the whole distance, with the exception of a portion in the Northern Territory, two or three times, and I can say that the line is better constructed than many lines in the settled districts. The northern country was difficult to travel through, but the line was constructed along the very best places, and there is no place in which a man might not travel at any time.

Todd admitted that he was not confident in the northern part of the line, much of which he had not personally seen. He asked for Burton's opinion, to which Burton replied, 'a more honest piece of work was never done'.

William McMinn admitted that the white ants were a problem, but for the wooden insulating pins, not the poles themselves. The ants would create tracks all the way up the poles to eat the pins. This was a far smaller problem than that implied by Patterson.

On that, Todd expressed doubt that Patterson had said the things he was reported to have said. Patterson had written to him, denying that he had 'authorised' the statements and Todd chose to believe him.

But Ayers did not believe Patterson. When the bonuses were paid to Todd and everyone else involved a week later, Patterson's payment—and *only* his payment—was withheld, until such time that 'enquiries have been made and satisfactory explanations given'.

Ayers chaired a closed-door enquiry the following year. Patterson denied making the most inflammatory comments either to the Brisbane *Telegraph* or to the politician Charles Mann, who had produced confidential, leaked information along similar lines. He pleaded that his only sin was to be too candid, too trusting, and too free with his sincerely held opinions.

Ayers pushed him for more. Did he say the things quoted in the Brisbane article? No, Patterson replied, he did not. He assured Ayers, 'when the *Register* reprinted the Queensland article, I at once wrote to the *Register* denying most positively that the Queensland Editor had obtained any of the information from me.'[6]

He apologised for any damage caused, but held that his views had been exaggerated and misunderstood. His abject, grovelling apology and denial were filed away, not made public. Patterson got his bonus.

After that, he should have let bygones be bygones, but Patterson was cursed with loathing and animosity that could not be quelled. In June the following year, he wrote to Blyth, then Ayers's chief secretary, lambasting the telegraph as a failure and disaster. In the letter, he claimed he had been right all along about 'the destructive effects of dry rot, and the ravages of the white ants on the wooden posts and pins'. He claimed that Todd 'had not the generosity to say a word in my defence'. He claimed it was his idea, not Todd's, to take steamships up the Roper River. He claimed that 'credit has been given where credit was not due, and that the same has been withheld from those rightly entitled to it'. Meaning himself.[7]

In his letter to Blyth, he even blamed Todd for having his bonus withheld, and for sullying his name generally. Furthermore, he noted that his dire predictions of cost blowouts had turned out to be true.

Patterson was ready to take on Todd, but he was not prepared for James Boucaut. After learning of Patterson's letter, Boucaut demanded in parliament that all official files on the topic be made public. Patterson complained that it was supposed to be private correspondence, but Boucaut was not interested. The papers, including Patterson's apology, were tabled on 4 August.[8]

All the private letters and memos between Patterson, Todd, and the government were declassified, open to the public's gaze. They cast Patterson in an even worse light. Todd, however, came out looking like an angel. It now transpired that, behind closed doors, Todd had defended Patterson all along.

Boucaut was fascinated by Patterson's never-before-seen written apology of the year before, the confidential memo that had gotten him his bonus. In that secret memo, Boucaut found that Patterson denied spreading rumours, and denied having spoken to the editor of the Brisbane paper. Yet now, a year later, he was taking credit for having said those same things!

Todd was compelled to reply. He said:

> His principal complaint is that I did not support him . . . if he means that I did not endorse his views as to the unreliability of the line, he is right. I never sympathised with his gloomy predictions; nor did I feel it my duty, publicly and wherever I went, to enlarge on the destructive effects of the white ants, and the

supposed insuperable difficulties in effecting repairs in the event of a break down during the wet season.

On cost blowouts, Todd pointed out that Patterson's claims were, once more, exaggerated. They simply were inaccurate. It was true that he had spent more money on iron poles, partly due to Patterson's urging, not because the line was failing, but because, with all those work teams in place throughout the centre, it was the most cost-effective time to do it.[9]

One paper commented, 'The attack on Mr Todd is in the worst possible taste.' It then said: 'Mr Patterson with his own pen has written his own condemnation.'[10]

Patterson, though publicly humiliated, at least retained his job, unlike his mate in the north, Government Resident Bloomfield Douglas. Rumours had reached Adelaide of the mismanagement of the Port Darwin settlement and of Douglas's decline. Douglas was spending large sums of money without explanation. Early in 1873, Douglas, highly intoxicated, was found on the roof of the residency with a firearm, threatening to shoot the police. He was coaxed down, then taken aboard the *Gulnare* to dry out.[11]

Ayers sent the Commissioner for Crown Lands, Thomas Reynolds, to investigate.

The inspector's report was scathing. Spending was extravagant and accounting non-existent. The streets were filled with rubbish and stank. The only permanent buildings in the whole place were the governor's residence, the police station, and the telegraph station. Behind Douglas's residence, Reynolds found an Aboriginal man kept prisoner, chained by his ankle.

Now, to be scrupulously fair, this last point was not quite as bad as it sounds. The Aboriginal man was known as 'Scotchman', an outcast from Larrakeeyah society who had murdered several Larrakeeyah people, was probably responsible for the death of at least two white men, had speared a horse, and tried to assassinate Government Resident Douglas himself. Douglas had tried him for the attempt on his own life, and—perhaps mercifully—had sentenced him to 'hard labour' as a servant at the residence. Douglas's children shuddered when they heard chains rattling around outside their bedrooms at night. Scotchman was hated by the Larrakeeyah and, four years later, when he tried to kill another of them, Larrakeeyah men speared him to death.

Be that as it may, having an Aboriginal man in chains at the back of your house is not a good look. That, combined with all the other problems, spelled the death of Douglas's career as Government Resident. His days as the Rajah of Port Darwin were over.

Douglas put his family on a ship to Adelaide, while he founded a mining company and then went inland to strike it rich. The company was a bust, and he returned to Adelaide, disgraced, jobless, and broke.[12]

56

The Fate of the Black Prince

Central Australia, 1872–74

When the line was complete and most of the others returned home, Andrew Hume stayed behind, working at the Powell Creek and Tennant Creek telegraph stations until October 1873. He was seen as a good worker and a skilled stockman.[1]

Opinions on Hume were mixed. Some thought he was a fraud, while others believed his stories and thought he was brave and clever. He wrote occasionally to east coast newspapers, providing reports of his adventures that had a tenuous link to reality.[2]

At Newcastle Waters, he ventured west, supposedly looking for Classon. Alfred Giles recalled cynically.

> He started and was away a week, turning up at Tennant's Creek with a plausible story of having been far to the west, where, the savages told him, Classon was still further west, but that there was a waterless desert across, which he could not face at the time of the year, and so on. He stated also that he had met some wonderful new savage tribes, who were wearing strings of pearls, precious stones, and shells around their necks and arms, but no clothes, and that they had idols carved out of trees with rubies and precious stones and profusion, and that they worshipped these, and so on, *ad nauseam*. It was most clearly proved that Hume had never been out of sight of the telegraph line, as between Powells Creek and Tennant's Creek he had kept a mile or so only west of the line and camped at different waters off it. He was an uneducated man; indeed, I do not think he could read or write.[3]

For months, nothing was heard of Hume on the east coast. Then, out of the blue, he arrived on 4 Feb 1874 at the Brisbane wharves aboard a ship from Port Darwin. He announced that he had found Classon, who was 'too decrepit' to return, but that Classon knew where to find the remains of Ludwig Leichhardt, and would be able to show the place to him when he next returned. He also announced that he had retrieved the saddlebag containing Leichhardt's quadrant and watch, and 75 pages of documents. The doubters were denounced. Hume's claims had been vindicated 'beyond all reasonable doubt'.[4]

Hume was asked if he had seen any sign of the Warburton expedition—an attempt led by Major Warburton to cross from Alice Springs to the west coast. He had indeed, he replied. He had met them when they were in Alice Springs, but then some months later, saw some of their camels near the telegraph line, indicating that the Warburton expedition had perished.

Todd was approached for comment. He said, 'Hume was *never* at Alice Springs, and I am certain he did not see Major Warburton's party at Alice Springs. Warburton had in the first instance less camels than the number Hume gives, and we know of several having returned.'[5]

Hume met Reverend Hassal, a respected Brisbane clergyman. He opened the bag to show Hassal the documents, but, as he needed to deliver them to Sydney, explained that he could not allow a thorough examination. When he arrived in Sydney two weeks later, his bag had been cut open and the contents were gone. Hume cried that someone had robbed him on the ship to Sydney. A likely story.[6]

Powerful people had egg on their face, but they still wanted to believe. Wealthy supporters sponsored Hume to lead an expedition west—overland this time—to find and retrieve Classon, find Leichhardt's remains and retrieve additional documents that Hume had reportedly left behind at the fabled tree.

Hume left Newcastle in July 1874, travelling north-west, with a serious, experienced team. But on Queensland's western plains, all but one of his companions quit and returned home. The one who stayed with him, a man named Thompson, appeared unexpectedly at a farmhouse in north-west Queensland in October, to report that the other two (they had recruited an additional person along the way) were dying of thirst. A search was made, and Hume and his last companion were both found dead.[7]

57
A Link to the West

Soon after the overland was completed, the Chief Telegraphist in Western Australia, James Fleming, approached Todd about building a line to connect Adelaide with Perth. There was already a line from Adelaide to Port Augusta, and in Western Australia, a line had been built to Albany on King George's Sound, where the mail steamers stopped on their way to the eastern colonies. All that remained, then, was to run a line between Albany and Port Augusta, via the border town of Eucla, a distance of about 1400 miles.

The Scottish-born James Fleming was convicted of defrauding tea-merchants in Glasgow in 1864, and was sentenced to seven years' transportation in Western Australia. He earned a ticket-of-leave only a year later, after which his wife and son emigrated to Perth to join him. He became headmaster of a boys' school, then worked as a journalist, then, thanks to technical skills learned in Scotland, became the colony's Chief Telegraphist in 1873.[1]

A deal was reached. Todd was responsible for getting the line to Eucla; Fleming would take it from there. Todd put out a call for tenders, but got no response. Much of the proposed route had not been surveyed and was too remote, going as it did through the long, lonely desert known as the Nullarbor Plain.

To make the contract more tempting, Todd divided the route into two sections then called for separate tenders on each. He found a contractor for the section from Port Augusta to Fowler's Bay, which was the easier part of the route, through settled country.

The second section, across the Nullarbor, again found no takers. Todd fell back on his friend and former travelling companion, Dick Knuckey, to manage the project on behalf of the government.

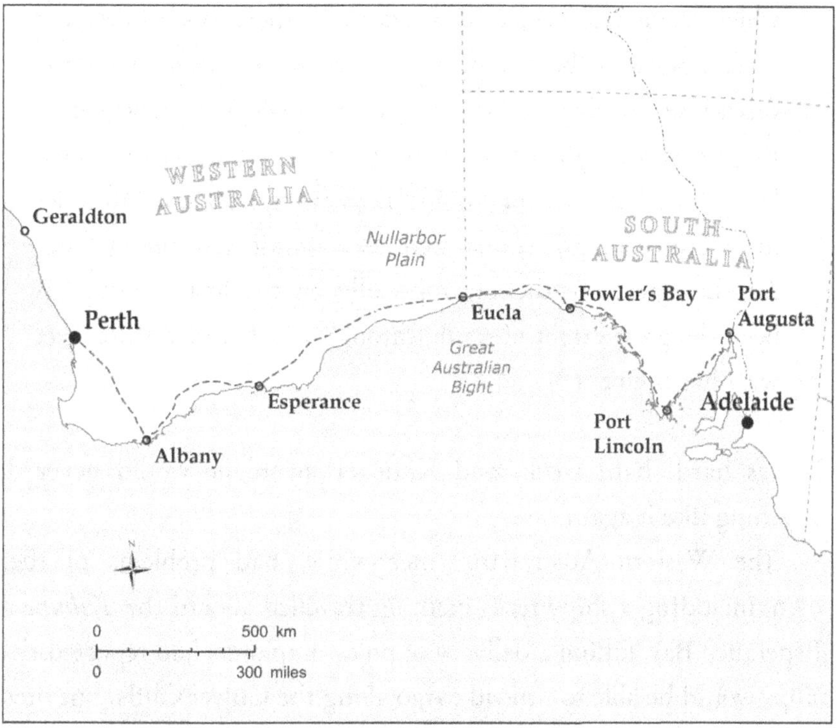

The telegraph line between Perth and Adelaide, completed in 1877

The logistical challenges were as daunting as ever. The Nullarbor Plain is utterly treeless. Timber poles could not be harvested along the way, so Todd ordered iron poles. And because the Nullarbor has no surface water, the poles could not be taken by bullock teams. The only way to transport them there was by ship, but even that was tough. The coastline adjacent to the Nullarbor consists of jagged cliffs, where the Southern Ocean thrashes the rocks. They were able to take shiploads of poles, supplies, and tanks of water to Fowler's Bay, the colony's furthest settlement almost 400 miles to the west, beyond which lay the desert.

The temperatures soared. Water was always at the forefront of Knuckey's mind.

The *Sydney Morning Herald* reported:

> The chief difficulty with which he has had to contend has been the want of water. Until the rains in the early part of the year,

> which facilitated operations wonderfully, there was scarcely any surface water to be found. The whole of the materials for the further section had to be carted from Fowler's Bay and before Eucla was reached, the constructors had to pass over two absolutely waterless tracts of country respectively 130 and 150 miles in length, which of course were also almost destitute of food. Another great obstruction, especially on the first section, has been the great extent of scrub, through which a road thirty feet wide has been cut.[2]

It was hard, hard work, and Knuckey swore he would never do anything like it again.

The Western Australians, meanwhile, had problems of their own, including a shipwreck. Fleming travelled aboard the *Tribune* to Esperance Bay, taking a delivery of poles. Explorers had reported that ships would be able to unload cargo along the Culver Cliffs, but those reports turned out to be wrong. Fleming's party explored rocky beaches and inlets by boat without success. That night, a wild sea smashed the anchored ship onto the rocks, then threw it onto a sandy beach. Fleming made an overland journey by foot of one hundred miles to Esperance Bay, where he procured a horse and returned to Perth.[3]

The line from Port Augusta to the border was completed on 16 July 1877, and the Western Australian part of the line finished in August.[4]

Due to the quirks of colonial politics, the east–west line had a peculiar arrangement at the border. The Western Australian Government insisted on retaining control of its own telegraph system, keeping it separate from the other colonies. Consequently, the station house at Eucla was actually partitioned into two stations. One was the terminus of South Australia's network, while the other was the terminus of Western Australia's network, and the staff on either side of the partition were mirror images of each other. On the South Australian side, Todd's telegraphists received and transcribed messages coming down the line from the east. They then poked those messages through holes in the wall, where someone in the Western Australian partition would collect them, read them and tap them out on the far side, sending them on their way west. And likewise, messages coming from the west would arrive through the holes, ready for transmission to the east.

This arrangement notwithstanding, the line was an instant success, carrying more than ten thousand messages in its first year.[5]

The absurd demarcation ended with Federation in 1901, when the partition was removed and the staff from both colonies combined into a single, smaller staff.

The Eucla station closed in 1927. Nothing remains of it but some half-buried brickwork in the shifting desert sands.

58
Barrow Creek
Barrow Creek, 1874

In December 1873, James Stapleton stopped at Barrow Creek while travelling down the line to Adelaide, making the same journey that Charles Todd had made the previous year. Johnston, the station's telegraphist, was sick, so Stapleton sent him south for treatment, offering to fill in until he returned or was replaced.

Barrow Creek Station, like other stations, was made of stone, with firearm loopholes in the walls. There was a courtyard surrounded on three sides by the building and double gates on the fourth. Stapleton sent a request to Charles Todd, asking for permission to give the local Aboriginal people, the Kaititja, flour and mutton from time to time. Todd approved.

On the afternoon of 23 February 1874, Kaititja men asked for flour, but were refused. Through the station's Aboriginal interpreter, Jemmy, Stapleton explained that he would only give flour to Kaititja who were sick or infirm, or who worked for the station. Late that afternoon, Stapleton and the other staff were smoking and chatting outside the station, in the building's shade to the east. Four young Kaititja men approached, demanding flour. Stapleton again refused, unless they worked. Three left, but one of them, a Kaititja youth named Umpassanna, stayed back, offering to work as a line repairer. Stapleton and the others talked to him about what duties he could perform.[1]

Just after sunset, without warning, a volley of spears rained upon them. Everyone started to rush to the eastern door, but were blocked by several Kaititja men. They turned and ran all the way around the building with the attackers pursuing them, to the courtyard gate, rushed through another volley and then through the door. Jemmy was speared in the thigh and was saved only by the others dragging him through a window. Others were injured. John Franks, a line repairer, was wounded. He staggered into the kitchen, then fell to the floor and died.

Stapleton remained outside longer to close and barricade the gates, which he succeeded in doing, but was hit by four spears. Once inside, three rifle shots were fired through the loopholes at nearby Kaititja men, who fled. Two more shots were fired at men in the distance.

An urgent message was sent south. When Stapleton was told that his wife had arrived at the Adelaide post office, he asked to be lifted to the desk so he could send a message to her himself. With his finger on the Morse key, he simply tapped, 'God bless you and the children.' He died the next day.[2]

With Jemmy's help, Trooper Samuel Gason, one of those wounded in the attack, compiled a list of assailants' names and descriptions. Arrest warrants were issued for all on the list. The Police Commissioner placed Trooper Gason in charge of the police response, and decided to bolster police presence at Barrow Creek. He was informed that there were no other police within hundreds of miles and that the four police in the Northern Territory goldfields could not be spared. Gason instead proposed a contingent from Adelaide, but was informed that they would take two months to get there by horseback.

The Commissioner asked Todd to send telegraph workers to Barrow Creek, where they would be sworn in as temporary 'special constables'. Todd sent a call to telegraphists at nearby stations to go at once to Barrow Creek, to report to Trooper Gason, where they would be 'assisting in the apprehension of the natives implicated in the attack'.[3]

Armed Kaititja men surrounded the station again the next morning, but two rifle shots were fired through the loopholes, 'probably' killing 'one or two' (according to Gason). The Kaititja men fled.

It was concluded at the time that the attack was provoked by the refusal to give the Aboriginal people food. Todd's understanding was that the attackers wanted 'flour and mutton' at the station. Water was another possibility. The region had been going through a long stretch without rain and many waterholes were dry. The site of the Barrow Creek station was chosen precisely because of its proximity to one of the best waterholes for miles around, and the Kaititja people believed that the white people had taken possession of an asset that was once theirs. Other explanations have been that the telegraph station was built on a sacred site, that telegraph workers had abducted Kaititja women, or that the Kaititja were retaliating after white men had dispersed their campsites. Or maybe their patience was simply exhausted and they just wanted the white men to leave their land. But these are all hypotheses. Their true reasons are unknown.

There was outrage in Adelaide. The *Evening Journal* wanted vengeance:

> To kill unoffending aboriginals in cold blood is an atrocious crime; to execute judgment upon assassins and the aiders and abettors of assassins is a duty that cannot be safely evaded. We hope that no false humanitarian notions will restrain the whites at Barrow's Creek in dealing with the belligerent savages by whom they are surrounded.[4]

Under the pseudonym 'Old Salt', a Port Adelaide resident wrote to the *Register*, proposing that the roof of every telegraph station should be fitted with a swivel howitzer or brass cannon, and that trees cleared to give a line of sight for a mile in every direction. Another offered to go up and sort things out, 'no questions asked'.

Others opposed these calls for violence. A correspondent mocked 'Old Salt's' proposal by suggesting that, in addition to cannons, a garrison of 50 men be sent to each station, and that they should march around the perimeter dressed in clerical garments to scare the Aboriginal men away. A lawyer named J.H. Gordon called for mercy, given the difficulties of both identifying suspects and proving their guilt, and arguing that reprisal was against the principles of British justice: 'No revenge. Anything like retaliation, indeed anything like severe punishment will seem to me to be cruel and unjust.'

The Governor believed that there must surely have been some kind of provocation. Todd privately expressed the same concern soon after the attack, although later publicly said that the motive, as far as he knew, was to gain access to the station's food. At any rate, arrest warrants had been issued, so all that could be done was to let the law take its course.

Yet no arrests were made. Over the following weeks and months, the general feeling in Adelaide was that the government's response was anaemic and timid. Then, in July, documents came to light that revealed that Trooper Gason had been very active indeed.

Gason had been at Barrow Creek that fateful night, and, though he survived, was one of the victims. He had ducked for cover as spears flew through the air; he had seen Franks and Stapleton die in front of him. He was therefore the wrong person to be in charge, but being the only officer of the law for hundreds of miles, he was the only one available.

The response was slow to start. Telegraph workers arrived on horseback, but because of the heat and lack of water, their horses were badly knocked up and needed rest. A team of line workers arrived on 27 February, reporting that they had had a 'brush' with a group of Aboriginal people about twenty miles away. Gason led a sortie there on 3 March, where they were themselves attacked. Gason reported to the Police Commissioner: 'On galloping up to where the natives were seen a large body of natives rushed out. They were evidently lying in ambush, all fully armed with spears.' There was a brief, bloody exchange, in which shots were fired and 'several' Kaititja killed before the others disappeared into the scrub.

On the next sortie they found a campsite, but its occupants scattered into the scrub as they approached. Gason persevered. After weeks of frustration, he decided that a suspect fleeing on foot was resisting arrest and he was therefore justified in shooting them.

On 13 April, Gason reported the results of a sortie to the Commissioner by telegraph. He said that his party had found an Aboriginal camp, which they attempted to disperse. When these people fled into the scrub, Gason and his men chased them, in order to arrest them. When three Aboriginal men fought back, they were shot dead.[5]

The Commissioner enquired whether any of the three dead Aboriginal men were named in the warrant. Gason replied that they were not, but they had been seen near Barrow Creek the day before the attack. The Commissioner asked why, if they did not participate in the attack and were not named in the warrant, Gason had tried to arrest them. Gason replied, 'They were with the attacking party.'

Gason had changed his story in private correspondence with the Commissioner, but he was not held to account. To protect himself against accusations of inaction, the Commissioner actually praised Gason for 'overawing' the Aboriginal people, such that they were unlikely to attack again.

The private diary entry of Robert Patterson two years earlier possibly reflected not just his own attitude, but the attitude of men like Samuel Gason: 'I much fear we shall have to shoot a score or so of them before we can establish a funk of the white man in the native mind.'

How many Kaititja men did Gason kill? By his own account, he and others killed 'some' during the evening attack, 'probably one or two' during the dawn attack, 'several' in early March, and three in April. Based on those four reports, one historian confidently claimed that Gason had killed eleven Kaititja men. Perhaps. But Gason spent months riding around the country with a loaded rifle, angry and upset, nursing wounds of the body and mind, hunting Kaititja men. The evidentiary trail is sparse and vague, but it is widely believed that the true number killed was much higher than eleven.[6] Barrow Creek caused a shift in attitudes regarding white control of Central Australia. In Adelaide, the view was widely held that kindness had been mistaken for weakness and that the policy of conciliation had failed. A more punitive era began.[7]

59

The Open Heart

The Adelaide to Port Darwin Telegraph Line, 1872 onwards

As he visited each station down the line, Todd had assigned the telegraphists a dual role as weather reporters. Todd had always been fascinated by weather, and meteorology was one of his first loves, when, as a boy, he had collected the daily rain gauge data at the British Observatory. That was why, when building the earlier line from Adelaide to Melbourne, he had ensured that telegraph stations doubled as weather stations. The more stations, the better and more useful the data. He was, among other things, a pioneer of meteorology in Australia.

Charles Todd collaborated with researchers across the country and around the world on weather patterns. He investigated connections between weather in Australia and in distant places such as India. This work on global climate connectivity was, a century later, acknowledged as an early contribution to weather science that led to later discoveries such as the El Niño effect.[1]

As soon as the line was operational, daily weather reports appeared in the major papers, describing conditions along the line. For the very first time, people in Adelaide could learn that on the previous day in Alice Springs, there had been a fresh southerly wind and a cloudy, stormy night, while in Port Darwin, it had been fine with a light easterly wind. Overnight, the continent's inland was demystified.

But the line was about more than just the weather. Australian farmers no longer needed to guess about the worth of produce in faraway markets. The days of gambling everything on a ship to London were over. Instead, markets could be monitored, fair prices sought, and deals made, all from Adelaide—or, for that matter, from any telegraph office in Australia. Trade boomed.

People with families and friends in Britain, or in any other country linked by telegraph, could learn of important news such as births, deaths, and marriages, arrange visits, send well wishes, and pay old debts. The news of the world was no longer stale by the time it reached the Australian shore, but as up-to-date as anywhere else.

The line's impacts, financial and social, were felt across the Australian colonies.[2]

The discovery of gold in the Northern Territory spurred the formation of gold companies in Adelaide, which then, by telegraph, sought finance from London. As the historian Geoffrey Blainey commented, 'The overland telegraph had opened the goldfields, and now was the magic instrument that raised the capital.'[3]

One observer, shocked at the hasty, slapdash arrangements, said, 'In the whole history of mining in the colonies, never before were claims floated by telegraph, without even a plan.'[4]

The Northern Territory goldrush eventually burned out. There was gold all right, and if the seams had been closer to major population centres, they might have paid handsomely. But the Northern Territory was too remote and the cost of extraction too high.[5]

The more the telegraph network was used, the more it expanded, and the more it expanded, the more it was used. In 1876, the British Australian Telegraph Company laid a cable from Sydney to Nelson, New Zealand, joining New Zealand to the network. Naturally, since all telegrams passed through Port Darwin, the New Zealand newcomer, like the other colonies, paid South Australia for the privilege of using its line.

Demand was insatiable, so in 1880, the British Australian Telegraph Company duplicated its cables between Port Darwin and Java, and between Java and Singapore.[6]

Todd was still on the track, riding down the line on his return to Adelaide, when he began pushing the government to use the telegraph stations as launching points for exploration. He believed that Alice Springs was the ideal place to start from. Expeditions were already being planned and by the end of 1872 two expeditions had begun.

Major Peter Warburton's expedition included (among others) two Afghan camel drivers, Sahleh and Halleem, and many camels, to explore the inland west of the line, and to search for a route from Alice Springs to Perth. When they arrived at the west coast town of Roeburne (now Karratha), nearly a thousand miles north of Perth, they were almost dead. Warburton was in such poor shape that the others had strapped him to a camel.[7]

Ernest Giles led another expedition, quickly abandoned, after a falling-out with others in his party. But he tried again, and eventually performed significant explorations of the inland.

But perhaps the most notable inland expedition of that time was made by William Gosse, who, in 1873, was the first white man to discover a gigantic, spectacular rock south-west of the MacDonnell Ranges. He named it Ayers Rock, after the premier, Henry Ayers, but it is now better known by its traditional name, Uluru.

Settlers followed the overland line looking for land to graze or hoping to strike it lucky with gold or tin, or just looking for work. The telegraph stations became the birthplaces of inland towns. Some of those places prospered, while others, like desert flowers, briefly bloomed then withered in the red dust.

The Afghan camel drivers played an iconic role, delivering mail along the line, until the railway line completed in 1929 put them out of business. That railway line from Adelaide to Darwin was named the 'Ghan' in their honour.

The telegraphists at Charlotte Waters, where the stony gibber plain receded to a shimmering horizon, nicknamed the place Bleak House. It was described by one visitor as the most desolate place she had ever seen. A telegraphist named Frank Gillen took an interest in the languages of the Aboriginal people, and spent years collecting notes on them. Those notes eventually found their way into the hands of Melbourne anthropologist Baldwin Spencer and became an indispensable record of Indigenous culture. The little settlement was born from the needs of technology, and when it was no longer needed, disappeared. The Ghan was later rerouted further west; and telegraphic innovations in the mid-twentieth century meant the repeater stations were no longer needed. Charlotte Waters, today, does not exist.[8]

But Alice Springs, in its picturesque valley in the MacDonnell Ranges further north, grew and prospered from the start. A township was gazetted there with the name of 'Stuart', after the explorer, but 'Stuart' did not stick; the name Whitfield Mills had given the place, after Charles Todd's wife, did stick, and was eventually made official.

She never went there. She was, after all, not much one for travel.

60

Charles and Alice

Adelaide

In 1875, after several years of declining health, Alice's mother, Charlotte Bell, died at their home at the observatory. Her funeral was held in Adelaide, but her will was executed in Cambridge by Alice's older brother, William, who had taken complete control of the family's assets and business. The Todds were shocked to receive a letter from William, stating that they owed money to Mrs Bell's estate.

William, apparently, was charging Alice for staying in the family home when she visited several years earlier, and was also deducting the expenses of Charlotte living in her own home, before she emigrated to Australia. Charles refused to pay the most egregious demands, but in a compromise, offered William a modest amount to quash the issue.[1]

That same year, the components for the post office clock arrived from England. In his instructions to the English bell maker, Todd had specified that when the bells chimed every quarter hour, they should sound exactly like the chimes of Great St Mary's, the university church in Cambridge, where Alice grew up. The post office's huge pendulums hung through several storeys of the tower. He then installed gas-powered lights to illuminate the clock face at night. From that day forth, every quarter hour, Alice could hear the sound of her childhood.[2]

Charles made that trip to England that he had talked about in 1885, but Alice did not go with him. Her decision to stay was understandable: her parents were gone; her beloved sister Sarah was gone; she was estranged from her brother William; and all her children were in Adelaide. Instead, their daughter, Lizzie, 30 years old and single, accompanied him.

In Cambridge, he caught up with his younger brother, Henry, who worked at the observatory there. Before leaving England, he had given Henry a job there and had personally trained him. When Charles arrived at the station, neither of them recognised each other, until Henry tentatively approached Charles, whom he expected to look much older.[3]

In Greenwich, Todd's old boss, George Airy, recently retired, greeted him like a long-lost son, and insisted on giving him a tour of changes to the observatory since he had gone.

England had changed in thirty years. When he and Alice left for Adelaide, rail was in it is infancy. Now, trains rattled through the tunnels of the London Underground, which had opened in 1863 and had been expanding since.

At the Inventions Exhibition in Kensington, he was entranced by a display of fifty thousand electric lights throughout the grounds, and a fountain that was illuminated by arc lights. He said later, 'It was a striking spectacle just as twilight was fading to see all the brilliant lights burst into illumination.'[4]

He was feted in London. Between business negotiations over the price of telegrams and letters, he had a busy schedule of private dinners and events held by institutions of science and learning. Cambridge University awarded him a Master of Arts degree, although he had never been a student at that—or any other—university. With the help of colleagues, he applied for the thing that he desired above all: a Fellowship of the Royal Society. His claim to membership included his meteorological work, his calculation of Australian longitude, astronomical observations that he had reported in English journals, and, of course, the overland telegraph. The process was slow, and he was not made a Fellow of the Royal Society until 1889, by which time he had long since returned to Adelaide.[5]

In an address to the Royal Colonial Institute, he told of the development of the telegraph in Australia. He reminded his audience that the telegraph and the steam engine 'have practically annihilated space and time'. He told them, 'By means of the telegraph, you in London can now communicate with distant Australia and New Zealand in less time than forty or fifty years ago you could communicate with Liverpool and Manchester . . .'

Telegraph, he said, was a great equaliser, globally and economically:

> We in Australia now know the result of the Derby, a boat-race or a cricket-match in the old country as soon almost as you know it yourselves. Our merchants can feel the pulse of your markets, and the other markets of the world, avail themselves of their fluctuations, and supply their requirements as readily as though they lived on the spot. Trade has thus been rendered safer, wild speculation has been checked by the rapid equalisation of prices . . . whilst the same conditions and facilities have placed men of small means in a better position to compete with their richer brethren.

He was generous in his praise for others, naming Samuel McGowan as the person who first brought telegraphy there, and James MacGeorge as the builder of South Australia's first line. He even said of MacGeorge: 'His enterprise, which obtained much sympathy and praise, deserved greater success than it met with.' He gave an unvarnished account of the problems, mentioning Patterson several times in a complimentary way. And he told of his ride home along the line.

When he finished speaking, one audience member commented, 'I listened to it as if I were hearing a romance of the Middle Ages, with this advantage—that I knew the story to be true, and saw the hero of the story before me.'[6]

Lizzie returned to Adelaide with him the following year, but not to stay, because in Cambridge, she had become engaged to lawyer Charles Squires. She packed her bags and said her goodbyes. Charles, in a letter to Oppenheimer, wrote, 'Lizzie prepares to leave. I will never see her again. This is awful.'[7]

In 1892, the Todds' daughter Maude visited England. While Maude was away, Alice wrote her three long letters. There were probably telegrams, too, although no record exists of them, and they would have been brief and businesslike. Because telegraphy was expensive, people reserved it for important matters, particularly over long distances. Most correspondence was still in the form of written letters, delivered by coach, train, and steamship.

Like many parents with an adult child travelling abroad, Alice and Charles worried about Maude running out of money, sending her more, just in case: 'Of course dear you must have some nice new dresses to wear when you pay your visits and a hat too and course you will need money to spend on travelling. The dear father would be vexed if you were to short yourself; he is going to send more money this mail.'[8]

Alice's letters reveal a happy and busy home life at the observatory. There were tennis parties, concerts, marriages, naughty children, and visits from friends.

She reported that their daughter Gwen and Gwen's husband, William, had been helping Charles sort his extensive library, separating books into work and non-work categories. They had a telephone, too: Alice interrupted one of her own letters to report, as if in real time, 'Fancy at half past four the Father telephoned to say he would bring Mr Shole a delightful man who dined with us on Friday to our family dinner again.' Then later, as if providing another instant update, 'Dinner was nice.'[9]

The following year, in 1893, Todd finally received the knighthood that was widely believed due to him. Thereafter, Charles was 'Sir Charles Todd' and Alice was 'Lady Alice'.

Alice died on 9 August 1898, at the age of 62, from complications after minor surgery. Various officials asked to attend the funeral, but Todd insisted that it be a small, private gathering, in keeping with her wishes and with her character. A photographic portrait taken of Todd two years later shows him looking sad and haggard, staring into space.[10]

After Federation in 1901, all the colonies' post office and telegraph departments were amalgamated. South Australia, it was discovered, was the only colony whose postal service ran a profit. The Federal takeover was not immediate, so Todd remained in charge, the benevolent dictator of the South Australia post.

He returned to astronomy, his first love. He published a pamphlet in 1903, titled *The Earth's Place in the Universe: Are There More Worlds Than One?* It was a response to a recent article by Alfred Russell Wallace, proposing that Earth was the only habitable planet in the universe, a position now known as the Rare Earth hypothesis. Todd paraphrased Wallace: 'the Creator has done so much for man that surely he must take a special interest in this world, whose position in the Universe he regards as special and unique'. Todd was no atheist, but he was unimpressed with Wallace's logic.

> I would ask are we justified in regarding our Earth . . . as the only habitable globe? May not alpha Centauri, a sun so much larger than ours, give light and heat to attendant planets equally favourably constituted for the development of intelligent organic life? We are not in a position to say yes, but we should be very rash and presumptive to say no . . .
>
> The subject is all engrossing and overwhelms our minds with awe, wonder and delight.[11]

Todd continued to work until 1905, retiring at the age of 79. In retirement, he enjoyed trips to Semaphore to watch the ships coming and going. On a walk by the water in 1910, he was struck by leg pain from a clot and died a day later.

The flag on the Adelaide post office tower was lowered to half-mast.

61
The End of the Line

The telegraph became such a vital part of Australian life that line interruptions were intolerable. Floods, fires, fallen poles, broken batteries, and wild storms could all knock out the line. On one occasion, Australia lost connection to the world because of a huge wasp's nest on the side of a pole. These breaks briefly plunged the colonies into the silent isolation of the past, but Todd's repair teams would typically fix them in a day or two.[1]

Outages in the Darwin-to-Java cable were less frequent but more serious, because a repair ship might spend weeks trawling the Timor Sea, searching for the break. To improve reliability and increase capacity, a duplicate cable was laid in 1879.

Other cables followed. New Zealand was connected to Sydney; Noumea to Brisbane; Java to Broome. In 1902, two important connections were made: a cable crossed the Indian Ocean from South Africa to Western Australia, landing in Fremantle after island-hopping via Mauritius and the Cocos (Keeling) Islands. And that same year, Brisbane was linked to Canada with a series of cables across the Pacific. Both of these Australia–London connections passed exclusively through British-controlled territories.

The telegraph was the lifeblood of commerce, the source of news, a conduit for culture, and a solace for lonely immigrants. It also strengthened Britain's cultural and legal grip on Australia.

Because of the telegraph, when Europe erupted into war in 1914, Australians followed events closely, and they knew which side they were on. When Australians died on the beaches of Gallipoli and in the fields of France and Belgium, reports of their deaths arrived by telegram. Those telegrams were hand-delivered to heartbroken parents and wives by telegram boys.

When the Imperial Japanese Army Air Force bombed Darwin in 1942, the overland telegraph line conveyed the news. And when Java was captured, Japan seized control of three of Australia's four western cables, putting Australia at risk of isolation. A British garrison was stationed on the Cocos (Keeling) Islands to guard the fourth cable and its daily tidings of death. Meanwhile, a new generation of telegram boys bicycled around the suburbs, delivering heartbreak to a new generation of parents.

The pace of change in communication sped up. After telegraph, there was revolution after exciting revolution: telephones; television; satellites; mobile phones; the internet. Telegraph modernised too, but it lost ground each year to newcomers. It faded away so gradually that when it ended, sometime in the 1980s (it's not clear exactly when), nobody noticed, because nobody used it anymore. Today, there are more underwater cables than ever, but they are fibre-optic internet cables. The original Darwin-to-Java telegraph cable rots on the ocean floor, connected to nothing. The telegraph exists no more.

Acknowledgements

A celebration of the 150th anniversary of the opening of the line was held in 2022. Connected with that celebration, a symposium was held, and several useful articles were written on different historical aspects of the building of the line. Mac Benoy, an organiser of those events, put me in touch with Stephen Gillam-Smith, a descendant of the Todd family. Stephen provided me with a document outlining Todd and Bell family histories, and some previously unknown letters written by Alice Todd. The historian Andrew Crouch, who has specialist expertise in the Overland Telegraph, and who was also involved in the anniversary events, provided feedback as a fact-checker.

At the Alice Springs telegraph station—now a museum well worth visiting—Mandy Galindo was helpful and enthusiastic. Mandy gave me access to a large number of historical documents held on site at the station. Jim Goulding, an Alice Springs historian, helped me better understand the nearby geography and Alice Springs history.

In Adelaide, the volunteer staff at the Royal Geographic Society of South Australia were marvellous. They are custodians of a unique collection of documents relating to Australian exploration, and it is there that I accessed the Symes Papers, the collected work of the historian Major-General George W. Symes.

Symes served in both world wars then emigrated to Adelaide. In his retirement, he became an avid historian, and began writing a history of the Overland Telegraph. He died in 1980 with his book incomplete, but leaving behind a large stack of files. His archive has been an indispensable resource for researchers of the telegraph ever since, and it was certainly invaluable to me. It is a motley collection of notes, clippings, files, newspaper articles, government documents, and personal essays on the topic of the telegraph. The one thing that was missing was the incomplete draft of his book. Other historians have mentioned its existence, but I did not find it there.

For the past few years, I have been fortunate to have been mentored by the editor and publisher Richard Walsh, who encouraged me to pursue this project, and gave valuable advice along the way.

The core team at Allen & Unwin was the same as for my previous two books, *Radio Girl* and *Nabbing Ned Kelly*: Elizabeth Weiss as publisher and Samantha Kent as editor.

Finally, thanks to Jenny Edwards, my biggest supporter.

Notes

The Lightning Line

1 W.T. Jeans, *Lives of the Electricians*, p. 145.

2 Kenneth Silverman, *Lightning Man*, p. 236.

Samuel McGowan

1 Samuel McGowan was born on 4 January 1829; he arrived in Melbourne aboard the *Glance* on 20 May 1883; 'Death of the Deputy Post-Master General,' *Argus*, 19 Apr 1877, p. 6.

2 See, for example, 'The Electric Telegraph', *Argus*, 6 Jul 1853, p. 2; 'Electric Telegraph', *Hobart Town Advertiser*, 2 Jul 1853, p. 2; Ann Moyal, *Clear Across Australia*, pp. 16–18.

3 A succinct description of Morse telegraph and how it was used in Australia is given by Richard Venus, 'How Did the Telegraph Work?'

4 See, for example, 'Geelong', *Age*, 29 Nov 1854, p. 5.

5 Ann Moyal, *Clear Across Australia*, p. 18.

Charles and Alice

1 Griffith Todd's life story is documented in births and deaths data, which can be found through sites such as ancestry.com and findmypast.com.

2 According to the census, Samuel and Mary King, and Elizabeth Todd resided at 19 Montpelier Row in Lewisham, only a short walk from the Todd parents at 61 Lea Terrace, where many of the girls seemed to be residing as well.

3 Too much should not be read into the presence of a servant. Servants for middle-class households were less glamorous than those for wealthy estates, and tended to do different kinds of tasks. A female servant in Victorian times were sometimes paid 'practically nothing', according to E. Griggs, 1983.

4 Other historians seem to have overlooked that Alice was boarding at the school where Charles Todd's sisters worked. No other Bell children, then in adulthood, had attended boarding schools and I don't know if they attended school at all, although they may well have.

5 Denis Cryle, *Behind the Legend*, pp. 34, 39.

6 There are several books about the Great Exhibition; the performance of the 'Hallelujah' chorus at the opening ceremony is mentioned in E. Bonython and A. Burton, *The Great Exhibitor*, p. 115.

7 Graham Dolan, 'The Deal Time Ball', www.royalobservatorygreenwich.org/articles.php?article=910, accessed 1 Jun 2023; the display can be found on p. 65 in the Great Exhibition catalogue, Class 10, exhibit 128, which describes it as 'electro-magnetic striking clocks, with large clock in the transept'. The inventor was Mr C. Shepherd of Leadenhall Street, London; G.W. Yapp and R. Ellis, *Official Catalogue of the Great Exhibition of the Works of Industry of All Nations*, p. 70.

8 Denis Cryle, *Behind the Legend*, p. 50.

9 I am sceptical of the version of events in which Charles rushed to Cambridge to seek Alice's advice, although it seems to have been a cherished family story. In 1900,

the *Register* published a feature article on Charles Todd with interview mixed with journalistic narration ('A Veteran Servant of the Queen,' 7 Jul 1900, p. 5). The article rather comically describes Airy telling Todd, 'Off you go, sir, and see her at once.' Unlikely. The two men would never have been so informal in a telegraph dialogue, and Airy would not have called a subordinate 'Sir'. I suspect that the journalist got this juicy gossip from Todd's adult daughter Lorna, still living in Adelaide at the time of the article. Todd would have been reeling after getting Airy's message. The extraordinary offer, carrying great opportunity yet also great sacrifice, would be just the sort of thing on which a trusted mentor could advise. That is why I conclude that the 'friend' was Breen. Lorna Todd, 'Telegraph Todd No. 3,' *Chronicle*, 18 Dec 1852, p. 11.

10 *South Australian Almanac*, 1857; *Charles Todd letter of appointment*, SLSA, PRG 630/14.

11 The scenario looks like a set-up; Mrs Bell raising the topic of marriage with her daughter hovering nearby, waiting to appear. It's a proposal (by Alice) and an arranged marriage (by Mrs Bell); an ambush of the most pleasant kind. If this anecdote is true—and it is plausible—then it completely undercuts claims that Todd had been 'courting' (some would say 'grooming') Alice since she was aged twelve. There is a less plausible variation on the story that a similar incident took place when Todd first met the family, with little Alice appearing and announcing, 'I will marry you, Mr Todd.' The story of Alice's proposal is the most plausible of the various family tales about Charles and Alice's early courtship, and it is inconsistent with Todd rushing back to Cambridge to ask Alice as soon as he received the job offer. Either he visited the Bell household to propose to Alice, or Alice proposed to him.

12 Denis Cryle, *Behind the Legend*, p. 52.

13 Ann Moyal, *Clear Across Australia*, p. 20.

14 Todd to Sturt, 1855, GRG 154/24; Ann Moyal, *Clear Across Australia*, p. 20.

Battle Lines

1 Denis Cryle, *Behind the Legend*, p. 55.

2 'The census,' *Register*, 4 Aug 1855, p. 2, http://nla.gov.au/nla.news-article49294107

3 'Telegraph Todd's Alice, No. 1,' *Chronicle*, 15 Oct 1953, p. 15; information about the Halls comes from various UK archives accessed via ancestry.com and findmypast.com.

4 *The Royal South Australian Almanack and General Directory for 1857*, pp. 27–32.

5 Frank Clune, *The Overland Telegraph*, p. 121.

6 'South Australia' *Argus*, 5 Jul 1853, p. 5. The *Argus*'s harsh judgement was not entirely fair. Tony Rogers and Judy Ferrente, in *The Weatherman from Greenwich*, describe some colourful episodes in the history of early Adelaide (see their Chapter 6 in particular).

7 Denis Cryle, *Behind the Legend*, p. 58; 'Committee on Estimates', *Adelaide Times*, 19 Jan 1856, p. 2; 'MacGeorge's Electric Telegraph', *Adelaide Times*, 22 Jan 1856, p. 3.

8 Sally O'Neill, 'Hart, John (1809–1873)', https://adb.anu.edu.au/biography/hart-john-3729, retrieved 1 Feb 2023

9 'The Telegraph on the City and Port Railway', *Register*, 31 Jan 1856, p. 2.

10 'Chess by Telegraph', *Register*, 21 Jan 1856, p. 3.
11 'St Luke's Church—Opening of the Bazaar', *Adelaide Observer*, 26 Jan 1856, p. 3.
12 F.R. Bradley, 'History of the Electric Telegraph in Australia', *Royal Australian Historical Society Journal and Proceedings*, pp. 239–63.
13 'The Rival Telegraphs', *Adelaide Observer*, 2 Feb 1856, p. 1.
14 The first train journey was on Saturday, 8 March; see 'Trial Trip on the Railway', *Register*, 10 Mar 1856, p. 2. The telegraph costs are given in: 'Advertising', *Register*, 19 Feb 1856, p. 1.
15 'The Telegraph in South Australia,' *Register*, 18 Jan 1856, p. 2, http://nla.gov.au/nla.news-article49745562
16 'The Magnetic Telegraph', *Adelaide Observer*, 26 Jan 1856, p. 7.
17 'The Rival Telegraphs' *Adelaide Observer*, 2 Feb 1856, p. 1. I have amended what appears to be a typo in the original quote. Also 'Legislative Council', *Register*, 26 Jan 1856, p. 2.
18 'Electric Telegraph', *Adelaide Times*, 29 Jan 1856, p. 3.
19 'Telegraph Charges', *Register*, 15 Feb 1856, p. 3.
20 Difference in appearance mentioned in 'Public Works', *Register*, 22 Apr 1856, p. 3.
21 'Telegraph to Gawler Town', *Register*, 8 Mar 1856, p. 3.
22 'Electric Telegraph', *Adelaide Times*, 6 Mar 1856, p. 2.
23 'The Electric Telegraph', *Adelaide Observer*, 15 Mar 1856, p. 6.
24 'Gawler Town', *Adelaide Times*, 20 Feb 1856, p. 2.
25 'The Cheap and Nasty Telegraph', *Adelaide Times*, 22 Feb 1856, p. 3.
26 'Magnetic and Electric Telegraph', *Register*, 2 Feb 1857, p. 2; 'The Times Exchange and Reading Room', *Adelaide Times*, 26 Mar 1857, p. 2.
27 'Sales By Auction This Day', *Register*, 5 Nov 1857, p. 2; Ann Moyal, *Clear Across Australia*, p. 20.
28 'Obituaries', *Adelaide Observer*, 4 Jan 1919, p. 33.

The Intercolonial Link

1 News reports of colonial parliamentary debates often convert first-person present tense into third-person past tense, so I sometimes unscramble the egg, as I have done here. 'Legislative Council', *Adelaide Observer*, 5 Apr 1856, p. 4.
2 'Rawnsley's Survey Party', *Adelaide Times*, 13 Sep 1851, p. 2.
3 'Legislative Council', *Adelaide Times*, 10 Oct 1851, p. 3.
4 Denis Cryle, *Behind the Legend*, p. 59.
5 'The Adelaide and Melbourne Electric Telegraph', *Adelaide Observer*, 25 Oct 1856, p. 5.
6 John Ewens, *Diary*, 19 Aug 1856.
7 'The Adelaide and Melbourne Electric Telegraph', *Adelaide Observer*, 25 Oct 1856, p. 5.

Todd's Progress

1 'The Magnetic Telegraph', *Adelaide Observer*, 23 May 1857, p. 2; 'Legislative Council', *Register*, 19 Nov 1856, p. 3; 'Parliamentary Summary', *Advertiser*, 4 Sep 1858, p. 2.
2 'The Magnetic Telegraph', *Register*, 10 Jun 1858, p. 2.
3 'The Telegraph to Melbourne', *Register*, 14 Jun 1858, p. 2.

4 'The Telegraph', *Register*, 15 Jun 1858, p. 2.
5 'The Intercolonial Telegraph', *Register*, 24 Jun 1858, p. 2.
6 'The Intercolonial Telegraph', *Register*, 24 June 1858, p. 2; 'Intercolonial Telegraph', *Register*, 28 Jun 1858, p. 2.
7 'The Intercolonial Telegraph', *Advertiser*, 22 Dec 1858, p. 2.
8 'The Boundary of the Colony,' *Advertiser*, 26 Aug 1868, p. 2.

The Race to Cable the World

1 Papers of Edward Henry Stanley, 'Interview with L. Gisborne on extension of telegraph to Australia', 24 Mar 1858.
2 'European and Australian Telegraph', *Sydney Morning Herald*, 3 Aug 1859, p. 5.
3 'European and Australian Telegraph,' *Sydney Morning Herald*, 3 Aug 1859, p. 5.
4 John Bailey's terrific book about John McDouall Stuart, *Mr Stuart's Track*, is well worth reading.
5 Charles Todd, 'European and Australian Telegraph,' *Sydney Morning Herald*, 3 Aug 1859, p. 5.
6 Sarah Murgatroyd, *The Dig Tree*, p. 46.
7 'The Overland Route to Europe,' *Argus*, 28 Dec 1858, p. 6.
8 'House of Assembly', *Adelaide Observer*, 25 Oct 1862, p. 2; this article describes the reward and states that it was announced in July 1859.
9 John Bailey, *Mr Stuart's Track*, pp. 167–8.
10 Sarah Murgatroyd's harrowing history of the Burke and Wills expedition, *The Dig Tree*, is an Australian classic.

Alice

1 Lorna Todd, 'Telegraph Todd and the Overland Line, No. 5', *Chronicle*, 1 Jan 1953, p. 9; for the Governor's guest list, see for example, 'The Queen's Birthday', *Adelaide Observer*, 29 May 1858, p. 1.
2 Denis Cryle, *Behind the Legend*, p. 66.
3 'Entertainment on Board the Irene', *Register*, 6 Jan 1857, p. 2.
4 Lorna Todd, 'Telegraph Todd's Alice, No. 1', *Chronicle*, 15 Oct 1953, p. 15.
5 Denis Cryle, *Behind the Legend*, p. 66.
6 Lorna Todd, 'Telegraph Todd's Alice, No. 1', *Chronicle*, 15 Oct 1953, p. 15.
7 Tracking Charles and Alice's sprawling family history was helped immensely by 'Profile of Bell, Gillam & Early Squires Families' provided by Stephen Gillam-Smith.
8 Lorna Todd, 'Telegraph Todd's Alice, No. 5', *Chronicle*, 12 Nov 1953, p. 14.
9 Lorna Todd claimed that the Todds were 'cash poor', although she was born some years later; Lorna Todd, 'Telegraph Todd's Alice No. 2', *Chronicle*, 22 Oct 1953, p. 14.
10 Letter from Alice Todd to her sister Sarah Squires, circa 1857, transcript in a document titled, 'Profile of Bell, Gillam & Early Squires Families,' provided to me by Stephen Gillam-Smith.
11 Lorna Todd, 'Telegraph Todd's Alice No. 2, Family Life in Adelaide during the Victorian Era', *Chronicle*, 22 Oct 1953, p. 14; letter from Alice to Charles, 28 Jun 1872, provided by Stephen Gillam-Smith.
12 Charles and Alice Todd, *Letters*, p. 7.

Escape Cliffs

1 'Northern Territory Land Act', 1863, https://nla.gov.au/nla.obj-488860926; there are numerous news articles from 1863 about the *Northern Territory Land Act*, e.g., 'The New Northern Territory', *Advertiser*, 27 Nov 1863, p. 2; and 'The Northern Territory', *Adelaide Observer*, 14 May 1864, p. 2.
2 'The Northern Territory', *Adelaide Observer*, 14 May 1864, p. 6.
3 'Melville Island', *Hobart Town Gazette*, 1 Apr 1825, p. 4; D. Pugh, 2022, 'Early Attempts to Establish Settlements: Fort Dundas', *ABC Education*, https://www.abc.net.au/education/early-attempts-to-establish-settlements-fort-dundas/13905892
4 G. Moodie, 2019, 'The Doomed Attempt to Claim Australia's North for the British Empire', *ABC News*, https://www.abc.net.au/news/2019-12-03/port-essington-worlds-end-failed-british-colonial-settlement/11730570
5 Frank Clune, *The Overland Telegraph*, p. 130.

The Cable Cometh

1 'Mr. Gisborne's Telegraph Scheme', *Register*, 16 Apr 1863.
2 Frank Clune, *The Overland Telegraph*, p. 114.
3 'India', *Geelong Advertiser*, 17 Mar 1865, p. 3.
4 'The Deep Sea Telegraph to Bombay', *Cornwall Chronicle (Tas)*, 23 Jun 1869, p. 2.
5 Frank Clune, *The Overland Telegraph*, p. 151; there is still a location near Darwin named Palmerston, but it is not on the site of the original settlement.
6 Frank Clune, *The Overland Telegraph*, p. 160.
7 'Mr Todd on Anglo–Australian Telegraphy', *Register*, 1 Sep 1869, p. 2.
8 'The Parliament,' *Register*, 14 Jan 1870, pp. 3, 6, 7.
9 Charles Todd, 1886, *Telegraphic Enterprise in Australasia*.

The Captain's Company

1 'Shipping Intelligence', *Register*, 12 Apr 1870, p. 4.
2 UK deaths register, 1875.
3 'Proposed Submarine and Land Telegraph Between Singapore and the Australian Colonies', *Sydney Morning Herald*, 19 May 1870, p. 2.
4 Commander Osborn's Adelaide address was the York Hotel, which I found in 'Letter from Commander Osborn', *Evening Journal*, 9 Jun 1870, p. 3.
5 Charles Todd, 1873, *Lecture*, SLSA, PRG 630/9
6 Osborn chaperoned by Todd: 'City Correspondence,' *Kapunda Herald and Northern Intelligencer*, 15 Apr 1870, p. 2; and 'Anglo-Australian Telegraph', *The Chronicle*, 23 Apr 1870, p. 8; their visit to botanic gardens: 'The Botanic Gardens', *Evening Journal*, 25 Apr 1870, p. 3.
7 Todd's report is printed in 'The Overland Telegraph', *Advertiser*, 25 Apr 1870, p. 2.
8 'The British Australian Telegraph', *Register*, 30 May 1870, p. 5.
9 'The Overland Telegraph Scheme', *Register*, 6 Jun 1870, p. 5.
10 'The Overland Telegraph', *Weekly Times* (Vic), 18 Jun 1870, p. 11.
11 'The Proposed British-Australian Telegraph', *The Queenslander*, 14 May 1870, p. 8.
12 'Proposed Submarine and Land Telegraph Between Singapore and the Australian Colonies', *Sydney Morning Herald*, 19 May 1870, p. 2.
13 'The Overland Telegraph Scheme', *Register*, 6 Jun 1870, p. 5; 'Letter from Commander Osborn', *Evening Journal*, 9 Jun 1870, p. 3.

14 'The Parliament', *Express & Telegraph*, 11 Jun 1870, p. 2.
15 'The Parliament', *Express & Telegraph*, 11 Jun 1870, p. 2
16 The bill passed on 10 June 1870, 'The Parliament,' *Express & Telegraph*, 11 Jun 1870, p. 2.
17 Osborn departed on 22 June aboard the *Aldinga* to Melbourne, and from there took the *City of Adelaide* to Sydney on 25 June. He had, during his time in Adelaide, already visited Melbourne for two weeks at the start of May; 'Shipping News', *Evening Journal*, 28 Apr 1870, p. 2, and 13 May 1870, p. 2; *Express & Telegraph*, 23 Jun 1870, p. 2; 'Shipping News', *The Herald*, 25 Jun 1870, p. 3.

To Port Darwin, and Quickly

1 'Mr. Douglas's Instructions', *Advertiser*, 23 May 1870, p. 3.
2 'Provisional Constitution for Port Darwin', *Evening Journal*, 30 Apr 1870, p. 2.
3 'Provisional Constitution for Port Darwin', *Evening Journal*, 30 Apr 1870, p. 2.
4 'Experimental Plant Nursery', *Adelaide Observer*, 26 Apr 1870, p. 2; 'First Impressions', *Chronicle*, 3 Sep 1870, p. 1; 'Plants Supplied to the *Gulnare*,' *The Queenslander*, 4 Jun 1870, p. 5.
5 'Plants Supplied to the *Gulnare*', *The Queenslander*, 4 June 1870, p. 5; Peter Taylor, *An End to Silence*, p. 45.
6 'Captain Douglas', *Advertiser*, 23 May 1870, p. 3; 'The Parliament', *Register*, 11 Aug 1870, p. 5.
7 P.L. Burns, 'Douglas, William Bloomfield' *Australian Dictionary of Biography*, https://adb.anu.edu.au/biography/douglas-william-bloomfield-3431/text5223
8 'The *Gulnare*', *Adelaide Observer*, 3 Sep 1870, p. 4.
9 'Threatened Attack by Hostile Natives', *Adelaide Observer*, 3 Sep 1870, p. 4.
10 Derek Pugh, *Darwin: Origin of a City*, p. 95.
11 Frank Clune, *The Overland Telegraph*, p. 166.

Double Deals

1 Though held in Melbourne, the conference was instigated by Tasmania. New Zealand was invited but declined; Queensland also did not send a delegate, for reasons unclear to me.
2 'The Double Negotiation and Rival Telegraphs', *Adelaide Observer*, 30 Jul 1870, p. 13; 'Douglas versus Dutton', *Register*, 29 Jul 1870, p. 5; Todd in attendance: 'Intercolonial Telegraphy', *Evening Journal*, 27 Jun 1870, p. 2.
3 'Parliamentary Paper', *Brisbane Courier*, 9 Jul, p. 5, and 13 Jul 1870, p. 3; Untitled, *Sydney Morning Herald*, 21 Jul 1870, p. 4.
4 'The Double Negotiation and Rival Telegraphs', *Adelaide Observer*, 30 Jul 1870, p. 13.
5 'Summary by the mail of colonial news', *Express* (WA), 27 Jul 1870, p. 3. http://nla.gov.au/nla.news-article256624250. Osborn's movements around Australia can be found in various shipping manifests for 1870 and 1871. He attended a dinner with Hart and others in July 1871.

First Contracts

1 The technical specifics and challenges involved in constructing the line are described in Andrew Crouch, 'The Building Process'; and Andrew Crouch & Richard Venus, 'The Overland Telegraph Line: How it was built'.

2 'Tenders', *Register*, 29 Jun 1870, p. 2; 'The Overland Telegraph', *Adelaide Observer*, 2 Jul 1870, p. 2.
3 John Rounsevell's initial offer was to build the southern part for £87,600; Darwent and Dalwood quoted £37,500, the smaller price reflecting the smaller distance of the northern part. Cost breakdowns are in 'Evening News', *Evening Journal*, 27 Jul 1870, p. 2.
4 'Latest news', *Evening News*, 23 July 1870, p. 2; 'Telegrams', *Border Watch*, 23 Jul 1870, p. 2; Peter Taylor, *An End to Silence*, p. 47; 'The Northern Telegraph', *Evening Journal*, 26 Jul 1870, p. 2; 'The Parliament', *Express & Telegraph*, 23 Jul 1870, p. 3.

Explorers for Hire

1 'The Overland Telegraph Route', *Evening Journal*, 4 Jul 1870, p. 2.
2 Cost breakdowns in 'Evening News', *Evening Journal*, 27 Jul 1870, p. 2.
3 'Starting of Overland Telegraph Parties', *Register*, 6 Sep 1870, p. 6; Alfed Giles, *Exploring in the Seventies*; Giles's book was quite useful in the writing of *this* book.
4 One prospector carted his copper 70 miles in a wheelbarrow. See 'Copper Mining at Beltana', *Register*, 1 Sep 1898, p. 6.
5 Elder's other station was Umberatana. Philip Jones & A. Kenny, *Australia's Muslim Cameleers*, p. 44; 'Topics for the Day', *Advertiser*, 3 Jul 1869, p. 2.
6 'The Overland Telegraph', *Register*, 13 Aug 1870, p. 5; Alfred Giles, *Exploring in the Seventies*, p. 15.
7 Alfred Giles, *Exploring in the Seventies*, p. 104.
8 'The Port Darwin Telegraph Expedition', *Chronicle*, 27 Aug 1870, p. 8.
9 Alfred Giles, *Exploring in the Seventies*, pp. 17–18.
10 'The Overland Telegraph', *Evening Journal*, 4 Nov 1870, p. 3.
11 Alfred Giles, *Exploring in the Seventies*, pp. 19–20.
12 Alfred Giles, *Exploring in the Seventies*, p. 22.
13 Alfred Giles, *Exploring in the Seventies*, p. 27.

The Plan

1 Peter Taylor, *An End to Silence*, p. 58.
2 'The Northern Telegraph', *Chronicle*, 6 Aug 1870, p. 11.
3 'The Overland Telegraph', *Register*, 1 Aug 1870, p. 4.
4 Departure of the *Omeo* reported in 'Northern Territory Telegraph Expedition', *Advertiser*, 22 Aug 1870, p. 3, and 'The Overland Telegraph', *Register*, 10 Sep 1870, p. 5.
5 'Instructions to Overseers' is in 'Overland Telegraph Papers,' SRSA, GRG 24/90/1/3
6 'Overland Telegraph Papers,' SRSA, GRG 24/90/1/3.

Go North, Young Man

1 'Overland Telegraph Expedition', *Chronicle*, 3 Sep 1870, p. 6; the three inspectors were A.T. Woods, G.R. McMinn and R.R. Knuckey. 'The Works on the Overland Telegraph Line', *Register*, 11 Oct 1870, p. 5.
2 'Starting of Overland Telegraph Parties', *Register*, 6 Sep 1870, p. 6. My description of Todd's speech at the stockyards is an amalgam of reports of two speeches he gave there within days of each other, presumably identical or nearly so.

3 'Starting of Northern Telegraph Parties', *Adelaide Observer*, 3 Sep 1870, p. 15; 'Overland Telegraph Expedition', *Chronicle*, 3 Sep 1870, p. 6.
4 'Rhynie', *Chronicle*, 10 Sep 1870, p. 7.
5 'The Week's News', *Adelaide Observer*, 17 Sep 1870, p. 7.
6 'Port Augusta', *Register*, 3 Sep 1870, p. 7; *The Australian Handbook and Almanac, and Shippers' and Importers' Directory for 1873*, p. 157; 'Starting of Northern Telegraph Parties,' *Adelaide Observer*, 3 Sep 1870, p. 15; 'Overland Telegraph Expedition,' *Chronicle*, 3 Sep 1870, p. 6.
7 'The Works on the Overland Telegraph' *Register*, 11 Oct 1870, p. 5.
8 John Rounsevell had gone ahead of them, having contracted to take supplies to The Peake; 'Country Letters', *Adelaide Observer*, 3 Sep 1870, p. 3.

A Surprise for Port Darwin

1 'Northern Territory', *Express & Telegraph*, 4 Jul 1871, p. 3; concertina playing mentioned in Derek Pugh, *Darwin: Origin of a City*, p. 55.
2 Sidney Herbert, *Reminiscences*, p. 18, described the method of landing the horses and bullocks.
3 'The Northern Territory', *Advertiser*, 5 Oct 1870, p. 2; 'Planting the First Pole of the Overland Telegraph at Port Darwin', *Illustrated Adelaide Post*, 1 Dec 1870, p. 4; 'Planting the First Telegraph Pole', *Register*, 21 Oct 1870, p. 6. Captain Sweet's photographic career is mentioned by Richard Venus, 'First and Last Poles'.
4 'The Northern Territory,' *Advertiser*, 5 Oct 1870, p. 2; 'Law Courts: Tuesday', *Chronicle*, 29 May 1875, p. 14.
5 The first group, closest to the settlement, was led by Charles Tymn; the second group at Tumbling Waters was led by Joseph Darwent, nephew of the contractor Joseph Darwent. Sidney Herbert, *Reminiscences*, p. 28.

From Port to Peake

1 'The Overland Telegraph Line', *Adelaide Observer*, 1 Oct 1870, p. 4.
2 'Parliament', *Register*, 8 Oct 1870, p. 6.
3 Peter Taylor, *An End to Silence*, p. 60.
4 'Planting the First Pole', *Evening Journal*, 5 Oct 1870, p. 2.
5 Richard Venus, 'The First and Last Poles'.
6 'The Works on the Overland Telegraph', *Register*, 11 Oct 1870, p. 5; 'Latest News', *Evening Journal*, 4 Oct 1870, p. 2; another article says that they travelled by express wagon: 'Overland Telegraph', *Evening Journal*, 11 Oct 1870, p. 3; although they were clearly on horseback from Beltana onwards.
7 Charles Todd, *Diary* 1, p. 82, SRSA, GRG 154/14/1
8 'The Overland Telegraph', *Evening Journal*, 4 Nov 1870, p. 3.
9 'The Overland Telegraph', *Evening Journal*, 3 Nov 1870, p. 2; 'The Overland Telegraph', *Evening Journal* 4 Nov 1870, p. 3 'The Overland Telegraph', *Register*, 8 Nov 1870, p. 4.
10 The junction of the Hugh and Finke rivers is at latitude and longitude of (–25.02, 134.16). The Peake station is at (–28.077, 135.906).
11 This description, in part, is derived from the *Symes Papers*, File 15.
12 'Starting of Overland Telegraph Parties', *Register*, 6 Sep 1870, p. 6.
13 'Starting of Overland Telegraph Parties,' *Register*, 6 Sep 1870, p. 6.

14 'The Northern Telegraph', *Express & Telegraph*, 2 Dec 1870, p. 2.
15 George Symes, *Exploring the MacDonnell Ranges*, Appendix B.
16 George Symes, *Exploring in the MacDonnell Ranges*, Appendix B.
17 Alfred Giles, *Exploring in the Seventies*, pp. 37–8, 44; Sidney Herbert, *Reminiscences*, p. 97, also describes the jerking method.
18 'The Overland Telegraph', *Evening Journal*, 3 Nov 1870, p. 2.
19 'The Port Augusta and Port Darwin Telegraph', *Express & Telegraph*, 18 Nov 1870, p. 2; 'The Northern Telegraph,' *Express & Telegraph*, 2 Dec 1870, p. 2.
20 Alfred Giles, *Exploring in the Seventies*, p. 38. Giles placed Charles Todd's arrival on 10 November but I trust Todd's own records on the date of his arrival. Even so, Giles provides much detail on various things.
21 'The Northern Telegraph', *Express & Telegraph*, 2 Dec 1870, p. 2; George Symes, *Exploring in the MacDonnell Ranges*, Appendix B, p. 1.

Poles in the Jungle

1 Sidney Herbert, *Reminiscences*, p. 63.
2 Sidney Herbert, *Reminiscences*, pp. 50, 53, 88.
3 Sidney Herbert, *Reminiscences*, p. 38.
4 Sidney Herbert, *Reminiscences*, pp. 37, 52.
5 Sidney Herbert, *Reminiscences*, p. 46.
6 Sidney Herbert, *Reminiscences*, pp. 38–48, 51, 52.
7 Sidney Herbert, *Reminiscences*, pp. 30–3, 35.
8 Sidney Herbert, *Reminiscences*, p. 62.
9 Sidney Herbert, *Reminiscences*, p. 23.
10 Sidney Herbert, *Reminiscences*, pp. 21–2.
11 'Law Courts: Tuesday', *Chronicle*, 5 Jun 1875, p. 14.
12 'Northern Territory,' *Advertiser*, 4 Jan 1871, p. 5.
13 Frank Clune, *The Overland Telegraph*, p. 198–9; 'News from the Northern Territory,' *Express & Telegraph*, 16 Dec 1870, p. 2.
14 'Arrival of the *Gulnare* from the Northern Territory,' *Express & Telegraph*, 8 Jul 1871, p. 2; the Whitting theory was mentioned in 'The Week's News', *Adelaide Observer*, 8 Jul 1871, pp. 7–8; McLachlan later declared that McMinn was wrong (see: 'Progress of the Northern Telegraph,' *Irish Harp and Farmers' Herald*, 30 Dec 1871), but I believe that McLachlan was wrong, partly because McMinn was a better surveyor and explorer, because there are other accounts of the discovered wheel tracks, and because those that saw them did not seem to be in any doubt about what they were seeing.
15 'Arrival of the *Gulnare* from the Northern Territory', *Express & Telegraph*, 8 Jul 1871, p. 2.

Number Two Depot

1 Sidney Herbert, *Reminiscences*, pp. 71–2, 79.
2 'Law Courts: Wednesday', *Chronicle*, 29 May 1875, p. 14; Sidney Herbert, *Reminiscences*, p. 73.
3 Sidney Herbert, *Reminiscences*, pp. 81–2.
4 Sidney Herbert, *Reminiscences*, pp. 84–5.
5 Sidney Herbert, *Reminiscences*, pp. 87–8.

Doubters

1 'Latest News', *Evening Journal*, 21 Dec 1870, p. 2; E. Mills, *W. Whitfield Mills*, p. 24; 'The Week's News', *Adelaide Observer*, 9 Mar 1872, p. 7.

2 'The Overland Telegraph', *Register*, 31 Dec 1870, pp. 4–5.

The Sweeping Plains

1 Knuckey's report to Todd is in SRSA, GRG 154/6/1.

2 'Charlotte of Charlotte Waters', *Walkabout*, 1 Feb 1944, pp. 28–9.

3 'To Ianthe, by George Gordon Byron,' *Poets and Lovers*, 30 Jun 2020, https://agapeta.art/2020/06/30/to-ianthe-by-george-gordon-byron/, accessed 19 Jan 2024.

4 'Lady Charlotte Bacon', *Register*, 7 Aug 1920, p. 10; 'Death of Lady Charlotte Bacon', *Adelaide Observer*, 20 Mar 1880, p. 8; 'Mr. A. Forster's Work and the Founders of the Colony', *Adelaide Observer*, 15 Dec 1866, p. 5; 'Anthony Bacon (1796–1864)', *Australian Dictionary of Biography*, https://adb.anu.edu.au/biography/bacon-anthony-1729

The Flooding Rains

1 Sidney Herbert, *Reminiscences*, p. 85.

2 Sidney Herbert, *Reminiscences*, pp. 85–6.

3 Sidney Herbert, *Reminiscences*, p. 90.

4 Sidney Herbert, *Reminiscences*, pp. 88, 90–1; in court it was testified that they reached the Katherine on the last day of December 1870, not the last day of January 1871 (as Herbert wrote); 'Law and Police Courts: Tuesday', *Adelaide Observer*, 5 June 1875, p. 10.

5 Sidney Herbert, *Reminiscences*, p. 49; 'Law Courts: Tuesday', *Chronicle*, 5 June 1875, p. 14.

6 Sidney Herbert, *Reminiscences*, p. 49.

The Ragged Mountain Ranges

1 Alfred Giles, *Exploring in the Seventies*, p. 62; Eliot Mills, *W. Whitfield Mills*, p. 28; The term 'Depot Junction' is from George Symes, *Exploring in the MacDonnell Ranges*.

2 George Symes, *Exploring the MacDonnell Ranges*, p. 10.

3 Woods's report, dated 26 Jan 1871, can be found in SRSA, GRG 154/6/1.

4 Alfred Giles, *Exploring in the Seventies*, p. 66.

5 G.R. McMinn, *Diary*, 16 Feb 1871, p. 38.

6 George Symes, *Exploring the MacDonnell Ranges*, p. 10. Whitfield Mills's report to Todd is in SRSA, GRG 154/6/1.

7 Alfred Giles, *Exploring in the Seventies*, p. 68.

8 They both left on 7 March 1871.

9 Alfred Giles, *Exploring in the Seventies*, p. 69; Mills report in SRSA GRG 154/6/1, p. 31.

10 Derek Pugh, *Twenty to the Mile*, p. 45.

11 There is a common misconception that the gap was named because Heavitree was Charles Todd's middle name. However, this is untrue. Charles Todd had no middle name at all. See Richard Venus, 'Charles Todd: Biographical Errors'.

12 Mills report, SRSA, GRG 154/6/1.

The Steady, Soaking Rain

1 'Law Courts: Tuesday', *Chronicle*, 5 June 1875, p. 14.
2 'The Overland Telegraph and Northern Territory', *Adelaide Observer*, 22 Jul 1871, p. 12; 'Law courts: Tuesday,' *Chronicle*, 5 June 1875, p. 14; Sidney Herbert, *Reminiscences*, p. 96.
3 'The Overland Telegraph and Northern Territory', *Adelaide Observer*, 22 July 1871, p. 12; 'Law courts: Wednesday,' *Chronicle*, 29 May 1875, p. 14.
4 Sidney Herbert, *Reminiscences*, p. 93.
5 Sidney Herbert, *Reminiscences*, p. 94, said the mood was 'mutinous'. Joseph Darwent said at one point at eleven workers went on strike on 14 March; a worker named William Carter testified that 'work was stopped'. 'Law courts: Tuesday,' *Chronicle*, 5 Jun 1875, p. 14 Beef jerking is from Herbert, pp. 96–7.
6 Sidney Herbert, *Reminiscences*, pp. 95–6.
7 'The Overland Telegraph and Northern Territory', *Adelaide Observer*, 22 July 1871, p. 12; Joseph Darwent said later that they were doing 'seven and a quarter miles a week with half the men.' In 'Law courts: Tuesday,' *Chronicle*, 5 Jun 1875, p. 14.
8 Sidney Herbert, *Reminiscences*, p. 96.
9 'Northern Territory', *Chronicle*, 8 Jul 1871, pp. 11–12.
10 Andrew Crouch, *Connecting the North*, p. 43; 'The *Gulnare*', *Advertiser*, 4 Mar 1871, p. 2.
11 Sidney Herbert, *Reminiscences*, p. 97.
12 'Mr. McMinn's Report', *Adelaide Observer*, 15 Jul 1871, p. 12; Alfred Giles, *Exploring in the Seventies*, p. 94.
13 'The Overland Telegraph and Northern Territory', *Adelaide Observer*, 22 Jul 1871, p. 12; 'Law Courts: Wednesday', *Chronicle*, 29 May 1875, p. 14.
14 'Law Courts: Wednesday', *Chronicle*, 29 May 1875, p. 14.
15 McMinn's report to Todd can be found in 'Arrival of the *Gulnare* from the Northern Territory,' *Express & Telegraph*, 10 Jul 1871, p. 3.
16 'The Overland Telegraph and Northern Territory,' *Adelaide Observer*, 22 Jul 1871, p. 12.
17 'Arrival of the *Gulnare* from the Northern Territory,' *Express & Telegraph*, 8 July 1871, p. 2.
18 McMinn's report to Todd, in: 'The Overland Telegraph: The Northern Territory Section', *Register*, 15 Jul 1871, p. 5.
19 'Arrival of the *Gulnare* from the Northern Territory', *Express & Telegraph*, 8 Jul 1871, p. 2.

A Wilful, Lavish Land

1 Alfred Giles, *Exploring in the Seventies*, pp. 72–3.
2 Alfred Giles, *Exploring in the Seventies*, p. 73.
3 Alfred Giles, *Exploring in the Seventies*, pp. 83–4.
4 Alfred Giles, *Exploring in the Seventies*, p. 86.

The Far Horizon

1 Andrew Crouch, *Building the Line*, p. 21.
2 'The Northern Telegraph Progress Report', *Advertiser*, 28 Mar 1871, p. 3.
3 'The Trans-Continental Telegraph', *Register*, 19 Jun 1871, p. 6.

4 'The Natives on the Telegraph Line', *Register*, 21 Jun 1871, p. 4.
5 'The Electric Telegraph in Queensland', *Queenslander*, 29 Apr 1871, p. 6.
6 'Queensland's Opposition to the Port Darwin Telegraph', *Chronicle*, 17 Jun 1871, p. 12.

The Grey Clouds Gather

1 *Symes Papers*, File 18.
2 'The Overland Telegraph and Northern Territory', *Register*, 17 Jul 1871, p. 3; 'Messrs Darwent and Dalwood's Contract', *Adelaide Observer*, 22 Jul 1871, p. 12.
3 'Mr. McMinn's Report', *Adelaide Observer*, 15 July 1871, p. 12.
4 'The Overland Telegraph', *Adelaide Observer*, 15 July 1871, p. 13; 'The Overland Telegraph', *Register*, 11 Jul 1871, p. 4; 'The Overland Telegraph: miscellaneous', *Register*, 7 Nov 1871, p. 4; Peter Taylor, *An End to Silence*, p. 92.
5 *Symes Papers*, File 18.
6 'The Australian Telegraph', *Australasian*, 6 Jul 1872, p. 20 (9); *Symes Papers*, File 19.
7 'The Australian Telegraph', *Australasian*, 6 Jul 1872, p. 20 (9).
8 'The Overland Telegraph', *Adelaide Observer*, 15 Jul 1871, p. 13.
9 Charles Todd, 1873, *Lecture*, p. 30.
10 'Heads of Intelligence', *Express & Telegraph*, 12 Aug 1871, p. 2.
11 William Crowder, *Diary*, p. 1.

The Ghost of Expeditions Past

1 The *Omeo* reached Port Darwin on 24 Aug 1871. 'Port Darwin', *Advertiser*, 29 Dec 1871, p. 2.
2 'Rough Notes from the Northern Territory,' *Advertiser*, 22 Dec 1871, p. 2.
3 'Northern Territory', *Express & Telegraph*, 4 Jul 1871, p. 3.
4 Alan Powell, *Far Country*, 1992, Kindle Locations 1957-1958. Melbourne University Press. Kindle Edition.
5 'Progress of the Northern Telegraph', *Irish Harp and Farmers' Herald*, 30 Dec 1871, p. 5.
6 'Rough Notes from the Northern Territory', *Advertiser*, 22 Dec 1871, p. 2.
7 A. Giles, *Exploring in the Seventies*, pp. 92, 101; 'Rough Notes from the Northern Territory,' *Advertiser*, 22 Dec 1871, p. 2.
8 'Northern Territory', *Express & Telegraph*, 4 Jul 1871, p. 3; Binmook's punishment mentioned in 'General News', *Express & Telegraph*, 26 Sep 1871, p. 2.
9 Derek Pugh, *Darwin: Origin of a City*, pp. 60, 94. Foelsche is believed to have been directly or indirectly involved in the killing of Aboriginal people in later years.
10 Alfred Giles, *Exploring in the Seventies*, pp. 104–5; 'The Overland Telegraph', *Express & Telegraph*, 6 Oct 1871, p. 2.
11 The representatives were Mr Finniss and Mr Squier. They chose a place called Mindil, also known as Fannie Bay. 'The Northern Territory', *Register*, 18 Jan 1872, p. 5; Harriet Douglas's marriage to Dan Daly comes from Alan Powell, *Far Country*, p. 101.
12 Alfred Giles, *Exploring in the Seventies*, p. 90.
13 Alfred Giles, *Exploring in the Seventies*, p. 107.
14 John Little, *Diary 1*, pp. 6–7.

15 Since bonuses were paid, we know this was the case, so it's reasonable to conclude that Robert Patterson knew it, too.
16 Alfred Giles, *Exploring in the Seventies*, p. 106.
17 John Little, *Diary 1*, pp. 5–7.

The Wreck of the *Gulnare*

1 'The Northern Territory', *Register*, 18 Jan 1872, p. 5.
2 That was the upshot of the findings of the enquiry. You can see a news summary of it here: 'Marine Board', *Advertiser*, 30 Jul 1872, p. 3; 'Port Darwin', *Express & Telegraph*, 12 Feb 1872, p. 3; the rumour about the captain being drunk is in William Crowder, *Diary*, 17 Dec 1871, p. 10.
3 'The Northern Territory', *Register*, 18 Jan 1872, p. 5.
4 John Little to Charles Todd, 12 Oct 1871, in *Symes Papers*, File 18.
5 'The Northern Territory,' *Register*, 18 Jan 1872, p. 5; 'Port Darwin,' *Express & Telegraph*, 12 Feb 1872, p. 3.
6 John Little, *Diary 1*, p. 24.
7 John Little, *Diary 1*, 26 Oct 1871.
8 John Little, *Diary 1*, 29 Oct 1871.

The Cable Has Landed

1 'Laying of the Singapore, Penang, and Madras Cables', *Launceston Examiner*, 13 May 1871, p. 3.
2 John Little, *Diary 1*, 28 Oct 1871.
3 'The Arrival of the *Investigator*', *Launceston Examiner*, 15 Apr 1869, p. 2.
4 'The Northern Territory', *Register*, 18 Jan 1872, p. 5.
5 John Little, *Diary 1*, 7 Nov 1871.
6 'The Northern Territory', *Register*, 18 Jan 1872, p. 5.
7 John Little, *Diary 1*, 10 Nov 1871.
8 John Little, *Diary 1*, 15 Nov 1871.

Heart of Darkness

1 Robert Patterson, *Diary*, pp. 3, 4, 25.
2 Robert Patterson, *Diary*, p. 16.
3 Robert Patterson, *Diary*, p. 5.
4 Robert Patterson, *Diary*, pp. 8–9.
5 Robert Patterson, *Diary*, p. 9.
6 Robert Patterson, *Diary*, p. 10.
7 Robert Patterson, *Diary*, p. 10. The early maps show Roper Creek as 'Stirling River'. Patterson's diary initially calls it the Stirling River, then without explanation mid-December, switches to Roper Creek, the name it is known by today.
8 Robert Patterson, *Diary*, p. 12; 6 Dec 1871, p. 14.
9 Alfred Giles, *Exploring in the Seventies*, p. 114.
10 Robert Patterson, *Diary*, p. 24; 'The South Australian Telegraph Expedition', *Empire* (NSW), 11 May 1872, p. 3; see also Charles Todd's letter to Harcus Snr, 10 Feb 1872, SRSA, GRG 154/23, p. 12.

The Voyage of the *Bengal*

1 William Crowder, *Diary*, 12 Dec, p. 9; 16 December, p. 11; cards mentioned by Crowder on p. 24.
2 The *Larrakeeyah* was lowered on 11 December 1871, see William Crowder, *Diary*, 11 Dec 1871, p. 9.
3 William Crowder, *Diary*, 11 Dec 1871, p. 9.
4 Robert Patterson, *Diary*, p. 12.
5 William Crowder, *Diary*, 15 Dec 1871, p. 10. They reached Maria Island on 15 December 1871.
6 William Crowder, *Diary*, p. 12.
7 William Crowder, *Diary*, p. 12. Missing front teeth described by Crowder on 28 Dec 1871, p. 14.
8 William Crowder, *Diary*, p. 12.
9 William Crowder, *Diary*, p. 13.
10 William Crowder, *Diary*, p. 14.
11 William Crowder, *Diary*, p. 17.
12 William Crowder, *Diary*, p. 14.

The Pitiless Blue Sky

1 Some news reports suggested that the telegraphists had rashly pressed forward, too eager to start work. However, Benjamin Clarke made the decision to send them on, as recorded in his personal diary on 2 Dec 1871.
2 'General News', *Express & Telegraph*, 6 Jan 1872, p. 2.
3 'The Overland Telegraph Route, No. VIII', *Evening Journal*, 16 Feb 1872, p. 3.
4 Ted Kraegen, 'Carl Kraegen's story'.
5 'The Overland Telegraph Route, No. VIII,' *Evening Journal*, 16 Feb 1872, p. 3.

Hart Tumbles

1 'The Parliament', *Express & Telegraph*, 4 Nov 1871, p. 2; 'House of Assembly', *Adelaide Observer*, 4 Nov 1871, p. 6; third person changed to first person, and tense adjusted for readability.
2 Boucaut's allegations of corruption worked against him as reported in 'The Crisis', *Register*, 4 Nov 1871, p. 4.
3 John Little, *Diary 1*, pp. 70–2.
4 'Death of Sir Charles Todd', *Evening Journal*, 31 Jan 1910, p. 2.
5 On the election, see, for example, 'South Australia', *Argus*, 25 Dec 1871, p. 7.

Tidings on Birdum Creek

1 Alfred Giles, *Exploring in the Seventies*, p. 115.
2 Robert Patterson, *Diary*, p. 15.

The Drovers

1 Ralph Milner, *First Overland Trek with Stock to Port Darwin*, SLSA, D7001(L), p. 1.
2 Arthur Ashwin, *From South Australia to Port Darwin*, p. 1; Ralph Milner, *First Overland Trek with Stock to Port Darwin*, pp. 1–4. The Milners also hired some other Aboriginal people, who quit before the group had crossed the border into the Northern Territory.

3 Arthur Ashwin, *From South Australia to Port Darwin*, p. 1.
4 John Milner, *First Overland Trek with Stock to Port Darwin*, p. 3.
5 Arthur Ashwin, *From South Australia to Port Darwin*, p. 8.
6 John Milner, *First Overland Trek with Stock to Port Darwin*, p. 1.
7 Arthur Ashwin, *From South Australia to Port Darwin*, pp. 8–12.
8 Ralph Milner, *First Overland Trek with Stock to Port Darwin*, pp. 1–2; Arthur Ashwin, *From South Australia to Port Darwin*, p. 13.

The *Bengal* or Bust

1 Robert Patterson, *Diary*, 18 Dec 1871.
2 Robert Patterson, *Diary*, 19 Dec 1871.
3 Robert Patterson, *Diary*, 10 Dec 1871.
4 Robert Patterson, *Diary*, 17 Dec 1871.
5 Robert Patterson, *Diary*, 25 Dec 1871.
6 Ralph Milner, *First Overland Trek with Stock to Port Darwin*, pp. 2–3.
7 Robert Patterson, *Diary*, 29 Dec 1871.
8 Robert Patterson, *Diary*, p. 29.
9 Robert Patterson, *Diary*, p. 29; William Crowder, *Diary*, p 15, says there were 40 men.
10 Robert Patterson, *Diary*, p. 29.
11 Robert Patterson, *Diary*, p. 30; William Crowder, *Diary*, p. 15. Crowder described the mast and sail in his diary, although Patterson neglected to mention them in his.
12 Robert Patterson, *Diary*, pp. 30, 32. The volunteers are named on p. 32 of Patterson's diary. They were Stretton (storekeeper), Burton (bullock driver), Dyke (bullock driver), Edwin Bayfield (stockman in charge of bullocks).
13 Robert Patterson, *Diary*, p. 31.
14 Robert Patterson, *Diary*, p. 31. Oars from bits of wood comes from Walter Rutt, 'Link in the Chain', *Register*, 10 Nov 2021, p. 4.
15 Robert Patterson, *Diary*, p. 31.
16 Robert Patterson, *Diary*, p. 32.
17 Robert Patterson, *Diary*, p. 32.
18 Robert Patterson, *Diary*, p. 32. The bushman's name was Burton, not to be confused with inland leader Robert Burton.
19 River in flood comes from Walter Rutt, 'Link in the Chain', *Register*, 10 Nov 2021, p. 4.
20 Robert Patterson, *Diary*, p. 32.
21 Robert Patterson, *Diary*, pp. 32–3.
22 Robert Patterson, *Diary*, p. 33.
23 Robert Patterson, *Diary*, p. 33.
24 Walter Rutt, 'Link in the Chain,' *Register*, 10 Nov 2021, p. 4.
25 Robert Patterson, *Diary*, pp. 33–34.
26 William Crowder, *Diary*, p. 21.

The Estafette

1 'Mr. Todd's Departure for Port Darwin', *Evening Journal*, 4 Jan 1872, p. 2.
2 'The Overland Telegraph', *Evening Journal*, 24 Aug 1871 p; 'Sudden Death on the Overland Telegraph', *Southern Argus*, 25 Aug 1871, p. 2.

3 'The Telegraph Constructors', *Evening Journal*, 1 Sep 1871, p. 3.
4 'The Overland Telegraph', *Evening Journal*, 31 Dec 1871, p. 2.
5 'Overland Telegraph', *Express and Telegraph*, 4 Jan 1872, p. 2.

The Black Prince

1 'The *Omeo*', *Register*, 1 Nov 1859, p. 2.
2 'The Steamship *Omeo*', *Age*, 7 Jan 1860, p. 5.
3 George Calder, *Stirring Events Ashore and Afloat*, pp. 75–6.
4 'A Trip to the Northern Territory', *Register*, 20 Mar 1872, p. 6.
5 'A Contradiction', *Ovens and Murray Advertiser*, 19 May 1874, p. 3.
6 'Mudgee', *Maitland Mercury*, 17 May 1866, p. 3; 'Horses and Cattle', *New South Wales Police Gazette*, 23 May 1866, p. 187; 'Wellington,' *Sydney Morning Herald*, 30 Jun 1866, p. 7.
7 'Relics of Leichhardt Alleged to Have Been Discovered', *Sydney Morning Herald*, 15 Aug 1871; 'Statement of Andrew Hume as to his Journey to the Western Coast', *Australian Town and Country Journal*, 9 Sep 1871, p. 15.
8 'The Fate of Leichhardt', *Kyneton Observer*, 26 Aug 1871, p. 3.
9 'Relics of Leichhardt—Hume's Tale', *Geelong Advertiser*, 30 Aug 1871, p. 3.
10 'Search for Traces of Leichhardt', *Sydney Mail*, 20 Jan 1872, p. 79; although his mission was public knowledge, Hume boarded the *Omeo* under the pseudonym 'Mr W. Freer', as recorded by Charles and Alice Todd, *Letters*, p. 32.

Todd's Fleet

1 Charles and Alice Todd, *Letters*, p. 18.
2 Charles and Alice Todd, *Letters*, p. 5; probably the failed 'Australian Eclipse Expedition'. See 'A Trip to the Northern Territory', *Register*, 20 Mar 1872, p. 6.
3 'A Trip to the Northern Territory', *Register*, 20 Mar 1872, p. 6.
4 Charles and Alice Todd, *Letters*, p. 8. Todd's written agreement with Calder can be found in Todd's outgoing letter book, SRSA, GRG 154/23.
5 'A Trip to the Northern Territory,' *Register*, 20 Mar 1872, p. 6.
6 Charles and Alice Todd, *Letters*, pp. 32, 36.
7 Charles and Alice Todd, *Letters*, p. 14.
8 The back-and-forth between Todd and Patterson can be found in a collection of Todd's correspondence, SRSA, GRG 154/23.
9 Robert Patterson, *Diary*, p. 38.

The Mighty Roper

1 Charles and Alice Todd, *Letters*, pp. 36–7.
2 Charles and Alice Todd, *Letters*, p. 10.
3 Charles and Alice Todd, *Letters*, p. 10.
4 Charles and Alice Todd, *Letters*, p. 36.
5 Charles and Alice Todd, *Letters*, p. 37; John Little, *Diary 1*, 17 Jan 1872, provides a description of the landing.
6 John Little, *Diary 1*, 17 Jan 1872.
7 Robert Patterson, *Diary*, 8 Feb 1872, p. 39.
8 Robert Patterson, *Diary*, 8 Feb 1872, p. 39.
9 Letter from Todd to Patterson dated 12 Feb 1872, SRSA, GRG 154/23, pp. 14–15.

10 'On the Roper,' *Advertiser*, 24 Apr 1872, p. 4.
11 Charles and Alice Todd, *Letters*, pp. 42–43.
12 John Little, *Diary*, 19 Feb 1872.
13 Charles and Alice Todd, *Letters*, p. 31.
14 William Crowder, *Diary*, p. 22.
15 William Crowder, *Diary*, p. 23. Todd report in *Symes Papers*, File 19.
16 Charles and Alice Todd, *Letters*, p. 37.

The Arrival of the *Tararua*

1 Charles and Alice Todd, *Letters*, p. 23.
2 Charles and Alice Todd, *Letters*, p. 28.
3 Charles and Alice Todd, *Letters*, p. 26.
4 Charles and Alice Todd, *Letters*, pp. 43–4.
5 Charles and Alice Todd, *Letters*, p. 45.
6 Charles and Alice Todd, *Letters*, p. 47.

Sending Supplies

1 'Search for the Leichhardt Relics', *Illawarra Mercury*, 15 Mar 1872, p. 2.
2 Charles Todd, 'Andrew Hume: to the Editor', *Advertiser*, 10 Jan 1874, p. 3; S. Herbert, *Reminiscences*, p. 126, mentions Hume passing through on his way south.
3 Alfred Giles, *Exploring in the Seventies*, pp. 155–6.
4 King's team left on 16 March 1872, Charles and Alice Todd, *Letters*, p. 47.
5 Charles and Alice Todd, *Letters*, p. 47.
6 Charles and Alice Todd, *Letters*, p. 45; William Crowder, *Diary*, pp. 24–5.
7 William Crowder, *Diary*, p. 25.
8 William Crowder, *Diary*, p. 25; Alfred Giles, *Exploring in the Seventies*, p. 130. Crowder says it was 18 pounds of meat, but that was by hearsay, whereas Giles, who was there on short rations, states that it was 6 pounds.
9 William Crowder, *Diary*, 28 Mar 1872, p. 25.
10 Charles and Alice Todd, *Letters*, pp. 50–1.

Providence Knoll

1 Robert Patterson, *Diary*, p. 54.
2 Walter Rutt, 'Link in the Chain,' *Register*, 10 Nov 2021, p. 4.
3 Walter Rutt, *Diary*, p. 52.
4 George Symes, 'The Lighter Side', *Symes Papers*, File 15.
5 Walter Rutt, *Diary*, p. 80; Sidney Herbert, *Reminiscences*, p. 129.
6 Sidney Herbert, *Reminiscences*, pp. 129–30.
7 Walter Rutt, *Diary*, p. 81.
8 See Livingston Chalmers, *Diary*, 6 Apr 1872, which was weeks before the end of their austerity.
9 Livingston Chalmers, *Diary*, 10 Mar 1872.
10 Livingston Chalmers, *Diary*, 3 Apr 1872.
11 Alfred Giles, *Exploring in the Seventies*, pp. 138–9.
12 Livingston Chalmers, *Diary*, 11 Apr 1871.

The Mystery of the Missing Boat

1 Charles and Alice Todd, *Letters*, p. 46.
2 Charles and Alice Todd, *Letters*, p. 55.
3 Charles and Alice Todd, *Letters*, pp. 55–7.
4 The missing boat incident is described in Charles and Alice Todd, *Letters*, pp. 55–62.
5 Charles and Alice Todd, *Letters*, p. 50. Considering the possibility of capturing a native prisoner, Todd added, 'I would perhaps give him a whipping as a punishment for his tribe stealing the boat.' As mentioned, none of this came to pass because Todd discovered that the tribe did not steal the boat.
6 Charles and Alice Todd, *Letters*, p. 50.
7 Charles and Alice Todd, *Letters*, p. 50.
8 Charles and Alice Todd, *Letters*, p. 51; 'North Australia to South Australia,' *Register*, 12 Dec 1872, p. 5.
9 Charles and Alice Todd, *Letters*, p. 49.
10 Charles and Alice Todd, *Letters*, p. 66.
11 Charles and Alice Todd, *Letters*, pp. 66–7.
12 Charles and Alice Todd, *Letters*, pp. 18, 64; Charles Todd to Squier, 16 May 1872, in Charles Todd, *Letters*, GRG 154/23.
13 Charles and Alice Todd, *Letters*, pp. 18, 64.
14 Derek Pugh, *Darwin: The Origin of a City*, p. 106.
15 Charles Todd to Robert Burton, 30 Mar 1872, in *Patterson Letters*, GRG 154/10.
16 Charles Todd to Francis Dutton, 22 May 1872, in Charles Todd, *Letters*, GRG 154/23.
17 Charles and Alice Todd, *Letters*, p. 65.
18 Charles and Alice Todd, *Letters*, p. 67.

Black and White

1 Robert Patterson, *Diary*, p. 65.
2 Derek Pugh, *Darwin: Origin of a City*, pp. 62–3.
3 William Crowder, *Diary*, 29 May 1872. Crowder's use of the word 'fit' employs an old meaning of that word that has fallen into disuse, namely 'fight' or 'conflict'.

To the End of the Line

1 Robert Patterson, *Diary*, 29 Apr 1872.
2 Charles Todd to Robert Patterson, 5 Jun 1872, in Charles Todd, *Outgoing Letter Book*, GRG 154/23.
3 Robert Patterson, *Diary*, 24 Apr 1872.
4 Robert Patterson, *Diary*, 13 Jun 1872.
5 Charles and Alice Todd, *Letters*, p. 2.
6 Robert Patterson, *Diary*, 22 June 1872; the wiring was competed to Daly Waters on 8 June 1872, and the telegraph station opened on 15 June 1872.
7 Robert Patterson, *Diary*, p. 73.
8 Livingston Chalmers, *Diary*, 14 Jul 1872.
9 Alfred Giles, *Exploring in the Seventies*, p. 155.
10 Robert Patterson, *Diary*, 17 Jun 1872, p. 80.
11 William Crowder, *Diary*, 18 Jul 1872.
12 Livingstone Chalmers, *Diary*, p. 50.

Across the Gap

1 Robert Patterson, *Diary*, 13 Jul 1872.
2 Charles Todd, *Diary*, 17 Jul 1872.
3 'North Australia to South Australia', *Evening Journal*, 15 Nov 1872, p. 3.
4 Robert Patterson, *Diary*, 31 Jul 1872.
5 This message is in the archive SLSA, GRG 154/16
6 These are from SRSA, GRG 154/17.
7 Most of the correspondence described in this chapter comes from a compilation of telegrams transmitted to and from Todd while he was travelling down the line, in SLSA, GRG 154/17.

The Join

1 William Crowder, *Diary*, 23 Aug 1872; 'The Overland Telegraph Line Just Finished,' *Evening Journal*, 22 Aug 1872, p. 2; Charles Todd, *Diary*, 22 Aug 1872.
2 Robert Patterson, *Diary*, 22 Aug 1872.
3 Walter Rutt, 'Link in the Chain,' *Register*, 10 Nov 2021, p. 4. Robert Patterson, *Diary*, 22 Aug 1872.
4 Robert Patterson, *Diary*, 22 Aug 1872.
5 'Congratulatory Messages,' *Register*, 23 Aug 1872, p. 5.
6 'The Gold Diggings,' *Register*, 23 Aug 1872, p. 5.
7 Robert Patterson, *Diary*, 22 Aug 1872.
8 William Crowder, *Diary*, 23 Aug 1872.
9 'The overland telegraph just finished,' *Evening Journal*, 22 Aug 1872, p. 2.
10 'Thirty-five years a civil servant,' *Advertiser*, 25 Jun 1908, p. 9.
11 Charles Todd, *Diary*, 20–23 Aug 1872.
12 'Congratulatory Messages', *Register*, 23 Aug 1872, p. 5.
13 Charles Todd, *Diary*, 22 Aug 1872.

The Long Ride Home

1 'North Australia to South Australia', *Register*, 18 Nov 1872, p. 6.
2 'Sydney', *Queensland Times*, 13 Aug 1872, p. 3.
3 'English News', *Alexandra Times*, 5 Oct 1872, p. 3.
4 'Arrival of the European Mail,' *The Queenslander*, 19 Oct 1872, p. 2.
5 Charles and Alice Todd converse over the line, Charles and Alice Todd, *Letters*, pp. 2, 13.
6 Charles Todd, *Diary*, 6 Sep and 9 Sep 1872.
7 'North Australia to South Australia,' *Register*, 18 Nov 1872, p. 6.
8 These quotes are mostly from Charles and Alice Todd, *Letters*. The quote that starts 'Sometimes when I think of your return' is from a transcript of a letter provided to me by Stephen Gillam-Smith.
9 Charles and Alice Todd, *Letters*, p. 16.
10 These letters were dated 20–29 Aug and 5 Sep 1872, as per Charles and Alice Todd, *Letters*, p. 3.
11 Charles and Alice Todd, *Letters*, p. 13.
12 Charles and Alice Todd, *Letters*, pp. 2–4.
13 'Repairs of the Submarine Cable', *Geelong Advertiser*, 21 Oct 1872, p. 3; 'Opening of the Submarine Cable, Communication Complete', *Australasian*, 26 Oct 1872, p. 14; 'The Java Submarine Cable,' *Weekly Examiner* (Tas), 26 Oct 1872, p. 11.

Goodbye to the Roper

1 Robert Patterson, *Diary*, p. 95.
2 Robert Patterson, *Diary*, p. 95.
3 Robert Patterson, *Diary*, p. 95.
4 Sidney Herbert, *Reminiscences*, p. 427; Robert Patterson, *Diary*, p. 96.
5 Robert Patterson, *Diary*, p. 97.
6 Robert Patterson, *Diary*, p. 97.
7 Sidney Herbert, *Reminiscences*, pp. 158–9.
8 Sidney Herbert, *Reminiscences*, p. 163.
9 Robert Patterson, *Diary*, 31 Oct–12 Nov 1872.
10 Untitled, *Telegraph*, 8 Nov 1872, p. 2.

Homecoming Hero

1 'Mr Charles Todd's Return', *Express & Telegraph*, 31 Oct 1872, p. 2.
2 'Topics', *Advertiser*, 31 Oct 1872, p. 2; this article also mentions that there happened to be a floral exhibition at Town Hall.
3 'Mr Todd and His Staff', *Express & Telegraph*, 2 Nov 1872, p. 3.
4 Richard Venus, 'Charles Knight: Pyrotechnician and Medical Galvanist'; 'The Telegraph Banquet', *Evening Journal*, 6 Nov 1872, p. 2; 'The Telegraph Demonstration', *Advertiser*, 6 Dec 1872, p. 4; 'Dinner and Presentations', *Advertiser*, 6 Dec 1872, p. 5.
5 The bill was passed on 29 Nov 1872, SRSA, GRG 154/90/3; nine years later, the reward money for capturing the Kelly gang was likewise apportioned to police according to rank.

Patterson's Curse

1 *Symes Papers*, File 25.
2 'The Overland Telegraph and Its Detractors,' *Evening Journal*, 13 Dec 1872, p. 2.
3 Charles Todd to Chief Secretary, Memorandum, 30 Jul 1874, in *Symes Papers*, File 25.
4 'The Overland Telegraph Line', *Evening Journal*, 17 Dec 1872, p. 2; *Symes Papers*, File 25.
5 'The Overland Telegraph Line', *Evening Journal*, 17 Dec 1872, p. 2; 'The Port August and Port Darwin Telegraph', *Express & Telegraph*, 17 Dec 1872, p. 2. I have taken the liberty of tweaking the tense and pronouns in statements in the articles to convert them into direct quotes, for better readability.
6 Robert Patterson, Memorandum, 29 Apr 1872, *Symes Papers*, File 25.
7 Patterson to Blyth, Memorandum, 3 Jun 1874, *Symes Papers*, File 25.
8 'House of Assembly', *Register*, 5 Aug 1874, p. 6.
9 Andrew Crouch, in his article 'Recriminations!', provides a more sympathetic view of Patterson than I have done. Crouch makes the point that with both the *Telegraph* journalist and the politician Charles Mann, Patterson was just being honest. With the *Telegraph*, he was naïve, whereas with Mann, he had a duty to be honest and forthright. Crouch also notes that the line *was* shoddy in places, and that poles *did* need to be replaced. Even so, Todd emphatically rejected Patterson's claims on both the detail and the overview. I have sided with Todd, so Crouch's view acts as a counterpoint to mine.
10 'Mr Patterson and the Overland Telegraph,' *Chronicle*, 22 Aug 1874, p. 12.

11 Derek Pugh, *Darwin: Origin of a City*, p. 107.
12 Derek Pugh, *Darwin: Origin of a City*, pp. 107–9; 'Northern Territory Affairs,' *Register*, 6 Jun 1873, p. 5.

The Fate of the Black Prince

1 Charles Johnston to Charles Todd, Telegram, 13 Aug 1872, in SRSA, GRG 154/17; Charles Todd, 'Andrew Hume: to the Editor', *Advertiser*, 10 Feb 1874, p. 3.
2 Alfred Giles, *Exploring in the Seventies*, pp. 156–7; 'Colonial Extracts', *Clarence and Richmond Examiner*, 31 Dec 1872, p. 4; 'Andrew Hume at Port Darwin', *Evening News*, 25 Sep 1873, p. 2; Livingston Chalmers, for one, admired and believed Hume, see his *Diary*, 4 Aug 1872.
3 Alfred Giles, *Exploring in the Seventies*, pp. 156–7; Hume wrote an account of his adventures from Newcastle Waters in a letter to the *Sydney Morning Herald*: 'In Search of Leichhardt's Records,' *Sydney Morning Herald*, 7 Nov 1872, p. 3.
4 'Discovery of a Companion of Leichhardt,' *Age*, 5 Feb 1874, p. 3; 'The Leichhardt Expedition,' *Empire*, 9 Feb 1874, p. 3; Untitled, *Evening News* (NSW), 10 Feb 1874, p. 2.
5 'Andrew Hume', *Express & Telegraph*, 11 Feb 1874, p. 2.
6 'The Leichhardt Relics—Andrew Hume's Statement', *Empire*, 21 Feb 1874, p. 2.
7 'Andrew Hume's Expedition', *Advocate* (Vic), 5 Dec 1874, p. 10.

A Link to the West

1 Ann Moyal, *Clear Across Australia*, pp. 28–9; 'James Coats Fleming', Western Australia, Telegrams Australia, https://telegramsaustralia.com/Forms/Special%20developments/People/Fleming%20James.html, accessed 20 Jan 2024.
2 *Sydney Morning Herald*, 24 Jul 1877.
3 'Eucla Telegraph Extension', *The Inquirer*, 10 Oct 1876, p. 1.
4 'Telegraph to Western Australia', *Register*, 9 Aug 1877, p. 4. A large amount of material on the east–west line can be found in Gavin Bienke, 'The Last Link'.
5 Ann Moyal, *Clear Across Australia*, p. 60.

Barrow Creek

1 The Barrow Creek attack is very well documented, with multiple sources from the white perspective, but, sadly, not from the Kaititja perspective. Detailed historical accounts are given in the following works: G. Reid, *A Picnic with the Natives: Aboriginal–European Relations in the Northern Territory to 1910*, pp. 61–6; M.C. Hartwig, *The Progress of White Settlement in the Alice Springs District and Its Effects upon the Aboriginal Inhabitants 1860–1894*, pp. 264–78. Derek Pugh also provides a detailed account in his 2021 book *Twenty to the Mile: The Overland Telegraph Line*, which also provides a harrowing account of the aftermath of a later attack at Daly Waters. There are also numerous articles newspaper articles on the topic from 1874 available online via the National Library of Australia's Trove service.
2 Peter Taylor, *An End to Silence*, pp. 167–8.
3 'The Barrow's Creek Affray', *Evening Journal*, 26 Feb 1874, p. 2; Todd's message was sent on 25 Feb 1874.
4 'The Barrow's Creek Affray', *Evening Journal*, 28 Feb 1874, p. 2.
5 'The Barrow Creek Natives', *Northern Territory Times and Gazette*, 12 Sep 1874, p. 3.

6 Some sources claim that Gason committed wholesale slaughter of over 90 Kaititja people at a place called 'Skull's Creek'. This claim may be right, but it seems to have arisen based on claims made by a white man, himself accused of atrocities, about 49 years after the events in question.

7 M.C. Hartwig, *The Progress of White Settlement in the Alice Springs District and Its Effects upon the Aboriginal Inhabitants 1860–1894*, p. 278. Suzie Herzberg provides an in-depth look at white–black relations along the line during and after the construction, including an exploration of Charles Todd's own views, in 'OT Construction—Relations with First Nations Peoples'.

The Open Heart

1 Denis Cryle, *Behind the Legend*, p. 144.

2 In 1873, its first year of operation, the cable carried a total of 8952 messages. By 1888 the total amount of international telegraphic messages was 34,382. These numbers come from Charles Todd's essay, 'Telegraphic Enterprise in Australasia'.

3 Geoffrey Blainey, *The Rush That Never Ended*, p. 208. Ann Moyal used this quote in *Clear Across Australia*, p. 61, which is where I first found it.

4 Geoffrey Blainey, *The Rush That Never Ended*, p. 92.

5 Geoffrey Blainey, *The Rush That Never Ended*, pp. 90–6.

6 Charles Todd, *Telegraphic Enterprise in Australia*, 1886.

7 Start of Warburton's expedition announced in: 'Exploration towards Western Australia,' *Register*, 23 Aug 1872, p. 4.

8 Rosamund Burton's *The Whispering Wire* and Alice Thomson's, *The Singing Line* are evocative modern explorations of the remnants of the Overland Telegraph line, the land it traversed, and the people who live there.

Charles and Alice

1 Todd's correspondence with William's lawyer about Charlotte Bell's estate can be found in 'Private letter book of Sir Charles Todd 1873–77', PRG 630/14, letter 33 and letter 34.

2 'The Post-Office Clock', *Register*, 7 Dec 1875, p. 5; *The Cyclopedia of South Australia*, p. 274.

3 Denis Cryle, *Behind the Legend*, p. 151.

4 'Banquet to Mr C. Todd, CMG,' *Register*, 1 Jun 1886, p. 7.

5 Denis Cryle, *Behind the Legend*, pp. 160–1.

6 Charles Todd, 1886, 'Telegraphic Enterprise in Australasia'.

7 Denis Cryle, *Behind the Legend*, p 164.

8 Letter from Alice Todd to Maude Todd, 3 Apr 1892; letter provided to me by Stephen Gillam-Smith.

9 Letters from Alice Todd to Maude Todd, 3, 11 and 17 Apr 1892; generously provided with transcriptions by Stephen Gillam-Smith.

10 'Topics of the Day,' *Herald* (Vic), 5 Jun 1893, p. 2.

11 Charles Todd, *The Earth's Place in the Universe*.

The End of the Line

1 This chapter made extensive use of the website telegramsaustralia.com, which has an abundance of information about the history of Australian telegraphy.

Bibliography

Books, pamphlets, journal articles

Bailey, John, 2006, *Mr Stuart's Track*, Pan Macmillan Australia: Sydney.

Blainey, Geoffrey, 1974, *The Rush That Never Ended*, Melbourne University Press: Melbourne.

Bonython, Elizabeth, and Burton, Anthony, 2003 *The Great Exhibitor: The Life and Work of Henry Cole*, V&A Publishing: London.

Bradley, F.R., 1934, 'History of the Electric Telegraph in Australia', *Royal Australian Historical Society Journal and Proceedings*, 20(4), pp. 239–63.

Burton, Rosamund, 2022, *The Whispering Wire: Tracing the Overland Telegraph Line through the Heart of Australia*, Wakefield: Hill End, SA.

Calder, George, 1897, *Stirring Events Ashore and Afloat*, E.W. Cole: Melbourne.

Clune, Frank, 1955, *The Overland Telegraph: The Story of a Great Australian Achievement and the Link Between Adelaide and Port Darwin*, Angus & Robertson: Sydney.

Crouch, Andrew, 2020, *Building the Line: The Construction of the Overland Telegraph Line*, Hesperian: Carlisle, Western Australia.

Crouch, Andrew, 2020, *Connecting the North: From the Diaries of the Overland Telegraph Expeditioners*, Andrew Crouch: St Marys, South Australia.

Cryle, Denis, 2017, *Behind the Legend: The Many Worlds of Charles Todd*, Australian Scholarly Publishing: North Melbourne.

Gardner's Directory: History, Gazetteer & Directory of Cambridge, 1851, Robert Gardner: Peterborough.

Giles, Alfred, 1926, *Exploring in the Seventies and the Construction of the Overland Telegraph Line*, W.K. Thomas & Co.: Adelaide.

Griggs, Edward, 1983, 'Domestic Servants and Households in Victorian England,' *Social History*, 8(2), pp. 201–10.

Hartwig, M.C., 1965, *The Progress of White Settlement in the Alice Springs District and Its Effects upon the Aboriginal Inhabitants 1860–1894*, Ph.D. thesis, University of Adelaide.

Jeans, William T., 1887, *Lives of the Electricians: Professors Tyndall, Wheatstone, and Morse*, Whittaker & Co.: London.

Jones, Philip, and Kenny, Anna, 2010, *Australia's Muslim Cameleers: Pioneers of the Inland, 1860s–1930s*, Wakefield Press: Kent Town, SA.

Lewis, John, 1922, *Fought and Won*, W.K. Thomas & Co., Adelaide.

Mills, Elliott Whitfield, 1993, *W. Whitfield Mills: Experiences with Darwin Survey & Overland Telegraph Parties and Discovery of Alice Spring: from SA to WA by Camel*, E.W. Mills: Glenside, SA.

Morse, Edward Lind, 1914, *Samuel Morse Letters and Journals*, Houghton Mifflin Co: Boston.

Moyal, Ann, 1984, *Clear Across Australia: A History of Telecommunications*, Nelson: Melbourne.

Murgatroyd, Sarah, 2010, *The Dig Tree: The Story of Bravery, Insanity and the Race to Discover Australia's Wild Frontier*, Text: Melbourne.

Powell, Alan, 1992, *Far Country: A Short History of the Northern Territory*, Melbourne University Press: Melbourne.

Pugh, Derek, 2019, *Darwin: Origin of a City*, Self-published.
Pugh, Derek, 2021, *Twenty to the Mile: The Overland Telegraph Line*, Self-published.
Reid, Gordon, 1990, *A Picnic with the Natives: Aboriginal–European Relations in the Northern Territory to 1910*, Melbourne University Press: Melbourne.
Rogers, Tony, and Ferrante, Judy, 2017, *The Weatherman from Greenwich: Charles Todd—1826 to 1910*, Australian Meteorological Association: Adelaide.
The Royal South Australian Almanack and General Directory for 1857, J. Allen: Adelaide.
Silverman, Kenneth, 2003. *Lightning Man: The Accursed Life of Samuel F.B. Morse*, Alfred A. Knopf: New York.
Symes, George W., 1960, *Exploring in the MacDonnell Ranges in 1870 to 1872*, Typed copy of a lecture given to the Historical Division, Royal Geographic Society, South Australia, in August 1960.
Taylor, Peter, 1980, *An End to Silence: The Building of the Overland Telegraph Line from Adelaide to Darwin*, Methuen Australia: Sydney.
Thomson, Alice, 1999, *The Singing Line*, Chatto & Windus: London.
Todd, Charles, 1873, Speech, State Library of South Australia PRG 630/9.
Todd, Charles, 1886, 'Telegraphic Enterprise in Australasia', Royal Colonial Institute, *Report of Proceedings* (17),1885–6, pp. 144–79.
Todd, Charles, 1903, *The Earth's Place in the Universe: Are There More Worlds Than One?* Adelaide: W.K. Thomas & Co. Held by the Royal Geographic Society of South Australia.
Yapp, George Wagstaffe, and Ellis, Robert (Commissioners for the Exhibition of 1851), *Official Catalogue of the Great Exhibition of the Works of Industry of All Nations*, Spicer Brothers: London.

Personal diaries, memoirs, letters

Please note that 'SLSA' means State Library of South Australia, and 'SRSA' means State Records of South Australia. Some, but not all, of these institutions' records are online.

Ashwin, Arthur, *From South Australia to Port Darwin*, SLSA D6992(L)
Chalmers, Livingston, *Diary*, SLSA, D 8057(L)
Clarke, Benjamin, *Diary of Benjamin Clarke*, SLSA, D 3378
Crowder, William, *Diary of W.A. Crowder*, SLSA, D 8065/1(L). Transcription by Ernest Roe, Helen Davies, and Kay Anson.
Ewens, John Reynolds, *Diary*, SLSA, D 8334 (L)
Gillam-Smith, Stephen, *Profile of Bell, Gillam & Early Squires Families.*
Herbert, Sidney W., *Reminiscences*, SLSA, D 69995(L)
Little, John, *Diary 1* and *Diary 2*, 1871–1872, SLSA, PRG 329
McMinn, Gilbert Rotherdale, *Diary of G.R. McMinn, 1870–1872*, SRSA, GRG 154/8/1
Milner, Ralph, *First Overland Trek with Stock to Port Darwin*, SLSA, D7001(L)
Patterson, Robert Charles, *Diary*, 1871–1872, D 8103/1/0/FC(L). Transcription by Andrew Crouch.
Rutt, Walter, *Diary of Walter Rutt*, SLSA, D 2575/FC(L)
Stanley, Edward Henry, *Papers*, 'Interview with L. Gisborne on extension of telegraph to Australia', 24 March 1858, *Australian Joint Copying Project*, http://nla.gov.au/nla.obj-903439952

Todd, Alice, *Letter to Charles Todd, 28 June 1872*, transcribed by Judy Munro, provided to the author by Stephen Gillam-Smith.
Todd, Alice, *Letters to Maude*, provided to the author by Stephen Gillam-Smith.
Todd, Charles, *Diary*, SRSA, four files: GRG 154/14/1, GRG 154/14/2, GRG 154/14/3, GRG 154/15
Todd, Charles, *Outgoing Letter Book of Charles Todd*, SRSA, GRG 154/23
Todd, Charles, *Private Letter Book of Charles Todd, 1873–77*, PRG 630/14. Transcription and annotation by Lyndall Fredericks and Kerrie Durrant.
Todd, Charles, and Todd, Alice, *Letters 1871–1872*, PRG 630/2. Transcription by Lyndall Fredericks.

OT150

As part of the commemoration of 150 years since the completion of the line, a website was created that hosted valuable source documents as well as articles and commentary. That website, ot150.net, was of immense help in the writing of this book. The following is a list of articles from ot150.net that have been cited in the endnotes. On 30 March 2024, they could be found at either https://www.ot150.net/l-telegrams.htm or https://www.ot150.net/l-monographs.htm.

Beinke, Gavin, 2022, 'The Last Link—The East West Telegraph', *OT-150 Monographs No. 8.*
Crouch, Andrew, 2021, 'Recriminations!', *OT-150 TELEGRAMS No. 6.*
Crouch, Andrew, 2022, 'The Building Process', *OT-150 TELEGRAMS No. 7.*
Crouch, Andrew, 2022, 'The Joining of the Wires', *OT-150 TELEGRAMS No. 4.*
Crouch, Andrew, & Venus, Richard, 2022, 'The Overland Telegraph Line: How It Was Built', *OT-150 TELEGRAMS No. 15.*
Herzberg, Suzie, 2022, 'OT Construction—Relations with First Nations Peoples', *OT-150 Monographs No. 6.*
Kraegen, Ted, 2022, 'Carl Kraegen's Story', *OT-150 TELEGRAMS No. 14.*
Venus, Richard, 2022, 'Charles Knight: Pyrotechnician and Medical Galvanist', *OT-150 TELEGRAMS No. 19.*
Venus, Richard, 2022, 'How Did the Telegraph Work?', *OT-150 TELEGRAMS No. 09.*
Venus, Richard, 2022, 'The First and Last Poles', *OT-150 TELEGRAMS No. 03.*

Other archival sources

Charles Todd letter of appointment, SLSA, PRG 630/14
Miscellaneous Telegrams of Charles Todd relating to the Progress of Work on the Overland Telegraph Line, SRSA, GRG 154/17
Overland Telegraph Papers, SRSA, GRG 24/90/1/3
Symes Papers: Collected Papers of George Symes, held by the Royal Geographic Society of South Australia.
Telegramsaustralia.com A website with a wealth of information on Australian telegraph history.
Todd Papers, SLSA, GRG 154/6/1
Trove. Almost all newspaper and magazine articles cited in this book were accessed through trove (trove.nla.gov.au), an invaluable online resource hosted by the National Library of Australia.

Index